The Embodied Mind

The Embodied Mind

Cognitive Science and Human Experience

Francisco J. Varela
Evan Thompson
Eleanor Rosch

The MIT Press
Cambridge, Massachusetts
London, England

Second printing, 1992

This book was set in Palatino by DEKR Corporation and was printed and bound in the United States of America.

Library of Congress Cataloging-in-Publication Data

Varela, Francisco J., 1945–
    The embodied mind : cognitive science and human experience /
Francisco J. Varela, Evan Thompson, Eleanor Rosch.
        p.   cm.   .
    Includes bibliographical references and index.
    ISBN 0-262-22042-3
    1. Cognition. 2. Cognitive science. 3. Experiential learning.
    4. Meditations—Buddhism. I. Thompson, Evan. II. Rosch, Eleanor. III. Title.
    BF311.V26   1991
    153.4—dc20   91-12438
                                                             CIP

Those who believe in substantiality are like cows;
those who believe in emptiness are worse.
Saraha (ca. ninth century CE)

Contents

8
Enaction: Embodied Cognition

9
Evolutionary Path Making and Natural Drift

V
WORLDS WITHOUT GROUND

10
The Middle Way

11
Laying Down a Path in Walking

Appendix A

Appendix B

x   Contents

Acknowledgments

The inspiration for this book began in the late seventies when Francisco Varela was teaching at the summer Science Program of the Naropa Institute in Boulder, Colorado. Naropa Institute tried to create an intellectual space for a dialogue between the cognitive sciences and the Buddhist traditions of meditative psychology and philosophy by offering a variety of courses and by gathering teachers and students for discussion in an informal atmosphere. In this enterprise and in the ideas that grew from it, the contributions of Newcomb Greenleaf, Robin Kornman, Jeremy Hayward, Michael Moerman, Joseph Goguen, and Charlotte Linde were invaluable. In 1979, the Alfred P. Sloan Foundation funded what was probably the very first conference on "Contrasting Perspectives on Cognition: Buddhism and the Cognitive Sciences." This conference, which gathered scholars from various universities in North America and Buddhist scholars from many schools and traditions, was so unsuccessful in establishing a genuine dialogue that we learned a great deal about how not to go about the exploration.

Over the next few years Francisco Varela continued to work privately on developing the dialogue between cognitive science and the Buddhist tradition, only occasionally presenting ideas in public. One particularly helpful discussion took place as a series of talks given in 1985 at Karma Choeling in Vermont.

The overall shape of this book first came into being when Evan Thompson, supported by a research grant from the Stiftung Zur Förderung der Philosophie (Germany), joined Francisco Varela at the Ecole Polytechnique in Paris in the summer of 1986. During this time a tentative first draft of the book was completed. We are grateful to the Stiftung and to Uri Kuchinsky for support during this period.

In the fall of 1987, the ideas of this first draft were presented at another conference on cognitive science and Buddhism, this one held at the Cathedral Church of St. John the Divine in New York City and organized by the Lindisfarne Program for Biology, Cognition, and Ethics. We are especially grateful to William I. Thompson and to the Very Reverend James Parks Morton for their interest and support of our work.

From 1987 to 1989, Varela and Thompson continued writing in Paris, supported by grants to the Lindisfarne Program for Biology, Cognition, and Ethics from the Prince Charitable Trusts of Chicago. In the fall of 1989, Eleanor Rosch, who had been teaching and doing research in both cognitive psychology and Buddhist psychology for many years at Berkeley, joined the project as a third author. In 1990–91, Varela, Thompson, and Rosch, working sometimes together and sometimes at a distance in Berkeley, Paris, Toronto, and Boston, produced several further drafts, resulting finally in this book.

Over the years, a great many people have encouraged and supported our work. William I. Thompson, Amy Cohen, and Jeremy Hayward were untiring in their advice, encouragement, and friendly criticism on virtually every aspect of the book. The comments and support of Mauro Cerutti, Jean-Pierre Depuy, Fernando Flores, Gordon Globus, and Susan Oyama were also especially helpful. Several other people read various drafts and/or portions of the manuscript and offered valuable comments: in particular, Dan Dennett, Gail Fleischaker, Tamar Gendler, Dan Goleman, and Lisa Lloyd. Finally, special thanks are due to Frank Urbanowski of The MIT Press for believing in this book, and to Madeline Sunley and Jenya Weinreb for their care in handling the revisions and production.

In addition to those already mentioned, each of us wishes to add several personal acknowledgments:

Francisco Varela especially thanks the late Chogyam Trungpa and Tulku Urgyen for personal inspiration. For financial support during the actual time of writing (1986–1990), thanks go to the Prince Charitable Trusts and to its chairman, Mr. William Wood Prince, and to the Fondation de France for a chair in Cognitive Science and Epistemology. The overall institutional support of the Centre de Recherche en Epistémologie Appliqué (CREA) at the Ecole Polytechnique and the Centre National de Recherche Scientifique (Institut des Neurosciences, URA 1199) is also gratefully acknowledged.

Evan Thompson wishes to thank Robert Thurman, now at Columbia University, for introducing him to Buddhist studies and comparative philosophy at Amherst College; and the Social Sciences and

Humanities Research Council of Canada for the generous doctoral fellowships that enabled him to write this book while also writing his doctoral dissertation in philosophy at the University of Toronto and for the postdoctoral fellowships that supported him during the completion of this work; thanks also for the hospitality of the Center for Cognitive Studies at Tufts University where this work was completed.

Eleanor Rosch wishes to thank Hubert Dreyfus, the Cognitive Science Program, and the Buddhist Studies Program of the University of California at Berkeley.

Introduction

This book begins and ends with the conviction that the new sciences of mind need to enlarge their horizon to encompass both lived human experience and the possibilities for transformation inherent in human experience. Ordinary, everyday experience, on the other hand, must enlarge its horizon to benefit from the insights and analyses that are distinctly wrought by the sciences of mind. It is this possibility for circulation between the sciences of mind (cognitive science) and human experience that we explore in this book.

If we examine the current situation today, with the exception of a few largely academic discussions cognitive science has had virtually nothing to say about what it means to be human in everyday, lived situations. On the other hand, those human traditions that have focused on the analysis, understanding, and possibilities for transformation of ordinary life need to be presented in a context that makes them available to science.

We like to consider our journey in this book as a modern continuation of a program of research founded over a generation ago by the French philosopher, Maurice Merleau-Ponty.[1] By *continuation* we do not mean a scholarly consideration of Merleau-Ponty's thought in the context of contemporary cognitive science. We mean, rather, that Merleau-Ponty's writings have both inspired and guided our orientation here.

We hold with Merleau-Ponty that Western scientific culture requires that we see our bodies both as physical structures and as lived, experiential structures—in short, as both "outer" and "inner," biological and phenomenological. These two sides of embodiment are obviously not opposed. Instead, we continuously circulate back and forth between them. Merleau-Ponty recognized that we cannot understand this circulation without a detailed investigation of its fundamental axis, namely, the embodiment of knowledge, cognition, and experience. For Merleau-Ponty, as for us, *embodiment* has this double sense: it encompasses both the body as a lived, experiential structure and the body as the context or milieu of cognitive mechanisms.

Embodiment in this double sense has been virtually absent from cognitive science, both in philosophical discussion and in hands-on research. We look to Merleau-Ponty, then, because we claim that we cannot investigate the circulation between cognitive science and human experience without making this double sense of embodiment the focus of our attention. This claim is not primarily philosophical. On the contrary, our point is that both the development of research in cognitive science and the relevance of this research to lived human concerns require the explicit thematization of this double sense of embodiment. This book is meant as a first step in this task.

Although we look to Merleau-Ponty for inspiration, we nonetheless recognize that our present-day situation is significantly different from his. There are at least two reasons for this difference, one from science and the other from human experience.

First, in the days when Merleau-Ponty undertook his work—the 1940s and 1950s—the potential sciences of mind were fragmented into disparate, noncommunicating disciplines: neurology, psychoanalysis, and behaviorist experimental psychology. Today we see the emergence of a new interdisciplinary matrix called cognitive science, which includes not only neuroscience but cognitive psychology, linguistics, artificial intelligence, and, in many centers, philosophy. Furthermore, most of cognitive technology, which is essential for the contemporary science of mind, has been developed only in the past forty years—the digital computer being the most significant example.

Second, Merleau-Ponty addressed the lived world of human experience from the philosophical standpoint elaborated in the tradition of phenomenology. There are many direct heirs to phenomenology in the contemporary scene. In France, the tradition of Heidegger and Merleau-Ponty is continued in authors such as Michel Foucault, Jacques Derrida, and Pierre Bourdieu.[2] In North America, Hubert Dreyfus has long been the Heideggerian gadfly of the cognitive science enterprise,[3] more recently joined in that critique by others who link it to various scientific domains, such as Terry Winograd, Fernando Flores,[4] Gordon Globus,[5] and John Haugeland.[6] In another direction, phenomenology as ethnomethodology has been recently pursued in the studies of improvisation by D. Sudnow.[7] Finally, phenomenology has given its name to a tradition within clinical psychology.[8] These approaches, however, are dependent upon the methods of their parent disciplines—the logical articulations of philosophy, interpretive analysis of history and of sociology, and the treatment of patients in therapy.

Despite this activity, phenomenology remains—especially in North America, where an important volume of current research in cognitive science is being done—a relatively uninfluential philosophical school. We believe that it is time for a radically new approach to the implementation of Merleau-Ponty's vision. What we are offering in this book is thus a new lineage of descent from the fundamental intuition of double embodiment first articulated by Merleau-Ponty.

What challenges does human experience face as a result of the scientific study of mind? The existential concern that animates our entire discussion in this book results from the tangible demonstration within cognitive science that the self or cognizing subject is fundamentally fragmented, divided, or nonunified. This realization is, of course, not new to Western culture. Many philosophers, psychiatrists, and social theorists since Nietzsche have challenged our received conception of the self or subject as the epicenter of knowledge, cognition, experience, and action. The emergence of this theme within science, however, marks a quite significant event, for science provides the voice of authority in our culture to an extent that is matched by no other human practice and institution. Furthermore, science—again unlike other human practices and institutions—incarnates its understanding in technological artifacts. In the case of cognitive science, these artifacts are ever more sophisticated thinking/acting machines, which have the potential to transform everyday life perhaps even more than the books of the philosopher, the reflections of the social theorist, or the therapeutic analyses of the psychiatrist.

This central and fundamental issue—the status of the self or cognizing subject—could, of course, be relegated to a purely theoretical pursuit. Nevertheless, this issue obviously touches our lives and self-understanding directly. It is therefore not at all surprising that those few eloquent books that do engage this issue, such as Hofstadter and Dennett's *The Mind's Eye* and Sherry Turkle's *The Second Self*, meet with considerable popularity.[9] In a more academic vein, the circulation between science and experience has surfaced in discussions of "folk psychology" or in forms of investigation such as "conversational analysis." An even more systematic attempt to address the relation between science and experience can be found in the recent book by Ray Jackendoff, *Consciousness and the Computational Mind*,[10] which addresses the relation between science and experience by attempting to provide a computational foundation for the experience of conscious awareness.

Although we share the concerns of these various works, we remain dissatisfied with both their procedures and their answers. Our view is that the current style of investigation is limited and unsatisfactory, both theoretically and empirically, because there remains no direct, hands-on, pragmatic approach to experience with which to complement science. As a result, both the spontaneous and more reflective dimensions of human experience receive little more than a cursory, matter-of-fact treatment, one that is no match for the depth and sophistication of scientific analysis.

How do we propose to remedy this situation? Considerable evidence gathered in many contexts throughout human history indicates both that experience itself can be examined in a disciplined manner and that skill in such an examination can be considerably refined over time. We refer to the experience accumulated in a tradition that is not familiar to most Westerners but that the West can hardly continue to ignore—the Buddhist tradition of meditative practice and pragmatic, philosophical exploration. Though considerably less familiar than other pragmatic investigations of human experience, such as psychoanalysis, the Buddhist tradition is especially relevant to our concerns, for, as we shall see, the concept of a nonunified or decentered (the usual terms are *egoless* or *selfless*) cognitive being is the cornerstone of the entire Buddhist tradition. Furthermore, this concept—although it certainly entered into philosophical debate in the Buddhist tradition—is fundamentally a firsthand experiential account by those who attain a degree of mindfulness of their experience in daily life. For these reasons, then, we propose to build a bridge between mind in science and mind in experience by articulating a dialogue between these two traditions of Western cognitive science and Buddhist meditative psychology.

Let us emphasize that the overriding aim of our book is pragmatic. We do not intend to build some grand, unified theory, either scientific or philosophical, of the mind-body relation. Nor do we intend to write a treatise of comparative scholarship. Our concern is to open a space of possibilities in which the circulation between cognitive science and human experience can be fully appreciated and to foster the transformative possibilites of human experience in a scientific culture. This pragmatic orientation is common to both partners in this book. On the one hand, science proceeds because of its pragmatic link to the phenomenal world; indeed, its validation is derived from the efficacy of this link. On the other hand, the tradition of meditative practice proceeds because of its systematic and disciplined link to human experience. The validation of this tradition is derived from its ability to transform progressively our lived experience and self-understanding.

In writing this book, we have aimed for a level of discussion that will be accessible to several audiences. Thus we have attempted to address not only working cognitive scientists but also educated laypersons with a general interest in the dialogue between science and experience, as well as those interested in Buddhist or comparative thought. As a result, members of these different (and, we hope, overlapping) groups may occasionally wish that we had devoted more time to some specific point in the scientific, philosophical, or comparative discussions. We have tried to anticipate a few of these points but have placed our comments in notes and appendixes so as not to detract from the flow of the discussion, which, once again, is intended for a wide audience.

Now that we have introduced the reader to the main theme of this book, let us outline how it unfolds into five parts:

• Part I introduces the two partners in our dialogue. We indicate what we mean by "cognitive science" and "human experience" and provide an overview of how the dialogue between these two partners will develop.

• Part II presents the computational model of mind, which gave rise to cognitive science in its classical form (cognitivism). Here we see how cognitive science uncovers the nonunity of the cognizing subject and how the progressive realization of a nonunified self provides the cornerstone of Buddhist meditative practice and of its psychological articulation.

• Part III addresses the issue of how the phenomena usually attributed to a self could arise without an actual self. Within cognitive science, this encompasses the concepts of self-organization and emergent properties of cognitive processes, especially in connectionist models. Within Buddhist psychology, it includes the emergent structure of mental factors within a single moment of experience and the emergence of the karmic causal patterning of experience over time.

• Part IV provides a further step, which consists in the presentation of a new approach in cognitive science. We propose the term *enactive* for this new approach. In the enactive program, we explicitly call into question the assumption—prevalent throughout cognitive science—that cognition consists of the representation of a world that is independent of our perceptual and cognitive capacities by a cognitive system that exists independent of the world. We outline instead a view of cognition as *embodied action* and so recover the idea of embodiment that we invoked above. We also situate this view of cognition within the context of evolutionary theory by arguing that evolution consists not in optimal adaptation but rather in what we call natural drift. This fourth step in our book may be the most creative contribution we have to offer to contemporary cognitive science.

• Part V considers the philosophical and experiential implications of the enactive view that cognition has no ultimate foundation or ground beyond its history of embodiment. We first situate these implications within the context of the contemporary Western critique of objectivism and foundationalism. We then present what was probably the most radically nonfoundationalist understanding in human history, the Madhyamika school of Mahayana Buddhism, the school on whose insights all major subsequent Buddhist thought has relied. We conclude our discussion by considering some of the more far-reaching ethical implications of the journey undertaken in this book. Part V may be the most creative contribution that we have to make within our larger cultural context.

We intend these five parts to express an ongoing conversation in which we explore experience and the mind within an expanded horizon that includes both the meditative attention to experience in daily life and the scientific attention to mind in nature. This conversation is ultimately motivated by a concern: without embracing the relevance and importance of everyday, lived human experience, the power and sophistication of contemporary cognitive science could generate a divided scientific culture in which our scientific conceptions of life and mind on the one hand, and our everyday, lived self-understanding on the other, become irreconcilable. Hence in our eyes, the issues at hand, though scientific and technical, are inseparable from deeply ethical concerns, ones that require an equally deep reunderstanding of the dignity of human life.

I
The Departing Ground

1
A Fundamental Circularity:
In the Mind of the Reflective Scientist

An Already-Given Condition

A phenomenologically inclined cognitive scientist reflecting on the origins of cognition might reason thus: Minds awaken in a world. We did not design our world. We simply found ourselves with it; we awoke both to ourselves and to the world we inhabit. We come to reflect on that world as we grow and live. We reflect on a world that is not made, but found, and yet it is also our structure that enables us to reflect upon this world. Thus in reflection we find ourselves in a circle: we are in a world that seems to be there before reflection begins, but that world is not separate from us.

For the French philosopher Maurice Merleau-Ponty, the recognition of this circle opened up a space between self and world, between the inner and the outer. This space was not a gulf or divide; it embraced the distinction between self and world, and yet provided the continuity between them. Its openness revealed a middle way, an *entre-deux*. In the preface to his *Phenomenology of Perception*, Merleau-Ponty wrote,

> When I begin to reflect, my reflection bears upon an unreflective experience, moreover my reflection cannot be unaware of itself as an event, and so it appears to itself in the light of a truly creative act, of a changed structure of consciousness, and yet it has to recognize, as having priority over its own operations, the world which is given to the subject because the subject is given to himself. . . . Perception is not a science of the world, it is not even an act, a deliberate taking up of a position; it is the background from which all acts stand out, and is presupposed by them: The world is not an object such that I have in my possession the law of its making; it is the natural setting of, and field for, all my thoughts and all my explicit perceptions.[1]

And toward the end of the book, he wrote, "The world is inseparable from the subject, but from a subject which is nothing but a project of the world, and the subject is inseparable from the world, but from a world which the subject itself projects."[2]

Science (and philosophy for that matter) has chosen largely to ignore what might lie in such an entre-deux or middle way. Indeed, Merleau-Ponty could be held partly responsible, for in his *Phenomenology* at least, he saw science as primarily unreflective; he argued that it naively presupposed mind and consciousness. Indeed, this is one of the extreme stances science can take. The observor that a nineteenth-century physicist had in mind is often pictured as a disembodied eye looking objectively at the play of phenomena. Or to change metaphors, such an observor could be imagined as a cognizing agent who is parachuted onto the earth as an unknown, objective reality to be charted. Critiques of such a position, however, can easily go to the opposite extreme. The indeterminacy principle in quantum mechanics, for example, is often used to espouse a kind of subjectivism in which the mind on its own "constructs" the world. But when we turn back upon ourselves to make our own cognition our scientific theme—which is precisely what the new science of cognition purports to do—neither of these positions (the assumption of a disembodied observor or of a dis-worlded mind) is at all adequate.

We will return to a discussion of this point shortly. At the moment, we wish to speak more precisely about this science that has come to take such a turn. What is this new branch of science?

What Is Cognitive Science?

In its widest sense the term *cognitive science* is used to indicate that the study of mind is in itself a worthy scientific pursuit.[3] At this time cognitive science is not yet established as a mature science. It does not have a clearly agreed upon sense of direction and a large number of researchers constituting a community, as is the case with, say, atomic physics or molecular biology. Rather, it is really more of a loose affiliation of disciplines than a discipline of its own. Interestingly, an important pole is occupied by artificial intelligence—thus the computer model of the mind is a dominant aspect of the entire field. The other affiliated disciplines are generally taken to consist of linguistics, neuroscience, psychology, sometimes anthropology, and the philos-

ophy of mind. Each discipline would give a somewhat different answer to the question of what is mind or cognition, an answer that
would reflect its own specific concerns. The future development of
cognitive science is therefore far from clear, but what has already been
produced has had a distinct impact, and this may well continue to be
the case.

From Alexandre Koyré to Thomas Kuhn, modern historians and
philosophers have argued that scientific imagination mutates radically
from one epoch to another and that the history of science is more like
a novelistic saga than a linear progression. In other words, there is a
human history of nature, a story that is well worth telling in more
than one way. Alongside such a human history of nature there is a
corresponding history of ideas about human self-knowledge. Consider, for example, Greek physics and the Socratic method or
Montaigne's essays and early French science. This history of self-
knowledge in the West remains to be fully explored. Nonetheless, it
is fair to say that precursors of what we now call cognitive science
have been with us all along, since the human mind is the closest and
most familiar example of cognition and knowledge.

In this parallel history of mind and nature, the modern phase of
cognitive science may represent a distinct mutation. At this time,
science (i.e., the collection of scientists who define what science must
be) not only recognizes that the investigation of knowledge itself is
legitimate but also conceives of knowledge in a broad, interdisciplinary perspective, well beyond the traditional confines of epistemology and psychology. This mutation, only some thirty years old, was
dramatically introduced through the "cognitivist" program (discussed
later), much as the Darwinian program inaugurated the scientific
study of evolution even though others had been concerned with
evolution before.

Furthermore, through this mutation, knowledge has become tangibly and inextricably linked to a technology that transforms the social
practices which make that very knowledge possible—artificial intelligence being the most visible example. Technology, among other
things, acts as an amplifier. One cannot separate cognitive science
and cognitive technology without robbing one or the other of its vital
complementary element. Through technology, the scientific exploration of mind provides society at large with an unprecedented mirror
of itself, well beyond the circle of the philosopher, the psycholo-

gist, the therapist, or any individual seeking insight into his own experience.

This mirror reveals that for the first time Western society as a whole is confronted in its everyday life and activities with such issues as: Is mind a manipulation of symbols? Can language be understood by a machine? These concerns directly touch people's lives; they are not merely theoretical. Thus it is hardly surprising that there is a constant interest in the media about cognitive science and its associated technology and that artificial intelligence has deeply penetrated the minds of the young through computer games and science fiction. This popular interest is a sign of a deep transformation: For millenia human beings have had a spontaneous understanding of their own experience—one embedded in and nourished by the larger context of their time and culture. Now, however, this spontaneous folk understanding has become inextricably linked to science and can be transformed by scientific constructions.

Many deplore this event, while others rejoice. What is undeniable is that the event is happening, and at an ever increasing speed and depth. We feel that the creative interpenetration among research scientists, technologists, and the general public holds a potential for the profound transformation of human awareness. We find this possibility fascinating and see it as one of the most interesting adventures open to everyone today. We offer this book as (we hope) a meaningful contribution to that transformative conversation.

Throughout this book, we will emphasize the diversity of visions within cognitive science. In our eyes, cognitive science is not a monolithic field, though it does have, as does any social activity, poles of domination so that some of its participating voices acquire more force than others at various periods of time. Indeed, this sociological aspect of cognitive science is striking, for the "cognitive revolution" of the past four decades was strongly influenced through specific lines of research and funding in the United States.

Nevertheless, our bias here will be to emphasize diversity. We propose to look at cognitive science as consisting of three successive stages. These three stages will be taken up in parts II, III, and IV respectively. But to help orient the reader, we will provide a short overview of these stages here. We have drawn them in the form of a "polar" map with three concentric rings (figure 1.1). The three stages correspond to the successive movement from center to periphery; each ring indicates an important shift in the theoretical framework

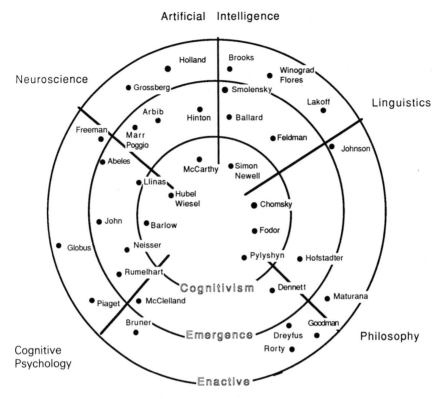

Figure 1.1
A conceptual chart of the cognitive sciences today in the form of a polar map, with the contributing disciplines in the angular dimensions and different approaches in the radial axis.

within cognitive science. Moving around the circle, we have placed the major disciplines that constitute the field of cognitive science. Thus we have a conceptual chart in which we can place the names of various researchers whose work is both representative and will appear in the discussion that follows.

We begin in part II with the center or core of cognitive science, known generally as *cognitivism*.[4] The central tool and guiding metaphor of cognitivism is the digital computer. A computer is a physical device built in such a way that a particular set of its physical changes can be interpreted as computations. A computation is an operation performed or carried out on symbols, that is, on elements that *represent* what they stand for. (For example, the symbol "7" represents the

Cognitivism

number 7.) Simplifying for the moment, we can say that cognitivism consists in the hypothesis that cognition—human cognition included—is the manipulation of symbols after the fashion of digital computers. In other words, cognition is *mental representation:* the mind is thought to operate by manipulating symbols that represent features of the world or represent the world as being a certain way. According to this cognitivist hypothesis, the study of cognition qua mental representation provides the proper domain of cognitive science, a domain held to be independent of neurobiology at one end and sociology and anthropology at the other.

Cognitivism has the virtue of being a well-defined research program, complete with prestigious institutions, journals, applied technology, and international commercial concerns. We refer to it as the center or core of cognitive science because it dominates research to such an extent that it is often simply taken to be cognitive science itself. In the past few years, however, several alternative approaches to cognition have appeared. These approaches diverge from cognitivism along two basic lines of dissent: (1) a critique of symbol processing as the appropriate vehicle for representations, and (2) a critique of the adequacy of the notion of representation as the Archimedes point for cognitive science.

The first alternative, which we call *emergence* and explore more fully in part III, is typically referred to as connectionism. This name is derived from the idea that many cognitive tasks (such as vision and memory) seem to be handled best by systems made up of many simple components, which, when connected by the appropriate rules, give rise to global behavior corresponding to the desired task. Symbolic processing, however, is localized. Operations on symbols can be specified using only the physical form of the symbols, not their meaning. Of course, it is this feature of symbols that enables one to build a physical device to manipulate them. The disadvantage is that the loss of any part of the symbols or the rules for their manipulation results in a serious malfunction. Connnectionist models generally trade localized, symbolic processing for distributed operations (ones that extend over an entire network of components) and so result in the emergence of global properties resilient to local malfunction. For connectionists a representation consists in the correspondence between such an emergent global state and properties of the world; it is not a function of particular symbols.

Emergence → Connectionist search for alternatives to symbolic processing.

The second alternative, which we explore and defend in part IV, is born from a deeper dissatisfaction than the connectionist search for alternatives to symbolic processing. It questions the centrality of the notion that cognition is fundamentally representation. Behind this notion stand three fundamental assumptions. The first is that we inhabit a world with particular properties, such as length, color, movement, sound, etc. The second is that we pick up or recover these properties by internally representing them. The third is that there is a separate subjective "we" who does these things. These three assumptions amount to a strong, often tacit and unquestioned, commitment to realism or objectivism/subjectivism about the way the world is, what we are, and how we come to know the world.

Even the most hard-nosed biologist, however, would have to admit that there are many ways that the world is—indeed even many different worlds of experience—depending on the structure of the being involved and the kinds of distinctions it is able to make. And even if we restrict our attention to human cognition, there are many various ways the world can be taken to be.[5] This nonobjectivist (and at best also nonsubjectivist) conviction is slowly growing in the study of cognition. As yet, however, this alternative orientation does not have a well-established name, for it is more of an umbrella that covers a relatively small group of people working in diverse fields. We propose as a name the term *enactive* to emphasize the growing conviction that cognition is not the representation of a pregiven world by a pregiven mind but is rather the enactment of a world and a mind on the basis of a history of the variety of actions that a being in the world performs. The enactive approach takes seriously, then, the philosophical critique of the idea that the mind is a mirror of nature but goes further by addressing this issue from within the heartland of science.[6]

Cognitive Science within the Circle

We began this chapter with a reflection on the fundamental circularity in scientific method that would be noted by a philosophically inclined cognitive scientist. From the standpoint of enactive cognitive science, this circularity is central; it is an epistemological necessity. In contrast, the other, more extant forms of cognitive science start from the view that cognition and mind are entirely due to the particular structures of cognitive systems. The most obvious expression of this view is

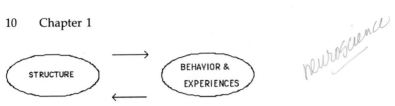

Figure 1.2
Interdependence or mutual specification of structure and behavior/experience.

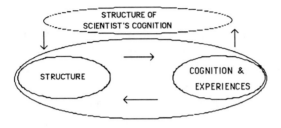

Figure 1.3
Interdependency of scientific description and our own cognitive structure.

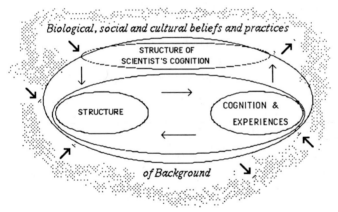

Figure 1.4
Interdependency of reflection and the background of biological, social, and cultural beliefs and practices.

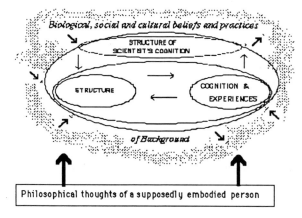

Figure 1.5
Interdependency of the background and embodiment.

found in neuroscience, where cognition is investigated by looking at the properties of the brain. One can associate these biologically based properties with cognition only through behavior. It is only because this structure, the brain, undergoes interactions in an environment that we can label the ensuing behavior as cognitive. The basic assumption, then, is that to every form of behavior and experience we can ascribe specific brain structures (however roughly). And, conversely, changes in brain structure manifest themselves in behavioral and experiential alterations. We may diagram this view as in figure 1.2. (In this diagram and those that follow, the double arrows express interdependence or mutual specification.)

Yet upon reflection we cannot avoid as a matter of consistency the logical implication that by this same view any such scientific description, either of biological or mental phenomena, must itself be a product of the structure of our own cognitive system. We may diagram this further understanding as in figure 1.3.

Furthermore, the act of reflection that tells us this does not come from nowhere; we find ourselves performing that act of reflection out of a given background (in the Heideggerian sense) of biological, social, and cultural beliefs and practices.[7] We portray this further step as in figure 1.4.

But then yet again, our very postulation of such a background is something that *we* are doing: we are *here*, living embodied beings, sitting and thinking of this entire scheme, including what we call a background. So, in all rigor, we should caption our entire endeavor with yet another layer indicating this embodiment here and now as in figure 1.5.

Plainly, this kind of layering could go on indefinitely, as in an Escher drawing. This last move makes it evident that, rather than adding layers of continued abstraction, we should go back where we started, to the concreteness and particularity of our own experience—even in the endeavor of reflection. The fundamental insight of the enactive approach as explored in this book is to be able to see our activities as reflections of a structure without losing sight of the directness of our own experience.

The Theme of This Book

This book is devoted to the exploration of this deep circularity. We will endeavor throughout to keep in mind our theoretical constructs about structure without losing sight of the immediacy of our experience.

Some aspects of the basic circularity of our condition have been discussed by philosophers in various ways at least since Hegel. The contemporary philosopher Charles Taylor refers to it when he says that we are "self-interpreting animals" and so wonders "whether features which are crucial to our self-understanding as agents can be accorded no place in our explanatory theory."[8] The usual response on the part of cognitive scientists is well put by Daniel Dennett when he writes that "every cognitivist theory currently defended or envisaged . . . is a theory of the sub-personal level. It is not at all clear to me, indeed, how a psychological theory—as distinct from a philosophical theory—could fail to be a sub-personal theory."[9] For Dennett, our self-understanding presupposes cognitive notions such as believing, desiring, and knowing but does not explain them. Therefore, if the study of mind is to be rigorous and scientific, it cannot be bound to explanations in terms of features essential to our self-understanding.

For the moment we wish simply to emphasize the deep tension in our present world between science and experience. In our present world science is so dominant that we give it the authority to explain even when it denies what is most immediate and direct—our everyday, immediate experience. Thus most people would hold as a fundamental truth the scientific account of matter/space as collections of atomic particles, while treating what is given in their immediate experience, with all of its richness, as less profound and true. Yet when we relax into the immediate bodily well-being of a sunny day or of the bodily tension of anxiously running to catch a bus, such accounts of space/matter fade into the background as abstract and secondary.

When it is cognition or mind that is being examined, the dismissal of experience becomes untenable, even paradoxical. The tension comes to the surface especially in cognitive science because cognitive science stands at the crossroads where the natural sciences and the human sciences meet. Cognitive science is therefore Janus-faced, for it looks down both roads at once: One of its faces is turned toward nature and sees cognitive processes as behavior. The other is turned toward the human world (or what phenomenologists call the "life-world") and sees cognition as experience.

[handwritten margin note: Cognition as (1) Behavior + (2) Experience]

When we ignore the fundamental circularity of our situation, this double face of cognitive science gives rise to two extremes: we suppose either that our human self-understanding is simply false and hence will eventually be replaced by a mature cognitive science, or we suppose that there can be no science of the human life-world because science must always presuppose it.

[handwritten margin note: Problem of Folk Psych.]

These two extremes summarize much of the general philosophical debate surrounding cognitive science. At one end stand philosophers such as Stephen Stich and Paul and Patricia Churchland who argue that our self-understanding is simply false.[10] (Note the Churchlands' suggestion that we might come to refer to brain states instead of experiences in actual daily discourse.) At the other end stand philosophers such as Hubert Dreyfus and Charles Taylor who seriously doubt the very possibility of cognitive science (perhaps because they often seem to accept the equation of cognitive science with cognitivism).[11] The debate thus recapitulates—though with new twists—the typical oppositions within the human sciences. If, in the midst of this confusion, the fate of human experience has been left to the philosophers, their lack of agreement does not bode well.

Unless we move beyond these oppositions, the rift between science and experience in our society will deepen. Neither extreme is workable for a pluralistic society that must embrace both science and the actuality of human experience. To deny the truth of our own experience in the scientific study of ourselves is not only unsatisfactory; it is to render the scientific study of ourselves without a subject matter. But to suppose that science cannot contribute to an understanding of our experience may be to abandon, within the modern context, the task of self-understanding. Experience and scientific understanding are like two legs without which we cannot walk.

We can phrase this very same idea in positive terms: it is only by having a sense of common ground between cognitive science and human experience that our understanding of cognition can be more complete and reach a satisfying level. We thus propose a constructive task: to enlarge the horizon of cognitive science to include the broader panorama of human, lived experience in a disciplined, transformative analysis. As a constructive task, the search for this expansion becomes motivated by scientific research itself, as we will see throughout this work.

2

What Do We Mean "Human Experience"?

Science and the Phenomenological Tradition

Our formulation in the previous chapter obviously owes much to the philosophy of Merleau-Ponty. We invoke him because in our Western tradition he seems to be one of the few whose work was committed to an exploration of the fundamental entre-deux between science and experience, experience and world. Another reason is that Merleau-Ponty was committed to seeing this circularity from the vantage point of what corresponded to cognitive science in his time—the emerging work in neuropsychology that was being pioneered in France. In his first major work, *The Structure of Behavior*,[1] Merleau-Ponty argued for the mutual illumination among a phenomenology of direct lived experience, psychology, and neurophysiology. Clearly this complementary style of work, the backbone of our concern in this book, was not taken up much further. The scientific tradition moved west to a predominantly positivist environment in the United States, and it is from there that the modern cognitive sciences familiar to us today were formed. We will come back to these formative years of cognitive science in the next chapter.

Throughout his writings, Merleau-Ponty drew on the earlier work of the German philosopher, Edmund Husserl. Husserl emphasized the importance of a direct examination of experience in a way that was radical, and yet deeply tied to the Western philosophical tradition. Descartes had seen the mind as a subjective consciousness that contained ideas that corresponded (or sometimes failed to correspond) to what was in the world. This view of the mind as representing the world reached its culmination in Franz Brentano's notion of *intentionality*. According to Brentano, all mental states (perception, memory, etc.) are *of* or *about* something; in his words, mental states necessarily have "reference to a content" or "direction toward an object" (which is not necessarily a thing in the world).[2] This directed-

ness or intentionality, Brentano claimed, was the defining characteristic of the mind. (This use of *intentional* should not be confused with
its use to mean "doing something on purpose.")

Husserl was a student of Brentano's and greatly extended his work.
In one of his major works, *Ideas: General Introduction to a Pure Phenomenology*,[3] published in 1913, Husserl tried to develop a specific procedure for examining the structure of intentionality, which was the
structure of experience itself, without any reference to the factual,
empirical world. He called this procedure "bracketing" (*epoché*), for it
required that one put out of action, as if in brackets, one's ordinary
judgments about the relation between experience and the world. The
standpoint from which these ordinary judgments are made Husserl
called the "natural attitude"; it is the attitude generally known as
"naive realism," which consists in the conviction not only that the
world is independent of mind or cognition but that things generally
are the way they appear. By bracketing the thesis of the natural
attitude, Husserl claimed to be able to study the intentional contents
of the mind purely internally, that is, without tracing them back to
what they seemed to refer to in the world. By this procedure he
claimed to have discovered a new domain that was prior to any
empirical science. In *Ideas*, Husserl set out to explore this new domain
by reflecting purely upon consciousness and discerning its essential
structures. In a sort of philosophical introspection—which he called
the "intuition of essences" (*Wesenschau*)—Husserl tried to reduce experience to these essential structures and then show how our human
world was generated from them.

Husserl thus took the first step of the reflective scientist: he claimed
that to understand cognition, we cannot take the world naively but
must see it instead as having the mark of our own structure. He also
took the second step, at least partially, in realizing that that structure
(the first step) was something that he was cognizing with his own
mind. In the philosophical fashion of his Western tradition, however,
he did not take the further steps we discussed in chapter 1. He began
with a solitary individual consciousness, took the structure he was
seeking to be entirely mental and accessible to consciousness in an
act of abstract philosophical introspection, and from there had great
difficulty in generating the consensual, intersubjective world of
human experience.[4] And having no method other than his own philosophical introspection, he certainly could not take the final move
which would return him to his experience, back to the beginning of

the process. The irony of Husserl's procedure, then, is that although he claimed to be turning philosophy toward a direct facing of experience, he was actually ignoring both the consensual aspect and the direct embodied aspect of experience. (In this Husserl followed Descartes: he called his phenomenology a twentieth-century Cartesianism.) It is not surprising, therefore, that younger European philosophers turned increasingly away from pure phenomenology to embrace existentialism.

Husserl recognized some of these problems in his later work. In his last work, *The Crisis of European Sciences and Transcendental Phenomenology*,[5] he once more took up the task of articulating the basis and method of phenomenological reflection. Here, however, he explicitly focused on the experience of consciousness in what he called the "lived-world." The lived world is not the naive, theoretical conception of the world found in the natural attitude. It is, rather, the everyday social world, in which theory is always directed toward some practical end.[6] Husserl argued that all reflection, all theoretical activity, including science, presupposes the life-world as a background. The task of the phenomenologist now became the analysis of the *essential relation* between consciousness, experience, and this life-world.

For Husserl, this analysis had to be undertaken for an additional reason: the role of the life-world had become obscured by the dominance of the objectivist conception of science. Husserl refered to this view as the "Galilean style" in science, for it consists in taking the idealized formulations of mathematical physics as descriptions of the way the world really is independent of the knowing subject. He disputed the equation of science in general with this specific style. But his argument was not directed against the scientific description of the world per se. Indeed, he wished to revitalize the natural sciences against what he perceived to be the rising tide of irrationalism in philosophy (which he took to be symptomatic of the "crisis" of European life in general). It was the equation of the Galilean style with all of science that obscured the relation between science and the life-world and so made impossible any philosophical grounding of the claims of the empirical sciences.

The solution to the problem, Husserl thought, was to expand the notion of science to include a new science of the life-world—pure phenomenology—which would link science and experience without succumbing to the objectivism of the Galilean style on the one hand and the irrationalism of existentialism on the other.

The Breakdown of Phenomenology

Even in *The Crisis*, Husserl insisted that phenomenology is the study of essences. Thus the analysis of the life-world that he undertook there was not anthropological or historical; it was philosophical. But if all theoretical activity presupposes the life-world, what, then, of phenomenology? It is a distinctly theoretical pursuit; indeed, Husserl claimed it is the very highest form of theory. But then phenomenology too must presuppose the life-world, even as it attempts to explicate it. Thus Husserl was being haunted by the untraversed steps of the fundamental circularity.

Husserl recognized some of this circularity and tried to deal with it in an interesting way. He argued that the life-world was really a set of sedimented, background *preunderstandings* or (roughly speaking) assumptions, which the phenomenologist could make explicit and treat as a system of beliefs. In other words, Husserl tried to break out of the circle by treating the background as consisting essentially of representations.[7] Once the life-world is construed in this way, however, Husserl's claim (indeed, the central claim of phenomenology) that the life-world is always prior to science becomes unstable. If the background consists of representations, what is to prevent scientific knowledge from permeating the background and contributing to its tacit store of beliefs? And if such permeation is possible, then what happens to the priority of phenomenology?

Husserl must have recognized these problems because he argued both that the life-world is prior to science and that our Western tradition is unique because our life-world is permeated by science. The task of the phenomenologist was to move back from an analysis of our scientifically permeated life-world to the "original" or "pre-given" life-world. But Husserl held on to the idea that this original life-world could be exhaustively accounted for by tracing it back to the essential structures of consciousness. He thus embraced the peculiar thought that the phenomenologist could stand both inside and outside of the life-world: he stood inside because all theory presupposed the life-world, and yet he stood outside because phenomenology alone could trace the genesis of the life-world in consciousness. Indeed, phenomenology was the highest form of theory for Husserl precisely because it was capable of such a peculiar contortion.[8]

Given this peculiar contortion, it is not surprising that Husserl's pure phenomenology was not (as he hoped it would be) cultivated and improved on from one generation to the next, unlike other methodological discoveries such as the methods for statistical inference. Indeed, it has been the headache of later commentators to find out just exactly how his method of "phenomenological reduction" is to proceed.

But there is a deeper reason for the failure of the Husserlian project that we wish to emphasize here: Husserl's turn toward experience and "the things themselves" was entirely *theoretical*, or, to make the point the other way around, it completely lacked any *pragmatic* dimension. It is hardly surprising, therefore, that it could not overcome the rift between science and experience, for science, unlike phenomenological reflection, has a life beyond theory. Thus although Husserl's turn toward a phenomenological analysis of experience seemed radical, it was, in fact, quite within the mainstream of Western philosophy.

Indeed, this criticism would hold even for Heidegger's existential phenomenology, as well as for Merleau-Ponty's phenomenology of lived experience. Both stressed the pragmatic, embodied context of human experience, but in a purely theoretical way. Despite the fact that one of Heidegger's chief arguments against Husserl was the impossibility of separating lived experience from the consensual background of cultural beliefs and practices, despite the fact that in a Heideggerian analysis one cannot, strictly speaking, speak of a human mind at all apart from that background, still Heidegger considered phenomenology the true method of ontology, a theoretical inquiry into human existence (*Dasein*) that was logically prior to any form of scientific investigation. Merleau-Ponty took Heidegger one step further by applying Heidegger's own criticism to phenomenology itself as well as to science. In Merleau-Ponty's view, both science and phenomenology explicated our concrete, embodied existence in a manner that was always after the fact. It attempted to grasp the immediacy of our unreflective experience and tried to give voice to it in conscious reflection. But precisely by being a theoretical activity after the fact, it could not recapture the richness of experience; it could be only a discourse about that experience. Merleau-Ponty admitted this in his own way by saying that his task was infinite.[9]

Within our Western tradition, phenomenology was and still is *the* philosophy of human experience, the only extant edifice of thought that addresses these issues head-on. But above all, it was and still is philosophy as theoretical reflection. In most of the Western tradition since the Greeks, philosophy has been the discipline that seeks to find the truth, including the truth about the mind, purely by means of abstract, theoretical reasoning. Even philosophers who critique or problematize reason do so only by means of arguments, demonstrations, and—especially in our so-called postmodern era—linguistic exhibitions (i.e., by means of abstract thought). Merleau-Ponty's critique of science and phenomenology, that they are theoretical activities after the fact, can equally be applied to most of Western philosophy as theoretical reflection. In this way, the loss of faith in reason so rampant in current thought becomes simultaneously a loss of faith in philosophy.

But if we turn away from reason, if reason is no longer taken as the method for knowing the mind, what can be used instead? One alternative is *un*reason, and, in the form of psychoanalytic theory, it has probably come to have more influence on our Western folk conception of the mind than any other single cultural factor. People—certainly middle-class North Americans and Europeans—have come to believe that they have an unconscious that is developmentally and symbolically primitive. They believe that both dreams and much of their waking life—motives, fantasies, preferences, aversions, emotions, behaviors, and pathological symptoms—are explainable by means of this unconscious. Thus, in the folk view, to know the mind "from the inside" is to use some version of psychoanalytic method to delve into the unconscious.

This "folk psychoanalytic" view is subject to the same critique that Merleau-Ponty made of science and phenomenology. The psychoanalytic method works within an individual's conceptual system. Whether an individual is commenting on a free association or using mathematical logic, having an ordinary waking conversation or dealing with the highly convoluted symbolic language of dreams, that person is knowing the mind and commenting on it in an after-the-fact fashion. The "professional" psychoanalyst knows, however, that he has to work within an individual's conceptual system and that a method that no theory can substitute for is required to go beyond this stage. What we find particularly interesting about psychoanalysis is that despite its great differences from cognitive science—despite the fact that it deals with phenomena of mind that are quite different from the normal subject matter of cognitive science and studies them by

patently different methods—we see some of the same stages of evolution that we identify in cognitive science mirrored in psychoanalytic
theory. We shall point to the convergences in future chapters. We
hasten to add that such pointing will only be in the spirit of providing
place markers, as it were, not carefully constructed bridges, since we
do not have firsthand experiences in a psychoanalytic process.

We are still in need of a method, however. Where can we turn for
a tradition that can provide an examination of human experience in
both its reflective and its immediate, lived aspects?

A Non-Western Philosophical Tradition

At this point, a bold step needs to be taken, one that takes us to the
heart of what we have to present: we need to enlarge our horizon to
encompass non-Western traditions of reflection upon experience. If
philosophy in the West no longer occupies a privileged, foundational
position with respect to other cultural activities such as science or art,
then a full appreciation of philosophy and its importance for human
experience requires that we examine the role of philosophy in cultures
other than our own. In our culture, cognitive science has caused great
excitement among philosophers (and the public at large) because it
has enabled them to see their tradition in a new light. Were we to
entertain the idea that there is no hard-and-fast distinction between
science and philosophy, then philosophers such as Descartes, Locke,
Leibniz, Hume, Kant, and Husserl would take on a new significance:
they could be seen, among other things, as protocognitive scientists.
(Or as Jerry Fodor puts it, "In intellectual history, everything happens
twice, first as philosophy and then as cognitive science."[10]) Might this
not also be the case for philosophical traditions with which we are
less familiar?

In this book we will focus on one such tradition, that which derives
from the Buddhist method of examining experience called *mindfulness
meditation*. We believe that the Buddhist doctrines of no-self and of
nondualism that grew out of this method have a significant contribution to make in a dialogue with cognitive science: (1) The no-self
doctrine contributes to understanding the fragmentation of self portrayed in cognitivism and connectionism. (2) Buddhist nondualism,
particularly as it is presented in the Madhyamika (which literally
means "middle way") philosophy of Nagarjuna, may be juxtaposed

with the entre-deux of Merleau-Ponty and with the more recent ideas of cognition as enaction.[11]

It is our contention that the rediscovery of Asian philosophy, particularly of the Buddhist tradition, is a second renaissance in the cultural history of the West, with the potential to be equally important as the rediscovery of Greek thought in the European renaissance. Our Western histories of philosophy, which ignore Indian thought, are artificial, since India and Greece share with us an Indo-European linguistic heritage as well as many cultural and philosophical preoccupations.[12]

There is, however, a more important reason for our interest. In the Indian tradition, philosophy never became a purely abstract occupation. It was tied ("yoked," as is traditionally said) to specific disciplined methods for knowing—different methods of meditation. In particular, within the Buddhist tradition, the method of mindfulness was considered fundamental. Mindfulness means that the mind is present in embodied everyday experience; mindfulness techniques are designed to lead the mind back from its theories and preoccupations, back from the abstract attitude, to the situation of one's experience itself.[13] Furthermore, and equally of interest in the modern context, the descriptions and commentaries on mind that grew out of this tradition never became divorced from living pragmatics: they were intended to inform an individual as to how to handle his mind in personal and interpersonal situations, and they both informed and became embodied in the structure of communities.

We are currently, in the West, in an ideal position to study Buddhism in its fully embodied aspects. First, the current trend for global integration and the growing impact of non-Western traditions have made it possible to appreciate that the designation and delineation of "religion" in the West is itself a cultural artifact that may, if taken literally, seriously hamper our understanding of other traditions. Second, in the last two decades Buddhism has actually taken root in Western countries and has begun to flourish as a living tradition. We have a historically unique situation in which the many culturally diverse forms that Buddhism assumed have been transplanted to the same geographical locations and are interacting with each other and with their host cultures. For example, in some of the large cities of North America and Europe, within walking distance of each other one might find centers representing all of the major forms of Buddhism in the world—the Theravadin traditions of Southeast Asia, the

Mahayana forms from Vietnam, China, Korea, and Japan, and the Vajrayana of Japan and Tibet. Whereas some centers represent religious institutions of a particular ethnic immigrant population, many are composed of Westerners who, under the guidance of traditionally sactioned teachers, are practicing and studying the form of Buddhism with which they are connected and are experimenting with how their particular teachings are to be acted out individually and communally in the sociocultural context of the modern Western world.

These factors are a great boon to the contemporary study of Buddhism, whether by interested individuals, scholars, or by the social and cognitive sciences. Unlike the initial introduction of Greek thought during the Renaissance, we are not dependent for our knowledge of Buddhist practices and ideas on the interpretation of a few fragmentary, historical, hermeneutically isolated texts—we can observe what texts are actually taught, how they are interpreted and used, and how, in general, the meditations, practices, and explicit teachings of Buddhism are being transmitted within the living practices of these developing Buddhist communities. We will rely not only on scholarship but also on these indigenous teachings in the presentations that follow.[14]

Examining Experience with a Method: Mindfulness/Awareness

There are many human activities of body and mind, both Buddhist and non-Buddhist. The word *meditation* in its general usage in modern America has a number of different prominent folk meanings:[15] (1) a state of concentration in which consciousness is focused on only one object; (2) a state of relaxation that is psychologically and medically beneficial; (3) a dissociated state in which trance phenomena can occur; and (4) a mystical state in which higher realities or religious objects are experienced. These are all altered states of consciousness; the meditator is doing something to get away from his usual mundane, unconcentrated, unrelaxed, nondissociated, lower state of reality.

Buddhist mindfulness/awareness practice is intended to be just the opposite of these. Its purpose is to become mindful, to experience what one's mind is doing as it does it, to be present with one's mind. What relevance does this have for cognitive science? We believe that if cognitive science is to include human experience, it must have some method for exploring and knowing what human experience is. It is for this reason that we are focusing on the Buddhist tradition of mindfulness meditation.

To get a sense of what mindfulness meditation is, one must first realize the extent to which people are normally not mindful. Usually one notices the tendency of the mind to wander only when one is attempting to accomplish some mental task and the wandering interferes. Or perhaps one realizes that one has just finished an anticipated pleasurable activity without noticing it. In fact, body and mind are seldom closely coordinated. In the Buddhist sense, we are not present.

How can this mind become an instrument for knowing itself? How can the flightiness, the nonpresence of mind be worked with? Traditionally, texts talk about two stages of practice: calming or taming the mind (Sanscrit: *shamatha*) and the development of insight (Sanscrit: *vipashyana*).[16] Shamatha, when used as a separate practice, is in fact a concentration technique for learning to hold ("tether" is the traditional term) the mind to a single object. Such concentration could eventually lead to states of blissful absorption; although such states were assiduously cataloged within Buddhist psychology, they were not generally recommended. The purpose of calming the mind in Buddhism is not to become absorbed but to render the mind able to be present with itself long enough to gain insight into its own nature and functioning. (There are many traditional analogies for this process. For example, to be able to see paintings on the wall of a dark cave, one needs a good light protected from the wind.) Most present-day schools of Buddhism do not practice shamatha and vipashyana as separate techniques but rather combine the functions of calming and of insight into a single meditation technique. (Some of the terminological confusions that result are, we hope, clarified in appendix A). We will refer here to these types of meditation by their more experiential designations as mindfulness/awareness meditation.

The description of mindfulness/awareness meditation that follows is based on the writings and oral presentations of traditional teachers and on observations, interviews, and discussions with present-day students of Buddhism from the major Buddhist traditions. Typically mindfulness/awareness is trained by means of formal periods of sitting meditation. The purpose of such periods is to simplify the situation to the bare minimum. The body is put into an upright posture and held still. Some simple object, often the breath, is used as the focus of alert attention. Each time the meditator realizes that his mind is wandering unmindfully, he is to acknowledge nonjudgmentally that wandering (there are various instructions as to how this is to be done) and bring the mind back to its object.

Breathing is one of the most simple, basic, ever-present bodily activities. Yet beginning meditators are generally astonished at how difficult it is to be mindful of even so uncomplex an object. Meditators discover that mind and body are not coordinated. The body is sitting, but the mind is seized constantly by thoughts, feelings, inner conversations, daydreams, fantasies, sleepiness, opinions, theories, judgments about thoughts and feelings, judgments about judgments—a never-ending torrent of disconnected mental events that the meditators do not even realize are occurring except at those brief instants when they remember what they are doing. Even when they attempt to return to their object of mindfulness, the breath, they may discover that they are only thinking about the breath rather than being mindful of the breath.

Eventually, it begins to dawn on the meditators that there is an actual difference between being present and not being present. In daily life they also begin to have instants of waking up to the realization that they are not present and of flashing back for a moment to be present—not to the breath, in this case, but to whatever is going on. Thus the first great discovery of mindfulness meditation tends to be not some encompassing insight into the nature of mind but the piercing realization of just how disconnected humans normally are from their very experience. Even the simplest or most pleasurable of daily activities—walking, eating, conversing, driving, reading, waiting, thinking, making love, planning, gardening, drinking, remembering, going to a therapist, writing, dozing, emoting, sightseeing—all pass rapidly in a blur of abstact commentary as the mind hastens to its next mental occupation. The meditator now discovers that the abstract attitude which Heidegger and Merleau-Ponty ascribe to science and philosophy is actually the attitude of everyday life when one is not mindful. This abstract attitude is the spacesuit, the padding of habits and preconceptions, the armor with which one habitually distances oneself from one's experience.

From the point of view of mindfulness/awareness meditation, humans are not trapped forever in the abstract attitude. The dissociation of mind from body, of awareness from experience, is the result of habit, and these habits can be broken. As the meditator again and again interrupts the flow of discursive thought and returns to be present with his breath or daily activity, there is a gradual taming of the mind's restlessness. One begins to be able to see the restlessness as such and to become patient with it, rather than becoming automatically lost in it.[17] Eventually meditators report periods of a more panoramic perspective. This is called awareness. At this point the breath is no longer needed as a focus. In one traditional analogy, mindfulness is likened to the individual words of a sentence, whereas awareness is the grammar that encompasses the entire sentence. Meditators also report experiencing space and spaciousness of mind. A traditional metaphor for this experience is that mind is the sky (a nonconceptual background) in which different mental contents, like clouds, arise and subside. Experience of panoramic awareness and of space are natural outgrowths of mindfulness/awareness meditation, since they begin to occur in meditators not only in Buddhist traditions where they have doctrinal significance and where they are thus encouraged but also in those traditions where they are discouraged (some Theravadin schools) and where specific antidotes to them then need to be applied. In those traditions, the development of practice is focused on increased intensity of mindfulness.

How is it that mindfulness/awareness can develop? There are two traditional approaches to talking about this. In one, the development is treated as the training of good habits. The mental fact of mindfulness is being strengthened like the training of a muscle that can then perform harder and longer work without tiring. In the other approach, mindfulness/awareness is considered part of the basic nature of the mind; it is the natural state of mind that has been temporarily obscured by habitual patterns of grasping and delusion. The untamed mind constantly tries to grasp some stable point in its unending movement and to cling to thoughts, feelings, and concepts as if they were a solid ground. As all these habits are cut through and one learns an attitude of letting go, the mind's natural characteristic of knowing itself and reflecting its own experience can shine forth. This is the beginning of wisdom or maturity (*prajña*).

It is important to realize that such maturity does not mean assuming the abstract attitude. As Buddhist teachers often point out, knowledge, in the sense of prajña, is not knowledge *about* anything. There is no abstract knower of an experience that is separate from the experience itself. Buddhist teachers often talk of becoming one with one's experience. What, then, are the contents or discoveries of this wisdom?

The Role of Reflection in the Analysis of Experience

If the results of mindfulness/awareness practice are to bring one closer to one's ordinary experience rather than further from it, what can be the role of reflection? One of our popular cultural images of Buddhism is that the intellect is destroyed. In fact, study and contemplation play a major role in all Buddhist schools. The spontaneous action, much dramatized in the popular image of the Zen master, is not contradictory to the use of reflection as a mode of learning. How can this be?

This question brings us to the methodological heart of the interaction between mindfulness/awareness meditation, phenomenology, and cognitive science. What we are suggesting is a change in the nature of reflection from an abstract, disembodied activity to an embodied (mindful), open-ended reflection. By *embodied*, we mean reflection in which body and mind have been brought together. What this formulation intends to convey is that reflection is not just *on* experience, but reflection *is* a form of experience itself—and that reflective form of experience can be performed with mindfulness/awareness. When reflection is done in that way, it can cut the chain of habitual thought patterns and preconceptions such that it can be an open-ended reflection, open to possibilities other than those contained in one's current representations of the life space. We call this form of reflection *mindful, open-ended reflection.*

In our usual training and practice as Western scientists and philosophers, we obviously proceed differently. We ask, "What is mind?", "What is body?" and proceed to reflect theoretically and to investigate scientifically. This procedure gives rise to a gamut of claims, experiments, and results on various facets of cognitive abilities. But in the course of these investigations we often forget just who is asking this question and how it is asked. By not including ourselves in the reflection, we pursue only a partial reflection, and our question becomes disembodied; it attempts to express, in the words of the philosopher Thomas Nagel, a "view from nowhere."[18] It is ironic that it is just this attempt to have a disembodied view from nowhere that leads to having a view from a very specific, theoretically confined, preconceptually entrapped somewhere.

The phenomenological tradition, from Husserl on, complained bitterly about this lack of self-included reflection but was able to offer in its place only a project of theoretical reflection *on* experience. The other extreme is to include the self but abandon reflection altogether

Self included reflection

in favor of a naive, subjective impulsivity. Mindfulness/awareness is neither of these; it works directly with, and so expresses, our basic embodiment.

Let us see how the difference in the theoretical and the mindfulness traditions of reflection manifest in an actual issue—the so-called mind-body problem. From Descartes on, the guiding question in Western philosophy has been whether body and mind are one or two distinct substances (properties, levels of description, etc.) and what the ontological relation between them is. We have already seen the simple, experiential, pragmatic approach taken in mindfulness/aware-ness meditation. It is a matter of simple experience that our mind and body can be dissociated, that the mind can wander, that we can be unaware of where we are and what our body or mind are doing.[19] But this situation, this habit of mindlessness, can be changed. Body and mind can be brought together. We can develop habits in which body and mind are fully coordinated. The result is a mastery that is not only known to the individual meditator himself but that is visible to others—we easily recognize by its precision and grace a gesture that is animated by full awareness. We typically associate such mind-fulness with the actions of an expert such as an athlete or musician.

We are suggesting that Descartes's conclusion that he was a think-ing thing was the product of his question, and that question was a product of specific practices—those of disembodied, unmindful re-flection. Husserlian phenomenology, though it embraced experience in a radical way, nonetheless continued the tradition by reflecting only upon the essential structures of thought. And even though it has recently become quite fashionable to criticize or "deconstruct" this standpoint of the *cogito*, philosophers still do not depart from the basic *practice* responsible for it.

Theoretical reflection need not be mindless and disembodied. The basic assertion of this progressive approach to human experience is that the mind-body relation or modality is not simply fixed and given but can be fundamentally changed. Many people would acknowledge the obvious truth of this conviction. Western philosophy does not deny this truth so much as ignore it.

To expand this point: As is the case with mindfulness in general, there are two ways of talking about the development of embodied reflection. One way—a preliminary or beginner's approach—is to liken it to the development of a skill. Take learning to play a flute. The description goes thus: One is shown the basic positions of the fingers, perhaps directly or in the form of a fingering chart. One then practices these notes in various combinations over and over until a basic skill is acquired. In the beginning, the relation between mental intention and bodily act is quite undeveloped—mentally one knows what to do, but one is physically unable to do it. As one practices, the connection between intention and act becomes closer, until eventually the feeling of difference between them is almost entirely gone. One achieves a certain condition that phenomenologically feels neither purely mental nor purely physical; it is, rather, a specific kind of mind-body unity. And, of course, there are many levels of possible interpretation, as can be seen in the variety of accomplished performers.

Although such examples may seem compelling and although meditation instructions for beginners sometimes make mindfulness sound like the development of a skill, description of the process only in these terms can actually be quite misleading. Contemplative traditions from around the world agree that if one thinks the point of meditative practice is to develop special skills and make oneself into a religous, philosophical, or meditative virtuoso, then one is engaging in self-deception and is actually going in the opposite direction. In particular, the practices involved in the development of mindfulness/awareness are virtually never described as the training of meditative virtuosity (and certainly not as the development of a higher, more evolved spirituality)[20] but rather as the letting go of habits of mindlessness, as an *un*learning rather than a learning. This unlearning may take training and effort, but it is a different sense of effort from the acquiring of something new. It is precisely when the meditator approaches the development of mindfulness with the greatest ambitions—the ambition to acquire a new skill through determination and effort—that his mind fixates and races, and mindfulness/awareness is most elusive. This is why the tradition of mindfulness/awareness meditation talks about effortless efforts and why it uses the analogy for meditation of tuning, rather than playing, a stringed instrument—the instrument must be tuned neither too tightly nor too loosely. When the mindfulness meditator finally begins to let go rather than to struggle to achieve some particular state of activity, then body and mind are found to be naturally coordinated and embodied. Mindful reflection is then found to be a completely natural activity. The importance of the distinction between skill and letting go should become increasingly apparent as we continue our story.

In summary it is because reflection in our culture has been severed from its bodily life that the mind-body problem has become a central topic for abstract reflection. Cartesian dualism is not so much one competing solution as it is the formulation of this problem. Reflection is taken to be distinctively mental, and so the problem arises of how it could ever be linked to bodily life. Although contemporary discussions of this problem have become quite sophisticated—largely because of the development of cognitive science—they have nevertheless not departed from the essentially Cartesian problematic of trying to understand how two seemingly distinct things are related.[21] (Whether these things are substances, properties, or merely levels of description rarely makes a difference to the basic structure of the discussion.)

From the standpoint of a mindful, open-ended reflection the mind-body question need not be, What is the ontological relation between body and mind, regardless of anyone's experience?—but rather, What are the relations of body and mind in actual experience (the mindfulness aspect), and how do these relations develop, what forms can they take (the open-ended aspect)? As the Japanese philosopher Yasuo Yuasa remarks, "One starts from the experiential assumption that the mind-body modality changes through the training of the mind and body by means of cultivation (*shugyo*) or training (*keiko*). Only after assuming this experiential ground does one ask what the mind-body relation is. That is, the mind-body issue is not simply a theoretical speculation but it is originally a practical, lived experience (*taiken*), involving the mustering of one's whole mind and body. The theoretical is only a reflection on this lived experience."[22]

We may notice that this viewpoint is resonant with pragmatism, a view in philosophy that is having a modern revival.[23] The body and mind relation is known in terms of what it can do. When one takes the more abstract attitude in philosophy or science, one might think that questions about the body-mind relation can be answered only after one first satisfactorily determines what is body and what is mind in isolation and abstraction. In the pragmatic, open-ended reflection, however, these questions are not separate from "the mustering of one's whole mind and body." Such involvement prevents the question, What is mind? from becoming disembodied. When we include in our reflection on a question the asker of the question and the process of asking itself (recall the fundamental circularity), then the question receives a new life and meaning.

Perhaps the closest discipline familiar to Westerners that verges on a pragmatic, open-ended view toward knowledge is psychoanalysis. We have in mind not so much the content of psychoanalytic theory but rather the idea that the very conception of mind and of the subject who is undergoing analysis is understood to change as the web of representations in which the self is entangled is slowly penetrated through analysis. What we believe traditional psychoanalytic methods lack, however, is the mindfulness/awareness component of reflection.

Experimentation and Experiential Analysis

The form most closely allied to pragmatism in science is the experimental method. If one wants to know how many teeth a horse has, one counts the teeth. More elaborate hypotheses are theoretically reduced to possible observations by means of deductive inferences. Although the philosophical theory of such experimentation has been historically tied to an objectivist, disembodied view of knowledge, it need not be.

Can mindfulness/awareness meditation be considered a kind of experimentation that makes discoveries about the nature and behavior of mind—a kind of experimentation that is embodied and open-ended? As we have already mentioned, in mindfulness/awareness meditation one does not begin by trying to attain some specific state (as in concentrations, relaxations, trances, or mystically oriented practices); rather, the goal is to be mindful of the mind as it takes its own course. By letting go of the mind in this way, the natural activity of the mind to be alert and observant becomes apparent.

Buddhist doctrines lay claim to being simply the observations that mind makes when it is allowed to be naturally observant. Indeed, all of the Buddhist assertions (lack of self, the codependent arising of experience, and so on) are treated by Buddhist teachers as discoveries rather than creeds or doctrines. Buddhist teachers are fond of pointing out that students are always invited, indeed required, to doubt such assertions and to test them directly in their own experience rather than to accept them as beliefs. (Of course if they come up with a drastically deviant answer, they might be invited to look again— much as it happens with scientific teaching in its normal form.)

There are two objections that could be raised to the claim that mindfulness/awareness is a means of discovery about the nature of experience. In the first place, one might wonder about the relationship between knowledge gained by means of meditation and the activity that we call introspection. After all, introspectionism as a school of psychology, made popular by the nineteenth-century psychologist Wilhelm Wundt, failed definitively to provide a basis for experimental psychology. There was no agreement at all among different laboratories of introspection on what results were yielded by the introspectionist method—the very antithesis of science. But what was this method called introspection? Each laboratory began with a theory that experience was decomposable into certain kinds of elements, and subjects were trained to decompose their experience in that fashion. A subject was asked to look at his own experience as an outside observer would. This is, in fact, what we usually think of as introspection in daily life. This is the very essence of what Merleau-Ponty and Heidegger called the abstract attitude of the scientist and the philosopher. The mindfulness meditator would say that the introspectionists were not actually aware of mind at all; they were just thinking about their thoughts. Such an activity, would, of course, serve only to display whatever preconceptions one is holding about the mind—no wonder different laboratories disagreed with one another. It is precisely to cut through the attitude of introspection that mindfulness/awareness meditation exists.

The second objection that could be raised to mindfulness/awareness as a method of observation of the mind in situ is that by meditating or becoming mindful and aware, one is disrupting one's normal mode of being in the world, one's active involvement and one's taken for granted sense of the world's independent reality. How can mindfulness, then, give us any information about that normal mode of being that it disrupts? Our answer is that this question, to have meaning, must itself presuppose the abstract attitude; one is reflecting back upon the active involvement and saying it is or is not disrupted as though this could be perceived from some independent, abstract vantage point of knowledge. From the Buddhist perspective, it is only by means of natural mindfulness that Heidegger and Merleau-Ponty could ever have known about a normal mode of active involvement in the world in the first place. (Merleau-Ponty virtually says as much himself in his preface to *Phenomenology of Perception*.) What mindfulness disrupts is mindlessness—that is, being mindlessly involved without realizing that that is what one is doing. It is only in this sense that the observation changes what is being observed, and that is part of what we mean by open-ended reflection.

In conclusion, we have argued that it is necessary to have a disciplined perspective on human experience that can enlarge the domain of cognitive science to include direct experience. We suggest such a perspective already exists in the form of mindfulness/awareness meditation. Mindfulness/awareness practice, phenomenological philosophy, and science are human activities; each is an expression of our human embodiment. Naturally, Buddhist doctrine, Western phenomenology, and science are each heir to numerous doctrinal disputes and conflicting claims. Each, however, insofar as it is a form of experimentation, is open to everyone and may be examined with the methods of each of the others. Thus, we believe that mindfulness/awareness meditation can provide a natural bridge between cognitive science and human experience. Particularly impressive to us is the convergence that we have discovered among some of the main themes of Buddhist doctrine, phenomenology, and cognitive science—themes concerning the self and the relation between subject and object. It is to these themes that we now turn in our journey of discovery.

II
Varieties of Cognitivism

3

Symbols: The Cognitivist Hypothesis

The Foundational Cloud

Our exploration of cognitive science and human experience begins in this chapter with an examination of cognitivism—the center of our diagram in chapter 1—and its historical origins in the earlier, cybernetic era of cognitive science. The main idea to be presented in part II is that the analysis of mind undertaken by certain traditions of mindfulness/awareness provides a natural counterpart to present-day cognitivist conceptions of mind. This chapter presents the cognitivist perspective; in the next chapter we will discuss some conclusions, in some respects similar, reached by means of mindfulness/awareness.

Let us begin by looking at the historical roots of present-day cognitivism. This short historical excursion is necessary, for a science that neglects its past is bound to repeat its mistakes and will be unable to visualize its development. Our excursion here is, of course, not intended to be a comprehensive history but only to touch on those issues of direct relevance for our concerns here.[1]

In fact, virtually all of the themes in present-day debates were already introduced in the formative years of cognitive science from 1943 to 1953. History indicates, then, that these themes are deep and hard to pursue. The "founding fathers" knew very well that their concerns amounted to a new science, and they christened this science with the new name *cybernetics*. This name is no longer in current use, and many cognitive scientists today would not even recognize the family connections. This lack of recognition is not idle. It reflects the fact that to become established as a science in its clear-cut cognitivist orientation, the future cognitive science had to sever itself from its roots, which were complex and entangled but also rich with possibilities for growth and development. Such a severance is often the case in the history of science: it is the price of passing from an exploratory stage to a full-fledged research program—from a cloud to a crystal.

The cybernetics phase of cognitive science produced an amazing array of concrete results, in addition to its long-term (often underground) influence:

- The use of mathematical logic to understand the operation of the nervous system
- The invention of information-processing machines (such as digital computers), thereby laying the basis for artificial intelligence
- The establishment of the metadiscipline of systems theory, which has had an imprint in many branches of science, such as engineering (systems analysis, control theory), biology (regulatory physiology, ecology), social sciences (family therapy, structural anthropology, management, urban studies), and economics (game theory)
- Information theory as a statistical theory of signal and communication channels
- The first examples of self-organizing systems

This list is impressive: we tend to consider many of these notions and tools an integral part of our lives. Yet they were all nonexistent before this formative decade, and they were all produced by an intense exchange among people of widely different backgrounds. Thus the work during this era was the result of a uniquely and remarkably successful interdisciplinary effort.

The avowed intention of this cybernetics movement was to create a science of mind. In the eyes of the leaders of this movement, the study of mental phenomena had been far too long in the hands of psychologists and philosophers. In contrast, these cyberneticians felt a calling to express the processes underlying mental phenomena in explicit mechanisms and mathematical formalisms.[2]

One of the best illustrations of this mode of thinking (and its tangible consequences) was the seminal 1943 paper by Warren McCulloch and Walter Pitts, "A Logical Calculus of Ideas Immanent in Nervous Activity."[3] Two major leaps were taken in this article: first, the proposal that logic is the proper discipline with which to understand the brain and mental activity, and second, the claim that the brain is a device that embodies logical principles in its component elements or neurons. Each neuron was seen as a threshold device, which could be either active or inactive. Such simple neurons could then be connected to one another, their interconnections performing the role of logical operations so that the entire brain could be regarded as a deductive machine.

These ideas were central for the invention of digital computers.[4] At that time, vacuum tubes were used to implement the McCulloch-Pitts neurons whereas today we find silicon chips, but modern computers are still built on the same so-called von Neumann architecture that has been made familiar with the advent of personal computers. This major technological breakthrough also laid the basis for the dominant approach to the scientific study of mind that was to crystalize in the next decade as the cognitivist paradigm.

In fact, Warren McCulloch, more than any other figure, can serve as an exemplar of the hopes and the debates of these formative years. As can be gleaned from his collected papers in *Embodiments of Mind*,[5] McCulloch was a mysterious and paradoxical figure whose tone was often poetic and prophetic. His influence seemed to wane during the later years of his life, but his legacy is being reconsidered as cognitive science becomes more aware that a thorough intertwining of the philosophical, the empirical, and the mathematical, which McCulloch's investigations exemplified, seems the best way to continue working. His favorite description for his enterprise was "experimental epistemology"—an expression not favored by current usage. It is one of those remarkable simultaneities in the history of ideas that in the 1940s the Swiss psychologist Jean Piaget coined the expression "genetic epistemology" for his influential work, and the Austrian zoologist Konrad Lorenz started to speak of an "evolutionary epistemology."

There was, of course, considerably more to this creative decade. For instance, there was extensive debate over whether logic is indeed sufficient to understand the brain's operations, since logic neglects the brain's distributed qualities. (This debate continues today, and we will consider it in more detail later, especially as it relates to the question of "levels of explanation" in the study of cognition.) Alternative models and theories were put forth, which for the most part were to lie dormant until they were revived in the 1970s as an important alternative in cognitive science.

By 1953 the main actors of the cybernetics movement, in contrast to their initial unity and vitality, were distanced from each other, and many died shortly thereafter. It was mainly the idea of mind as logical calculation that continued.

Defining the Cognitivist Hypothesis

Just as 1943 was clearly the year in which the cybernetics phase was born, so 1956 was clearly the year that gave birth to cognitivism. During this year, at two meetings held at Cambridge and Dartmouth, new voices (such as those of Herbert Simon, Noam Chomsky, Marvin Minsky, and John McCarthy) put forth ideas that were to become the major guidelines for modern cognitive science.[6]

The central intuition behind cognitivism is that intelligence—human intelligence included—so resembles computation in its essential characteristics that cognition can actually be defined as computations of symbolic representations. Clearly this orientation could not have emerged without the basis laid during the previous decade. The main difference was that one of the many original, tentative ideas was now promoted to a full-blown hypothesis, with a strong desire to set its boundaries apart from its broader, exploratory, and interdisciplinary roots, where the social and biological sciences figured preeminently with all their multifarious complexity.

What exactly does it mean to say that cognition can be defined as computation? As we mentioned in chapter 1, a computation is an operation that is carried out or performed on symbols (on elements that represent what they stand for). The key notion here is that of representation or "intentionality," the philosopher's term for *aboutness*. The cognitivist argument is that intelligent behavior presupposes the ability to represent the world as being certain ways. We therefore cannot explain cognitive behavior unless we assume that an agent acts by representing relevant features of her situations. To the extent that her representation of a situation is accurate, the agent's behavior will be successful (all other things being equal).

This notion of representation is—at least since the demise of behaviorism—relatively uncontroversial. What is controversial is the next step, which is the cognitivist claim that the only way we can account for intelligence and intentionality is to hypothesize that cognition consists of acting on the basis of representations that are physically realized in the form of a symbolic code in the brain or a machine.

According to the cognitivist, the problem that must be solved is how to correlate the ascription of intentional or representational states (beliefs, desires, intentions, etc.) with the physical changes that an agent undergoes in acting. In other words, if we wish to claim that intentional states have causal properties, we have to show not only how those states are physically possible but how they can cause behavior. Here is where the notion of *symbolic computation* comes in. Symbols are both physical and have semantic values. Computations are operations on symbols that respect or are constrained by those semantic values. In other words, a computation is fundamentally semantic or representational—we cannot make sense of the idea of computation (as opposed to some random or arbitrary operation on symbols) without adverting to the semantic relations among the symbolic expressions. (This is the meaning of the popular slogan "no computation without representation.") A digital computer, however, operates only on the physical form of the symbols it computes; it has no access to their semantic value. Its operations are nonetheless semantically constrained because every semantic distinction relevant to its program has been encoded in the *syntax* of its symbolic language by the programmers. In a computer, that is, syntax mirrors or is parallel to the (ascribed) semantics. The cognitivist claim, then, is that this parallelism shows us how intelligence and intentionality (semantics) are physically and mechanically possible. Thus the hypothesis is that computers provide a mechanical model of thought or, in other words, that thought consists of physical, symbolic computations. Cognitive science becomes the study of such cognitive, physical symbol systems.[7]

To understand this hypothesis properly, it is crucial to realize the level at which it is proposed. The cognitivist is not claiming that if we were to open up someone's head and look at the brain, we would find little symbols being manipulated there. Although the symbolic level is physically realized, it is not reducible to the physical level. This point is intuitively obvious when we remember that the same symbol can be realized in numerous physical forms. Because of this nonreducibility it is quite possible that what corresponds to some symbolic expression at the physical level is a global, highly distributed pattern of brain activity. We will return to consider this idea later. For now the point to be emphasized is that in addition to the levels of physics and neurobiology, cognitivism postulates a distinct, irreducible symbolic level in the explanation of cognition. Furthermore, since symbols are semantic items, cognitivists also postulate a third distinctly semantic or representational level. (The irreducibility of this level too is intuitively obvious when we remember that the same semantic value can be realized in numerous symbolic forms.)[8]

This multilevel conception of scientific explanation is quite recent and is one of the major innovations of cognitive science. The roots and initial formulation of the innovation as a broad scientific idea can be traced back to the era of cybernetics, but cognitivists have contributed greatly to its further rigorous philosophical articulation.[9] We would like the reader to keep this idea in mind, for it will take on added significance when we turn to discuss the related—though still controversial—notion of *emergence*.

The reader should also notice that the cognitivist hypothesis entails a very strong claim about the relations between syntax and semantics. As we mentioned, in a computer program the syntax of the symbolic code mirrors or encodes its semantics. In the case of human language, it is far from obvious that all of the semantic distinctions relevant in an explanation of behavior can be mirrored syntactically. Indeed, many philosophical arguments can be given against this idea.[10] Furthermore, although we know where the semantic level of a computer's computations comes from (the programmers), we have no idea how the symbolic expressions supposed by the cognitivist to be encoded in the brain would get their meaning.

Since our concern in this book is with experience and cognition in its basic, perceptual modality, we will not take up such issues about language in detail here. Nonetheless, they are worth pointing out, since they are problems that lie at the heart of the cognitivist endeavor.

The cognitivist research program can be summarized, then, as answers to the following fundamental questions:

Question 1: What is cognition?

Answer: Information processing as symbolic computation—rule-based manipulation of symbols.

Question 2: How does it work?

Answer: Through any device that can support and manipulate discrete functional elements—the symbols. The system interacts only with the form of the symbols (their physical attributes), not their meaning.

Question 3: How do I know when a cognitive system is functioning adequately?

Answer: When the symbols appropriately represent some aspect of the real world, and the information processing leads to a successful solution of the problem given to the system.

Manifestations of Cognitivism

Cognitivism in Artificial Intelligence
The manifestations of cognitivism are nowhere more visible than in artificial intelligence (AI), which is the literal construal of the cognitivist hypothesis. Over the years many interesting theoretical advances and technological applications have been made within this orientation, such as expert systems, robotics, and image processing. These results have been widely publicized, and so we need not digress to provide specific examples here.

Because of wider implications, however, it is worth noting that AI and its cognitivist basis reached a dramatic climax in Japan's ICOT Fifth Generation Program. For the first time since the war there is a national plan involving the efforts of industry, government, and universities, launched in 1981. The core of this program is a cognitive device capable of understanding human language and of writing its own programs when presented with a task by an untrained user. Not surprisingly, the heart of the ICOT program was the development of a series of interfaces of knowledge representation and problem solving based on PROLOG, a high-level programming language for predicate logic. The ICOT program has triggered immediate responses from Europe and the United States, and there is little question that this is a major commercial concern and engineering battlefield. (It is also worth noting that the Japanese goverment has launched in 1990 the Sixth Generation Program based on connectionist models.) Although it is only one example, the ICOT program is a major illustration of the inseparability of science and technology in the study of cognition and of the effects that this marriage has on the public at large.

The cognitivist hypothesis has in AI its most literal construal. The complementary endeavor is the study of natural, biologically implemented cognitive systems, especially humans. Here, too, computationally characterizable representations have been the main explanatory tool. Mental representations are taken to be occurrences of a formal system, and the mind's activity is what gives these representations their attitudinal color—beliefs, desires, intentions, etc. Here, therefore, unlike AI, we find an interest in what the natural cognitive systems are really like, and it is assumed that their cognitive representations are *about* something *for* the system; they are said to be intentional in the sense indicated here.

Cognitivism and the Brain

Another equally important effect of cognitivism is the way it has shaped current views about the brain. Even though in theory the symbolic level of cognitivism is compatible with many views about the brain, in practice almost all of neurobiology (and its huge body of empirical evidence) has become permeated with the cognitivist, information-processing perspective. More often than not, the origins and assumptions of this perspective are not even questioned.[11]

The exemplar of this approach is the celebrated studies of the visual cortex, an area of the brain where one can easily detect electrical responses from neurons when the animal is presented with a visual image. It was reported early on that it was possible to classify cortical neurons, such as feature detectors, responding to certain attributes of the object being presented—its orientation, contrast, velocity, color, and so on. In line with the cognitivist hypothesis, these results have been seen as the biological basis for the notion that the brain picks up visual information from the retina through the feature-specific neurons in the cortex, and the information is then passed on to later stages in the brain for further processing (conceptual categorization, memory associations, and eventually action).[12]

In its most extreme form, this view of the brain is expressed in Barlow's "grandmother cell" doctrine, where there is a correspondence between concepts (such as the concept someone has of her grandmother) or percepts and specific neurons.[13] (This is equivalent to AI detectors and labeled lines.) This extreme view is waning in popularity now,[14] but the basic idea that the brain is an information-processing device that responds selectively to features of the environment remains as the dominant core of modern neuroscience and in the public's understanding.

Cognitivism in Psychology

Psychology is the discipline that most people assume to be the study of mind. Psychology predates cognitive science and cognitivism and is not coextensive with either of them. What influence has cognitivism had on psychology? To understand something of this, we need some historical background in psychology.

We have already mentioned introspectionism and its differences from mindfulness meditation. It may be that when anyone first thinks to inquire about the mind, there are a limited number of possibilities of how to proceed, and turning to one's own mind is one of the universal strategies that will occur. This track, developed by the meditative traditions of India, was aborted for psychology in the West when the nineteenth-century introspectionists, lacking a method of mindfulness, tried to treat the mind as an external object, with disastrous results for interobserver agreement. The breakdown of introspectionism into noncommensurable, warring laboratories left experimental psychology with a profound distrust of self-knowledge as a legitimate procedure in psychology. Introspectionism was replaced by the dominant school of behaviorism.

One obvious alternative to looking inward to the mind is to look outward at behavior; we even have the folk saying, "Actions speak louder than words." Behaviorism was particularly compatible with the early twentieth-century positivist zeitgeist of disembodied objectivism in science, for it eliminated mind entirely from its psychology. According to behaviorism, although one could objectively observe inputs to the organism (stimuli) and outputs (behavior) and could investigate the lawful relationships between inputs and outputs over time, the organism itself (both its mind and its biological body) was a black box that was methodologically unapproachable by behavioral science (hence no rules, no symbols, no computations). Behaviorism completely dominated North American experimental psychology from the 1920s until fairly recently.

The first signs of a postbehaviorist experimental cognitive psychology began to appear in the late 1950s. The trick of these early researchers who were still, strictly speaking, positivist, was to find experimental means for defining and measuring the effect of a given forbidden mentalistic phenomenon. Let us take mental images as an example.

A mental image is undisputably in the black box for a behaviorist; it is not publicly observable, so one cannot have observer agreement about it. Researchers, however, gradually devised demonstrations of the pragmatic effects of mental images. Instructing an experimental subject to hold a mental image during a signal detection task lowers the accuracy of the detection, and, furthermore, this effect is modality specific (a visual image interferes more in a visual detection task than an auditory task, and vice versa).[15] Such experiments legitimate im-

agery even in behaviorist terminology—imagery is a powerful inter-
vening variable. Furthermore, experiments began to explore the behavior of mental images in themselves, often showing that they had
properties like those of perceptual images. In delightfully ingenious
experiments, Kosslyn showed that mental visual images appear to be
scanned in real time,[16] and Shepard and Metzler showed that mental
images appear to be rotated in real time just as perceptual visual
images are.[17] Studies of other formerly mentalistic (now called cognitive) phenomena began to be performed in perception, memory,
language, problem solving, concepts, and decision making.

What influence did cognitivism have on this emerging experimental
investigation of the mind? Interestingly, the initial effect of cognitivism on psychology was extremely liberating. The computer metaphor of the mind could be used to formulate experimental hypotheses
or even to legitimate one's theory simply by programming it. Although the programs were almost entirely cognitivist (psychological
processes were modeled in terms of explicit rules, symbols, and
representations), the overall effect was to breach the constraints of
behaviorist orthodoxy and admit into psychology long-suppressed,
commonsense understanding of the mind. For example, developmental psycholinguistics could now explore openly the idea that
children learn the vocabulary and grammar of their language not as
reinforced, paired associates but as hypotheses about correct adult
speech that develop with their cognitive capacities and experience.[18]
Motivation could be understood as more than hours of deprivation;
one could now talk of cognitive representations of goals and plans.[19]
The social system was not just a complex stimulus; it could be modeled in the mind as representations of scripts and social schemas.[20]
One could speak of the human information processor as a lay scientist, testing hypotheses and making mistakes.[21] In short, the introduction of the computer metaphor in a very general, albeit implicitly
cognitivist, sense into cognitive psychology allowed an explosion of
commonsense theory and its operationalization into computer models
and human research.

Strict cognitivism in its explicit form, on the other hand, places
strong constraints on theory and has generated primarily philosophical debate. Let us return to mental imagery as an example. In cognitivism, mental imagery, like any other cognitive phenomenon, can
be no more than the manipulation of symbols by computational rules.
Yet Shepard's and Kosslyn's experiments have demonstrated that

mental images perform in a continuous fashion in real time, very like visual perception. Does this refute cognitivism? A hard-line cognitivist, such as Pylyshyn, argues that images are simply subjective epiphenomena (as they were for behaviorism) of more fundamental symbolic computations.[22] Attempting to bridge the rift between data and cognitivist theory, Kosslyn has formulated a model by which images are generated in the mind by the same rules that generate images in computer displays: the interaction of languagelike operations and picturelike operations together generate the internal eye.[23] One current view of the imagery debate is that since, at best, the imagery research demonstrates the similarity of imagery to perception, this simply points us to the need for a viable account of perception.[24]

Cognitivism and Psychoanalysis
We stated earlier that psychoanalytic theory had mirrored much of the development of cognitive science. In fact, psychoanalysis was explicitly cognitivist in its inception.[25] Freud attended Brentano's course in Vienna, as did Husserl, and he fully endorsed the representational and intentional view of the mind. For Freud, nothing could affect behavior unless it were mediated by a representation, even an instinct. "An instinct can never be an object of consciousness—only the idea that represents the instinct. Even in the unconscious, moreover, it can only be represented by the idea."[26] Within this framework, Freud's great discovery was that not all representations were accessible to consciousness; he never seemed to doubt that the unconscious, for all that it might operate on a different symbol system than the conscious, was fully symbolic, fully intentional, and fully representational.

Freud's descriptions of mental structures and processes are sufficiently general and metaphorical that they have proved translatable (with arguable degrees of loss of meaning) into the language of other psychological systems. In the Anglo-American world, one extreme was Dollard and Miller's hotly contested retheorizing of Freudian discoveries in terms of behaviorist-based learning theory.[27] More relevant for us was Erdelyi's rather placidly accepted (perhaps because of Freud's preexisting cognitivist "metaphysics") translation into cognitivist-based information-processing language.[28] For example, Freud's concept of repression/censorship becomes, in cognitivist terms, the matching of information from a perception or idea to a criterion level for acceptable accounts of anxiety: if it is above the criterion, it goes to a stop-processing/accessing information box, from whence it is shunted back to the unconscious; if below the criterion, it is allowed into the preconscious and, perhaps, then into the conscious. After another criterion match in the decision tree, it is either allowed into behavior or suppressed. Does such a description add anything to Freud? It certainly serves to translate such notions as the Freudian unconscious into what is taken to be a "scientific" currency of the day. It is also fair to say that many contemporary post-Freudian theorists in Europe—such as Jacques Lacan—would disagree: such theorizing misses the central spirit of the psychoanalytic journey—to move beyond the trap of representations, including those about the unconscious.

It is presently fashionable to say that Freud "decentered" the self; what he actually did was to divide the self into several basic selves. Freud was not a strict cognitivist in the Pylyshyn sense: the unconscious had the same type of representations as the conscious, all of which could, at least theoretically, become, or have been, conscious. Modern strict cognitivism has a far more radical and alienating view of unconscious processing. It is to this issue that we now turn as we discuss the meaning of cognitivism for our experience.

Cognitivism and Human Experience

What implications does this cognitivist research program have for an understanding of our experience? We wish to emphasize two related points: (1) cognitivism postulates mental or cognitive processes of which we are not only unaware but of which we cannot be aware, and (2) cognitivism is thereby led to embrace the idea that the self or cognizing subject is fundamentally fragmented or nonunified. These two points will become considerably intertwined as we proceed.

As the reader might recall, our first point has already appeared when we presented the tension between science and experience to which cognitive science gives rise. There we quoted Daniel Dennett's claim that all cognitivist theories are theories of what Dennett calls the "sub-personal level." By this phrase, Dennett means that cognitivism postulates mental (not just physical and biological) mechanisms and processes that are not accessible to the "personal level" of consciousness, especially self-consciousness. In other words, one cannot discern in conscious awareness or self-conscious introspection any of the cognitive structures and processes that are postulated to account for cognitive behavior. Indeed, if cognition is fundamentally symbolic computation, this discrepancy between personal and subpersonal immediately follows, since presumably none of us has any awareness of computing in an internal, symbolic medium when we think.

It is possible to overlook the depth of this challenge to our self-understanding, largely because of our post-Freudian belief in the unconscious. There is a difference, however, between what we usually mean by "unconscious" and the sense in which mental processes are said to be unconscious in cognitivism: we usually suppose that what is unconscious can be brought to consciousness—if not through self-conscious reflection, then through a disciplined procedure such as psychoanalysis. Cognitivism, on the other hand, postulates processes that are mental but that cannot be brought to consciousness at all. Thus we are not simply unaware of the rules that govern the generation of mental images or of the rules that govern visual processing; we could not be aware of these rules. Indeed, it is typically noted that if such cognitive processes could be made conscious, then they could not be fast and automatic and so could not function properly. In one formulation these cognitive processes are even considered to be "modular" (to comprise distinct subsystems that cannot be penetrated by conscious mental activity).[29] Thus cognitivism challenges our conviction that consciousness and the mind either amount to the same thing or there is an essential or necessary connection between them.

Of course, Freud too challenged the idea that the mind and consciousness are the same. Furthermore, he certainly realized that to distinguish between the mind and consciousness entails the disunity of the self or cognizing subject, a point to which we shall turn shortly. It is not clear, however, whether Freud took the further step of calling into question the idea that there is an essential or necessary connection between the mind and consciousness. As Dennett notes, Freud, in his argument for unconscious beliefs, desires, and motivations, left open the possibility that these unconscious processes belonged to a fragment of ourselves hidden in the depths of the psyche.[30] Although it is not clear the extent to which Freud meant such a fragmentation literally, it is clear that cognitive science does take a literal, if not homuncular, view. As Dennett puts it, "Although the new [cognitivist] theories abound with deliberately fanciful homunculus metaphors—subsystems like little people in the brain sending messages back and forth, asking for help, obeying and volunteering—the actual subsystems are deemed to be unproblematic *non*conscious bits of organic machinery, as utterly lacking in point of view or inner life as a kidney or kneecap."[31] In other words, the characterization of these "sub-personal" systems in "fanciful homunculus metaphors" is only provisional, for eventually all such metaphors are "discharged"—they are traded in for the storm of activity among such selfless processes as neural networks or AI data structures.[32]

Our pretheoretical, everyday conviction, however, is that cognition and consciousness—especially self-consciousness—belong together in the same domain. Cognitivism runs directly counter to this conviction: in determining the domain of cognition, it explicitly cuts across the conscious/unconscious distinction. The domain of cognition consists of those systems that must be seen as having a distinct representational level, not necessarily of those systems that are conscious. Some representational systems are, of course, conscious, but they need not be to have representations or intentional states. Thus for cognitivists, cognition and intentionality (representation) are the inseparable pair, not cognition and consciousness.

This theoretical division of the domain of cognition is considered by cognitivists to be "an empirical discovery of no small importance"[33] and indicates, again, the remarkable mutation wrought by cognitivism. But now a problem arises: we seem to be losing our grip on something that is undeniably close and familiar—our sense of self. If consciousness—to say nothing of self-consciousness—is not essential for cognition, and if, in the case of cognitive systems that are conscious, such as ourselves, consciousness amounts to only one kind of mental process, then just what is the cognizing subject? Is it the collection of all mental processes, both conscious and unconscious? Or is it simply one kind of mental process, such as consciousness, among all the others? In either case, our sense of self is challenged, for we typically suppose that to be a self is to have a coherent and unified "point of view," a stable and constant vantage point from which to think, perceive, and act. Indeed, this sense that we have (are?) a self seems so incontrovertible that its calling into question or denial—even by science—strikes us as absurd. And yet, if someone were to turn the tables and ask us to look for the self, we would be hard pressed to find it. Dennett, as usual, makes this point with flair: "You enter the brain through the eye, march up the optic nerve, round and round the cortex, looking behind every neuron, and then before you know it, you emerge into daylight on the spike of a motor nerve impulse, scratching your head and wondering where the self is."[34]

Our problem, however, goes even deeper. It is one thing to be unable to find a coherent and unified self amid the furious storm of subpersonal activity. This inability would certainly challenge our sense of self, but the challenge would be limited. We could still suppose that there really is a self but that we simply cannot find it in this fashion. Perhaps, as Jean-Paul Sartre held, the self is too close, and so we cannot uncover it by turning back upon ourselves. The cognitivist challenge, however, is much more serious. According to cognitivism, cognition can proceed without consciousness, for there is no essential or necessary connection between them. Now whatever else we suppose the self to be, we typically suppose that consciousness is its central feature. It follows, then, that cognitivism challenges our conviction that the most central feature of the self is needed for cognition. In other words, the cognitivist challenge does not consist simply in asserting that we cannot find the self; it consists, rather, in the further implication that the self is not even needed for cognition.

At this point, the tension between science and experience should be obvious and tangible. If cognition can proceed without the self, then why do we nonetheless have the experience of self? We cannot simply dismiss this experience without explanation.

Until recently, most philosophers nonchalantly shrugged off this problem by arguing that the perplexities surrounding it are just not relevant to the purposes of cognitive science.[35] This mood, however, has begun to change. Indeed, one prominent cognitive scientist, Ray Jackendoff, has recently published a book that attempts to address just these issues.[36] Jackendoff's work is important, for it squarely faces the problematic relations among consciousness, mind, and self uncovered by cognitivism. His work is also instructive for our purposes, for it provides a paradigm of how the purely theoretical treatment of the relation between science and experience is both methodologically and empirically incomplete. For these reasons, we will conclude this chapter with a brief consideration of Jackendoff's project.

Experience and the Computational Mind

We have now seen that, in the hands of cognitivism, the cognizing subject is split in two: cognition consists, on the one hand, of unconscious symbolic computation and, on the other hand, of conscious experience. Jackendoff's work focuses on the problematic relation between these two aspects of cognition, which he calls the *computational mind* and the *phenomenological mind*.

It is important to appreciate just how problematic the relation between the computational mind and the phenomenological mind is. The problem centers on how intentionality and consciousness are related. We have seen that cognitivism draws a sharp and fundamental distinction between these two aspects of cognition. Our cognition, however, seems to be directed toward the world in a way that intimately involves consciousness. Thus notice that our cognition is directed toward the world in a certain way: it is directed toward the world *as we experience it*. For example, we perceive the world to be three-dimensional, macroscopic, colored, etc.; we do not perceive it as composed of subatomic particles. Thus our cognition is directed toward an experiential world, or in the terms of phenomenology, toward a *lived* world. How, then, if intentionality and consciousness are fundamentally distinct, does cognition come to be about the world as we consciously experience it? This problem is paramount, for as Jackendoff notes, by postulating a computational mind that is inaccessible to consciousness, cognitivism "offers no explication of what a conscious experience is" (p. 20).

Jackendoff calls this problem the "mind-mind problem," for it centers on the relation between the computational mind and the phenomenological mind. In his words (p. 20),

> The upshot is that psychology now has not two domains to worry about, the brain and mind, but three: the brain, the computational mind, and the phenomenological mind. Consequently, Descartes' formulation of the mind-body problem is split into two separate issues. The "phenomenological mind-body problem". . . is, How can a brain have experiences? The "computational mind-body problem" is, How can a brain accomplish reasoning? In addition, we have the mind-*mind* problem, namely, What is the relationship between computational states and experience?

It should be apparent from our presentation of cognitivism that the motivation for the cognitivist hypothesis has been what Jackendoff calls the "computational mind-body problem," that is, the problem of how thought construed as reasoning is physically and mechanically possible. The "mind-mind problem," on the other hand, corresponds to the problem of intentionality and consciousness in its full-blown form: How is cognition as symbolic computation related to the world as experienced?

How, then, does Jackendoff propose to tackle this issue? His basic idea is that "the elements of conscious awareness are caused by/supported by/projected from information and processes of the computational mind" (p. 23). In other words, he proposes to consider conscious awareness "as an *externalization* or *projection* of some subset of elements of the computational mind" (p. 23). The research program, then, is to determine which elements "project" or "support" conscious awareness. Jackendoff argues that these elements correspond to *intermediate-level representations* in the computational mind (to representations that lie midway between the most "peripheral" or sensory level and the most "central" or thoughtlike level).

Jackendoff successively refines this "intermediate-level theory" throughout the course of his book. We shall return to one of these refinements after we have presented the enactive view of cognition. At this point we wish simply to emphasize two important consequences that follow from his basic idea of consciousness as a projection from intermediate levels of representation in the computational mind. The first consequence is that to develop his computational theory, Jackendoff requires experiential or phenomenological evidence. The second is that his theory reveals the disunity of the cognizing subject. These two consequences bring to the fore the necessity of complementing cognitive science with a pragmatic, mindful, open-ended approach to human experience, such as we find in the mindfulness/awareness tradition.

Consider first that according to Jackendoff's theory the organization of conscious awareness is determined by the computational mind. As Jackendoff puts it, "Every phenomenological distinction is caused by/supported by/projected from a corresponding computational distinction" (p. 24). It follows, then, that phenomenological distinctions constrain computational models. In other words, any computational model of the mind that purports to explain the phenomenological mind must have the resources to explain all of the distinctions that we make in conscious experience. Jackendoff is well aware of this consequence, for he writes, "The empirical force of this hypothesis is to bring phenomenological evidence to bear on the computational theory. The computational theory must be sufficiently expressive (must contain sufficient distinctions of the proper sorts) to make the world of awareness possible. Thus, if there is a phenomenological distinction that is not yet expressed by our current computational theory, the theory must be enriched or revised" (p. 25).

In this paragraph, we see again how the fundamental circularity with which we began this book comes to the fore. To explain cognition, we turn to investigate our structure—understood in the present context as our computational mind. But since it is also cognition as experience that we wish to explain, we must turn back and attend to the kinds of distinctions we draw in experience—the phenomenological mind. Having attended to experience in this way, we can then turn back to enrich and revise our computational theory, and so on. Our point is not at all that this circle is vicious. Rather, our point is that we cannot situate ourselves properly within this circle without a disciplined and open-ended approach from the side of experience.

To appreciate this point, let us ask, How are we to specify the appropriate phenomenological or experiential distinctions? Are these distinctions simply given to us by virtue of our being experiencing creatures? Jackendoff appears to think so, for although he admits that experiential evidence constrains his theory, he nonetheless treats experience as something that requires no disciplined procedure for its investigation beyond "the hope that disagreements about phenomenology can be settled in an atmosphere of mutual trust" (p. 275). This is quite an assumption for a field that saw the demise of introspectionism because of its total inability to agree on anything and that can readily see people and nations disagreeing constantly over the nature of even simple matters of experience. Jackendoff assumes that everyday—largely mindless—experience provides access to all the relevant phenomenological evidence and that the phenomenological quest is limited to just that largely mindless state. He considers neither the possibility that conscious awareness can be progressively developed beyond its everyday form (a strange omission considering his interest in musical cognition) nor that such development can be used to provide direct insight into the structure and constitution of experience. These are assumptions that Jackendoff is forced to make because our Western tradition neither provides a critique of mindless phenomenologizing nor provides any method, other than hit or miss hand waving, to investigate the phenomenological mind. We find this all the more telling because Jackendoff demonstrates such phenomenological acumen and brilliant synergistic theorizing. There is clearly the need for the disciplined, open-ended approach to experience if such matters are to be discussed.

The relevance of a mindful, open-ended stance toward experience again becomes apparent when we consider our second point, which is that Jackendoff's theory implies the disunity of the cognizing subject. We typically suppose that consciousness unifies and grounds all the disparate elements of one's self—one's thoughts, feelings, perceptions, etc. The phrase "unity of consciousness" refers to the idea that one understands all of one's experiences as happening to a single self. As Jackendoff rightly notes, however, there is an equally obvious *disunity* in consciousness, for the forms in which we can be consciously aware depend considerably on the modalities of experience. Thus visual conscious awareness is markedly distinct from auditory awareness, and both are markedly distinct from tactile awareness. Since, as we have just seen, Jackendoff's computational theory is constrained by phenomenological distinctions, he must give some account of this experiential disunity. Jackendoff suggests that each form of conscious awareness is derived or projected from a different set of representational structures in the computational mind (p. 52):

> The hypothesis that emerges from these considerations is that each modality of awareness comes from a different level or set of levels of representation. The disunity of awareness thus arises from the fact that each of the relevant levels involves its own special repertoire of distinctions. . . .
>
> [This theory] goes against the grain of the prevailing approaches to consciousness, which start with the premise that consciousness is unified and then try to locate a unique source for it. [This theory] claims that consciousness is fundamentally not unified and that one should seek multiple sources.

In the previous section, we saw that cognitivism implies the disunity of the cognizing subject because it draws a fundamental distinction between consciousness and intentionality. Jackendoff takes this disunity one step further, however, by claiming that consciousness itself is fundamentally disunified. Furthermore, his view is motivated not by the problem of how cognition is physically possible (the "computational mind-body problem") but rather by the problem of how the computational mind generates conscious experience (the "mind-mind" problem). For this reason Jackendoff does not simply assert the disunity of the cognizing subject on computational grounds; he also respects and attends to the phenomenological evidence for disunity. Indeed, it is precisely this disunity that Jackendoff uses to build a bridge between the computational mind and the phenomenological mind (p. 51).

This considerable advance, however, makes the tension between science and experience only more apparent. It must be remembered that Jackendoff attends to conscious experience because he holds that it results from an underlying computational organization. Thus for Jackendoff the distinctions present in the phenomenological mind are not *made* by the phenomenological mind; they are, rather, projected into the phenomenological mind by the computational mind. Indeed, Jackendoff explicitly rejects the idea that consciousness has any causal efficacy; instead he holds that all causality takes place at the computational level. He is thus led to embrace a consequence that he himself admits to be unpleasant: if consciousness has no causal efficacy, then it can have no effects and so "is not good for anything" (p. 26).

With this consequence we are confronted in a more extreme form with the effects of the cognitivist separation of intentionality and consciousness. If cognition can proceed without consciousness, if consciousness itself is "not good for anything," then why are we consciously aware, both of ourselves and of the world? Does cognitive science require that we treat experience as, in the end, simply epiphenomenal?

Some cognitive scientists appear to be willing to embrace just this conclusion. They shrug their shoulders and say, "So much the worse for experience," as if experience could be blamed for not living up to the demands of a theory. And yet what does such a conclusion mean to these very same scientists and philosophers, when not engaged in theoretical reflection? Does it change in any way the flow of lived experience? Is the philosophical conclusion itself, as we fear it is in most modern philosophy, an epiphenomenon?

We have already argued that these two responses—the dismissal of experience on the one hand and the unquestioned acceptance of it on the other—are extreme and lead to an impasse. In so arguing, we obviously imply the possibility of some other, middle way. The next several chapters are devoted to the exploration of such a middle way and have the experience of self as their theme. In the next chapter we turn to face directly the "I of the storm" in a reflection on selfless minds and human experience. As we will see, the disunity of the self and of conscious awareness, which modern-day cognitivism has uncovered, is in fact a focal point of the entire mindfulness/awareness tradition.

4

The I of the Storm

What Do We Mean by "Self"?

At every moment of our lives there is something going on, some experience. We see, hear, smell, taste, touch, think. We can be pleased, angry, afraid, tired, perplexed, interested, agonizingly self-conscious, or absorbed in a pursuit. I can feel that *I* am being overwhelmed by *my* own emotions, that I have greater worth when praised by another, that I am destroyed by a loss. What is this self, this ego-center, that appears and disappears, that seems so constant yet so fragile, so familiar and yet so elusive?

We are caught in a contradiction. On the one hand, even a cursory attention to experience shows us that our experience is always changing and, furthermore, is always dependent on a particular situation. To be human, indeed to be living, is always to be in a situation, a context, a world. We have no experience of anything that is permanent and independent of these situations. Yet most of us are convinced of our identities: we have a personality, memories and recollections, and plans and anticipations, which seem to come together in a coherent point of view, a center from which we survey the world, the ground on which we stand. How could such a point of view be possible if it were not rooted in a single, independent, truly existing self or ego?

This question is the meeting ground of everything in this book: cognitive science, philosophy, and the meditative tradition of mindfulness/awareness. We wish to make a sweeping claim: all of the reflective traditions in human history—philosophy, science, psychoanalysis, religion, meditation—have challenged the naive sense of self. No tradition has ever claimed to discover an independent, fixed, or unitary self within the world of experience. Let us give the voice for this to David Hume's famous passage: "For my part, when I enter most intimately into what I call *myself*, I always stumble on some particular perception or other, of heat or cold, light or shade, love or hatred, pain or pleasure. I never can catch *myself* at any time without a perception, and never can observe anything but the perception."[1] Such an insight directly contradicts our ongoing sense of self.

It is this contradiction, the incommensurability of the outcome of reflection and experience, that has provoked us on the journey in this book. We believe that many non-Western (even contemplative) traditions, and all Western traditions, deal with this contradiction simply by turning away from it, refusing to confront it, a withdrawal that can take one of two forms. The usual way is simply to ignore it. Hume, for example, unable to find the self as he reflected in his study, chose to withdraw and immerse himself in a game of backgammon; he resigned himself to the separation of life and reflection. Jean-Paul Sartre expresses this by saying that we are "condemned" to a belief in the self. The second tactic is to postulate a transcendental self that can never be known to experience, such as the *atman* of the Upanishads or the transcendental ego of Kant.[2] (Noncontemplative traditions, of course, can just not notice the contradiction—for example, self-concept theory in psychology.)[3] The major—and perhaps only— tradition that we know that directly confronts this contradiction and that has spoken to it for a long time arose from the practice of mindfulness/awareness meditation.

We have already described mindfulness/awareness practice as a gradual development of the ability to be present with one's mind and body not only in formal meditation but in the experiences of everyday life. Beginning meditators are usually amazed at the tumultuous activity of their mind as perceptions, thoughts, feelings, desires, fears, and every other kind of mental content pursue each other endlessly like a cat chasing its tail. As the meditators develop some stability of mindfulness/awareness so that they have periods when they are not constantly (to use traditional images) sucked into the whirlpool or thrown from a horse, they begin to have insight into what the mind, as it is experienced, is really like. Experiences, they notice, are impermanent. This is not just the leaves-fall, maidens-wither, and kings-are-forgotten type of impermanence (traditionally called gross impermanence) with which all people are hauntingly familiar but a personal penetrating impermanence of the activity of the mind itself. Moment by moment new experiences happen and are gone. It is a rapidly shifting stream of momentary mental occurrences. Furthermore, the shiftiness includes the perceiver as much as the perceptions. There is no experiencer, just as Hume noticed, who remains constant to receive experiences, no landing platform for experience. This actual experiential sense of no one home is called *selflessness* or *egolessness*. Moment by moment the meditator also sees the mind pulling away from its sense of impermance and lack of self, sees it grasping experiences as though they were permanent, commenting on experiences as though there were a constant perceiver to comment, seeking any mental entertainment that will disrupt mindfulness, and restlessly fleeing to the next preoccupation, all with a sense of constant struggle. This undercurrent of restlessness, grasping, anxiety, and unsatisfactoriness that pervades experience is called *Dukkha*, usually translated as suffering. Suffering arises quite naturally and then grows as the mind seeks to avoid its natural grounding in impermanence and lack of self.

The tension between the ongoing sense of self in ordinary experience and the failure to find that self in reflection is of central importance in Buddhism—the origin of human suffering is just this tendency to grasp onto and build a sense of self, an ego, where there is none. As meditators catch glimpses of impermanence, selflessness, and suffering (known as the three marks of existence) and some inkling that the pervasiveness of suffering (known as the First Noble Truth) may have its origin in their own self-grasping (known as the Second Noble Truth), they may develop some real motivation and urgency to persevere in their investigation of mind. They try to develop a strong and stable insight and inquisitiveness into the moment to moment arising of mind. They are encouraged to investigate: How does *this* moment arise? What are its conditions? What is the nature of "my" reactivity to it? Where does the experience of "I" occur?

The search for how the self arises is thus a way of asking, "What and where is mind?" in a direct and personal way. The initial spirit of inquisitiveness in these questions is actually not unlike Descartes's *Meditations*, though this statement might surprise some people since Descartes has received such bad press these days. Descartes's initial decision to rely not on the word of the Church fathers but rather on what his own mind could discern in reflection obviously partakes of the spirit of self-reliant investigation, as does phenomenology. Descartes, however, stopped short: His famous "I think, I am" simply leaves untouched the nature of the "I" that thinks. True, Descartes did infer that the "I" is fundamentally a thinking thing, but here he went too far: the only certainty that "I am" carries is that of being a thought. If Descartes had been fully rigorous, mindful, and attentive, he would not have jumped to the conclusion that I am a thinking *thing* (res cogitans); rather he would have kept his attention on the very *process* of mind itself.

In mindfulness/awareness practice, the awareness of thinking, emotions, and bodily sensations becomes quite pronounced in the basic restlessness that we normally experience. To penetrate that experience, to discern what it is and how it arises, some types of mindfulness meditation direct the meditator to attend to experience as precisely and dispassionately as possible. It is only through a pragmatic, open-ended reflection that we can examine systematically and directly this restlessness that we usually ignore. As the contents of experience arise—discursive thoughts, emotional tonalities, bodily sensations—the meditator is attentive not by becoming concerned with the contents of the thoughts or with the sense of *I* thinking but rather by simply noting "thinking" and directing his attention to the never-ceasing process of that experience.

Just as the mindfulness meditator is amazed to discover how mindless he is in daily life, so the first insights of the meditator who begins to question the self are normally not egolessness but the discovery of total egomania. Constantly one thinks, feels, and acts as though one had a self to protect and preserve. The slightest encroachment on the self's territory (a splinter in the finger, a noisy neighbor) arouses fear and anger. The slightest hope of self-enhancement (gain, praise, fame, pleasure) arouses greed and grasping. Any hint that a situation is irrelevant to the self (waiting for a bus, meditating) arouses boredom. Such impulses are instinctual, automatic, pervasive, and powerful. They are completely taken for granted in daily life. The impulses are certainly there, constantly occurring, yet in the light of the questioning meditator, do they make any sense? What kind of self does he think he has to warrant such attitudes?

The Tibetan teacher Tsultrim Gyatso puts the dilemma this way:

> To have any meaning such a self has to be lasting, for if it perished every moment one would not be so concerned about what was going to happen to it the next moment; it would not be one's "self" anymore. Again it has to be single. If one had no separate identity why should one worry about what happened to one's "self" any more than one worried about anyone else's? It has to be independent or there would be no sense in saying "I did this" or "I have that." If one had no independent existence

there would be no-one to claim the actions and experiences as its own . . . We all act as if we had lasting, separate, and independent selves that it is our constant preoccupation to protect and foster. It is an unthinking habit that most of us would normally be most unlikely to question or explain. However, all our suffering is associated with this pre-occupation. All loss and gain, pleasure and pain arise because we identify so closely with this vague feeling of selfness that we have. We are so emotionally involved with and attached to this "self" that we take it for granted. . . . The meditator does not speculate about this "self." He does not have theories about whether it does or does not exist. Instead he just trains himself to watch . . . how his mind clings to the idea of self and "mine" and how all his sufferings arise from this attachment. At the same time he looks carefully for that self. He tries to isolate it from all his other experiences. Since it is the culprit as far as all his suffering is concerned, he wants to find it and identify it. The irony is that however much he tries, he does not find anything that corresponds to the self.[4]

If there is no experienced self, then how is it that we think there is? What is the origin of our self-serving habits? What is it in experience that we take for a self?

Looking for a Self in the Aggregates

We now turn to some of the categories in the Buddhist teachings called the *Abhidharma*.[5] This term refers to a collection of texts that forms one of the three divisions of the Buddhist canon (the other two are the *Vinaya*, which contains ethical precepts, and the *Sutras*, which contain the speeches of the Buddha). Based on the Abhidharma texts and their later commentaries, there emerged a tradition of analytic investigation of the nature of experience, which is still taught and used in contemplation by most Buddhist schools. The Abhidharma contains various sets of categories for examining the arising of the sense of self. These are not intended as ontological categories, such as one finds, for example, in Aristotle's *Metaphysics*. Rather, these categories serve on the one hand as simple descriptions of experience and on the other hand as pointers toward investigation.[6]

The most popular set of these categories, one that is common to all Buddhist schools, is known as the five aggregates. (The Sanscrit term translated as "aggregate" is *skandha*, which literally means "heap." The story goes that when the Buddha first taught this framework for examining experience, he used piles of grain to stand for each aggregate.) The five aggregates are

1. Forms
2. Feelings/sensations
3. Perceptions (discernments)/impulses
4. Dispositional formations
5. Consciousnesses[7]

The first of the five aggregates is considered to be based on the physical or material; the remaining four are mental. All five together constitute the psychophysical complex that makes up a person and that makes up each moment of experience.[8] We will examine the way in which we take each of these to be ourselves and will query whether we can find something in the aggregates that will answer to our basic, emotional, reactional conviction in the reality of self. In other words, we will be looking for a full-blown, really existing ego-self—some lasting self that would serve as the object of our emotional conviction that there really is a ground underneath the dependent, impermanent, everyday personality.

Forms

This category refers to the body and the physical environment. It does so, however, strictly in terms of the senses—the six sense organs and the corresponding objects of those organs.[9] They are the eye and visible objects, the ear and sounds, the nose and smells, the tongue and tastes, the body and touchables, and the mind and thoughts. The sense organs do not refer to the gross external organ but to the actual physical mechanism of perception. The mind organ (there is debate in the tradition as to just what physical structure that is) and thoughts are treated as a sense and its object because that is how they appear in experience: we feel that we perceive our thoughts with our mind just as we perceive a visible object with our eye.

We might point out that even at this level of analysis we have already departed from the usual idea of an abstract, disembodied observer who, like a cognitive entity parachuted into a ready-made world, encounters matter as a separate and independent category. Here, as in Merleau-Ponty's phenomenology, our encounter with the physical is already situated and embodied. Matter is described experientially.

Is our body our self? Think how important our body and possessions are to us, how terrified we become if the body or important
possessions are threatened, how angry or depressed we become if
they are damaged. Think of how much effort, money, and emotion
we spend on feeding, grooming, and caring for the body. Emotionally
we treat the body as though it were ourself. Intellectually we may do
so also. Our circumstances and moods may change, but the body
appears stable. The body is the location point of the senses; we look
at the world from the vantage point of the body, and we perceive the
objects of our senses to be related spatially to our body. Though the
mind may wander, sleeping or daydreaming, we count on returning
to the same body.

Yet do we really think of the body as the same as the self? As upset
as we might be at the loss of a finger (or any other body part), we
would not feel that we had thereby lost our identity. In fact, even in
normal circumstances, the entire makeup of the body changes rapidly, as seen by the turnover of one's cells. Let us take a brief philosophical excursion on this point.

We might ask, "What do the cells that make up my body now have
in common with the cells that will make up my body in, say, seven
years?" And, of course, the question contains its own answer: what
they have in common is that they both make up my body and therefore make up some kind of pattern through time that is supposedly
my self. But we still don't know what that pattern qua the self *is;* we
have simply gone round in a circle.

Philosophers will recognize this little vignette as a variation on the
example of the ship of Theseus, which, every so often, has all of its
planks replaced. The question is, Is it the same ship or not? And
philosophers, being more sophisticated than most of the rest of us,
deftly reply that there really isn't any fact of the matter one way or
the other. It all depends on what you want to say. In one sense, yes,
it is the same ship, and in another sense, no, it isn't the same ship.
It all depends on what your criteria of identity are. For something to
be the same (to have some kind of invariant pattern or form) it must
suffer some change, for otherwise one would not be able to recognize
that it had stayed the same. Conversely, for something to change
there must also be some kind of implicit permanance that acts as a
reference point in judging that a change has occurred. So the answer
to the quandary is both yes and no, and the details of any specific

yes or no answer will depend on one's criteria of identity in the given situation.[10]

But surely the self—*my* self—can't depend on how someone chooses to look at it; it is, after all, a self in its own right. Perhaps, then, the ego-self is the owner of the body, of this form that can be seen in so many ways. Indeed, we do not say "I am a body" but "I *have* a body." But just what is it that I have? This body, which I seem to own, is also the home for numerous microorganisms. Do I own them? A strange idea, since often they seem to get the best of me. But who is it that they get the best of?

Perhaps the most definitive argument that we do not take our body as our self is that we can imagine a total body transplant, that is, the implantation of our mind in someone else's body (a favorite theme in science fiction), yet we would still count as ourselves. Perhaps, then, we should leave the material and look to the mental aggregates for the basis of the self.

Feelings/Sensations

All experiences have some kind of feeling tone, classifiable as pleasant, unpleasant, or neutral, and as either bodily feeling or mental feeling. We are very concerned about our feelings. We strive endlessly to seek pleasure and avoid pain. Our feelings are certainly self-relevant, and at moments of strong feeling we take ourselves as our feelings. Yet are they our self? Feelings change from moment to moment. (Awareness of these changes can be made even more precise in mindfulness/awareness practice: one develops firsthand experience of the momentary arising of feelings and sensations as well as their changes.) Though feelings affect the self, no one would say that these feelings *are* the self. But what/who is it, then, that feelings are affecting?

Perceptions/Impulses

This aggregate refers to the first moment of recognition, identification, or discernment in the arising of something distinct, coupled with the activation of a basic impulse for action toward the discerned object.

Within the context of mindfulness/awareness practice, the coupling of discernment and impulse in a moment of experience is especially important. There are said to be three root impulses—passion/desire (toward desirable objects), aggression/anger (toward undesirable ob-

jects), and delusion/ignoring (toward neutral objects). Insofar as beings are caught up in habits of ego clinging, physical or mental objects
are discerned, even at the first instant, in relation to the self—either
as desirable, undesirable, or irrelevant to the self—and in that very
discernment is the automatic impulse to act in the relevant fashion.
These three basic impulses are also called the three poisons because
they are the beginnings of actions that will lead to further ego grasping. But who is this ego who is grasping?

Dispositional Formations
This next aggregate refers to habitual patterns of thinking, feeling,
perceiving, and acting—habitual patterns such as confidence, avarice,
laziness, worry, etc. (see appendix B). We are now in the domain of
the kinds of phenomena that could well be called cognitive in the
language of cognitive science or personality traits in personality psychology.

   We are certainly heavily self-invested in our habits and traits—our
personality. If someone criticizes our behavior or makes a favorable
comment about our personality, we feel that she is referring to our
self. As in each of the other aggregates, our emotional response
indicates that we take this aggregate as our ego-self. But again when
we contemplate the object of that response, our conviction falls apart.
We do not normally identify our habits with our self. Our habits,
motives, and emotional tendencies may change considerably over
time, but we still feel a sense of continuity as if there were a self
distinct from these personality changes. Where could this sense of
continuity come from, if not from a self that is the basis of our present
personality?

Consciousnesses
Consciousness is the last of the aggregates, and it contains all of the
others. (Indeed, each of the aggregates contains those that precede it
in the list.) It is the mental experience that goes with the other four
aggregates; technically it is the experience that comes from the contact
of each sense organ with its object (together with the feeling, impulse,
and habit that is aroused). Consciousness, as a technical term *vijñana*,
always refers to the dualistic sense of experience in which there is an
experiencer, an object experienced, and a relation (or relations) binding them together.

Let us turn for a moment to the systematic description of consciousness made by one of the Abhidharma schools (see appendix B). The mental factors are the relations that bind the consciousness to its object, and at each moment a consciousness is dependent on its momentary mental factors (like the hand and its fingers).[11] Note that the second, third, and fourth aggregates are included here as mental factors. Five of the mental factors are omnipresent; that is, in every moment of consciousness the mind is bound to its object by all five of these factors. There are *contact* between the mind and its object; a specific *feeling* tone of pleasantness, unpleasantness, or neutrality; a *discernment* of the object; an *intention* toward the object; and *attention* to the object. The rest of the factors, including all the dispositions that make up the fourth aggregate, are not always present. Some of these factors can be present together in a given moment (such as confidence and diligence), others are mutually exclusive (such as alertness and drowsiness). The combination of mental factors that are present make up the character—the color and taste—of a particular moment of consciousness.

Is this Abhidharma analysis of consciousness a system of intentionality along Husserlian lines? There are similarities in that there is no consciousness without an object of consciousness and a relation. (Mind [sems] in the Tibetan tradition is often defined as "that which projects itself to other.") But there are differences. Neither the objects of consciousness nor the mental factors are representations. Most important, consciousness (vijñana) is only one mode of knowing; prajña does not know by means of a subject/object relationship. We might call the simple experiential/psychological observation that conscious experience takes a subject/object form *protointentionality*.[12] Husserl's theory is based not only on protointentionality but also on Brentano's notion of intentionality as subsequently elaborated by Husserl into a full-fledged representational theory.[13]

The temporal relationship between a consciousness and its object was the subject of great dispute among the Abhidharma schools: some held that the occurrence of the object and of mind was simultaneous; others, that the object occurred first, followed in the succeeding moment by the mind (first a sight, then the seeing consciousness). A third claim was that mind and object were simultaneous for sight, sound, smell, taste, and touch but that the thinking consciousness took as its object the preceding moment of thought. This disupte became integral to philosophical debates about what things actually existed. There were also disputes about which factors to include and how they were to be characterized.

Despite the atmosphere of debate that surrounded some issues, there was unanimous agreement on the more experientially direct claim that each of the senses (eye, ear, nose, tongue, body, and mind) had a different consciousness (recall Jackendoff)—that is, at each moment of experience there was a different experiencer as well as a different object of experience. And of course there was agreement that no actual self was to be found in consciousness, either in the experiencer, the object of experience, or the mental factors binding them together.

In our habitual and unreflective state, of course, we impute continuity of consciousness to all our experience—so much so that consciousness always occurs in a "realm," an apparently cohering total environment with its own complete logic (of aggression, poverty, etc.).[14] But this apparent totality and continuity of consciousness masks the discontinuity of momentary consciousnesses related to one another by cause and effect. A traditional metaphor for this illusory continuity is the lighting of one candle with a second candle, a third candle from that one, and so on—the flame is passed from one candle to the next without any material basis being passed on. Taking this sequence as a real continuity, however, we cling tenaciously to this consciousness and are terrorized by the possibility of its termination in death. Yet when mindfulness/awareness reveals the disunity of this experience—a sight, a sound, a thought, another thought, and so on—it becomes obvious that consciousness as such cannot be taken as that self we so treasure and for which we are now searching.

We seem unable to find a self anywhere in each aggregate when we take them one by one. Perhaps, then, all the aggregates combine in some way to form the self. Is the self the same as the totality of the aggregates? This idea would be quite attractive if only we knew how to make it work. Each aggregate taken singly is transitory and impermanent; how, then, are we to combine them into something lasting and coherent? Perhaps the self is an *emergent* property of the aggregates? In fact, many people when pressed to define the self (perhaps in a psychology class) will use the concept of an emergent as a solution. Indeed, given the contemporary scientific interest in the emgerent and self-organizing properties of certain complex aggregates, this idea is even plausible. At this point, however, the idea is of no help. Such a self-organizing or synergistic mechanism is not evident in experience. More important, it is not the abstract idea of an emergent self that we cling to so fiercely as our ego; we cling to a "real" ego-self.

When we recognize that no such real self is given to us in our experience, we may swing to the opposite extreme, which is to say that the self must be radically different from the aggregates. In the Western tradition, this move is best exemplified in the Cartesian and Kantian claim that the observed regularity or pattern of experience requires that there be an agent or mover behind the pattern. For Descartes, this mover was the *res cogitans*, the thinking substance. Kant was more subtle and precise. In his *Critique of Pure Reason*, he wrote, "Consciousness of self according to the determinations of our state in inner perception is merely empirical, and always changing. No fixed and abiding self can present itself in this flux of inner appearances. . . . [Thus] there must be a condition which precedes all experience, and which makes experience itself possible. . . . This pure original unchangeable consciousness I shall name *transcendental apperception*."[15] *Apperception* basically means awareness, especially awareness of the process of cognition. Kant saw quite clearly that there was nothing given in this experience of awareness that corresponded to the self, and so he argued that there must be a consciousness that is transcendental, that precedes all experience and makes that experience possible. Kant also thought that this transcendental awareness is responsible for our sense of unity and identity through time, thus his full term for the transcendental ground of the everyday self was "the transcendental unity of apperception."

Kant's analysis is brilliant, but it only heightens the predicament. We are told that there really is a self, but we can never know it. Furthermore, this self hardly answers to our emotional convictions: it is not *me* or *my* self; it is just the idea of a self in general, of some impersonal agent or mover behind experience. It is pure, original, and unchangeable; I am impure and transitory. How could such a radically different self have any relation with my experience? How could it be the conditon or ground of all of my experiences and yet remain untouched by those experiences? If there truly is such a self, it can be relevant to experience only by partaking of the world's fabric of dependency, but to do so would obviously violate its pristine, absolute conditon.

We may present the difference between the Kantian and the mindfulness/awareness views of self in the form of a diagram (see figures

4.1–4.3). In both the Kantian and the mindfulness/awareness traditions, there is, as we have seen, a recognition of the absence of a
substantial self in the momentariness of experience (figure 4.1). The
Kantian move avoids confronting the puzzle of our tendency to believe in a self in the face of this momentariness by positing a pure,
original, and unchangeable consciousness as a ground—the transcendental ego (figure 4.2). In the mindfulness/awareness tradition, the
attitude is to hold the puzzle of this momentariness vividly in mind
by considering that the grasping toward a self could occur within any
given moment of experience (figure 4.3).

At this point the reader will probably become rather irritated and
say, "Fine, the self isn't really a lasting and coherent thing; it is just

Figure 4.1
The momentariness of experience.

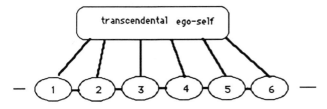

Figure 4.2
Postulation of a transcendental self as a ground for the momentariness of experience.

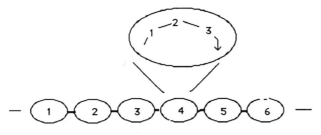

Figure 4.3
The grasping toward an ego-self as occuring within a given moment of experience.

the continuity of the stream of experience. It is a process and not a thing. What's the big deal?" But remember, we have been looking for a self that answers to our emotional/reactional convictions. At this immediate experiential level, we do not feel as if the self is *merely* the stream of experience. Indeed, even to call it a stream reveals our grasping after some sense of solidity, for this metaphor implies that experience flows continuously. But when we subject this continuity to analysis, we seem able to find only discontinuous moments of feeling, perception, motivation, and awareness. We could, of course, redefine the self in all sorts of ways to get around these problems, perhaps even by following contemporary analytic philosophers who use quite sophisticated logical techniques, such as possible world semantics, but none of these new accounts would in any way explain our basic reactional behavior and everyday tendencies.

The point is not whether we can redefine the self in some way that makes us comfortable or intellectually satisfied, nor is it to determine whether there really is an absolute self that is nonetheless inaccessible to us. The point is rather to develop mindfulness of and insight into our situation as we experience it here and now. As Tsultrim Gyamtso remarks, "Buddhism is not telling anyone that he should believe that he has a self or that he does not have a self. It is saying that when one looks at the way one suffers and the way one thinks and responds emotionally to life, *it is as if one believed there were a self that was lasting, single and independent and yet on closer analysis no such self can be found.* In other words, the aggregates (*skandhas*) are empty of a self."[16]

Momentariness and the Brain

Nonmeditating modern readers may be feeling somewhat frustrated at this point. "But what about the brain?" they may ask. It is a general trend in our scientific culture to shunt questions about the mind and consciousness to the brain: if we can assume the functioning of the brain to be continuous and unified, then we can assume our mind to be continuous. We are not talking here about a philosophical assumption (which would be inflammatorily debatable) but about a psychological attitude. Although, strictly speaking, in the Abhidharma context we have already taken care of this question with our discussion of the first aggregate of form, the possibility of a dialogue about momentariness with neuroscience has been left completely open—is there any evidence for momentariness in the functioning of the brain?

Let us be clear about what we are investigating. An examination of experience with mindfulness/awareness reveals that one's experience is discontinuous—a moment of consciousness arises, appears to dwell for an instant, and then vanishes, to be replaced by the next moment.[17] Is this description of experience (the kind of description of actual human experience that we have been asking for) consonant or not consonant with descriptions that we get from neuroscience? Notice that we are not talking about a direction of causality. And we are not dependent on neuroscience to validate experience; that would be scientific imperialism. We are simply interested, in as open a way as possible, in what neuroscience has to say about the issue of momentariness.

There is a literature in neuroscience and psychology that can be referred to as "perceptual framing," which deals with sensorimotor rhythmicity and parsing. One of the most well known phenomena studied in this literature is called "perceptual simultaneity" or "apparent motion." For example, if two lights are shown successively with an interval less than a period of 0.1–0.2 seconds, they will be seen as simultaneous, or in apparent simultaneity. If the interval is slightly increased, the flashing lights will appear to be in rapid motion. If the interval is increased further, the appearance of motion becomes distinctly sequential. There are examples of this phenomenon that are quite familiar: advertisment displays often have a row of flashing lights with the last light shaped as an arrow. One set of lights turns on, and then the next, and the next, giving one the impression that the lights are jumping from one place to the other in the direction of the arrow.

It is well known that the brain has a periodic rhythm of activity, which is detectable in the electroencephalogram (EEG). Since the dominant rhythm for the visual cortex is also about 0.15 seconds, it is natural to assume that there is a relationship between temporal framing and cortical alpha rhythm.

This relationship can be tested experimentally.[18] Figure 4.4 displays the experimental design. A subject was taken and fitted with surface electrodes so that the dominant 0.1 seconds rhythm (the so-called alpha rhythm) could be extracted from the electrical activity in his cortex. That rhythm was then used to trigger on and off the lights that are depicted in front of the subject. It is well known that if one puts the on-off timing of those lights within a certain range, the subject will say that the lights are on simultaneously. And depending on how much one enlarges the interval, the subject will say either that the lights move from one position to another or are sequential. If the interstimulus interval (the time between the first light being on and the second being on) is less than 50 milliseconds, then the lights are reported as simultaneous. If it is over 100 milliseconds, then the lights are reported as sequential. In between these two intervals the lights appear to move.

In this experiment, however, the subject was asked how he saw the set of lights at different moments of his *own* cortical rhythm. Figure 4.5 presents some of the results. Of the three bars in figure 4.5, the middle bar represents what the subject saw when there was no correlation between his brain rhythm and the lights. Here the interval between the lights is set so that there there is an almost chance level of seeing them as either simultaneous or in apparent motion. On either side of the middle bar, there is a correlation between the perception of the lights and the cortical rhythm at two of its phases—the positive peak and the negative peak. If the two lights are started at the negative peak, the subject sees them almost always as simultaneous. If they are started at the positive peak, then the subject sees them in apparent motion. The temporal distance between the lights has not been changed; all that has been changed is the moment at which the subject has been presented with the lights.

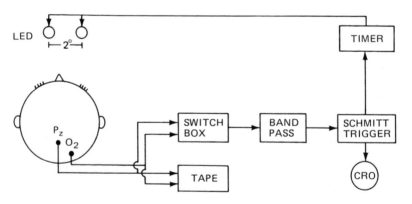

Figure 4.4
Experimental setup to investigate the natural parsing of perceptual events. See text for description. From Varela et al., Perceptual framing and cortical alpha rhythm.

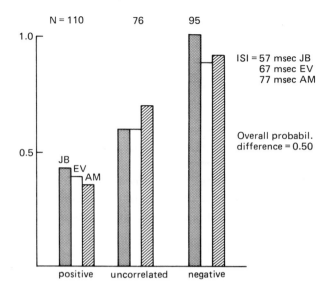

Figure 4.5
Results of experiments revealing temporal parsing of perceptual events around 100–150 msec. See text for more details.

Experiments such as these suggest that there is a natural parsing in the visual frame and that such framing is at least partially and locally related to the rhythm of one's brain in the range of duration of about 0.1–0.2 seconds at its minimum. Roughly stated, if the lights are presented at the beginning of the frame, the likelihood of seeing them occur simultaneously is much greater than if they are presented toward the end of the frame: when they are presented toward the end of the visual frame, the second light can fall, as it were, in the next frame. Everything that falls within a frame will be treated by the subject as if it were within one time span, one "now."

Such neural parsing is to be expected given the fact that the brain is not a sequence of relay stations from the retina to the muscles. At each level there are strong reciprocal and branching connections, so that the entire network can operate only by a large amount of cooperative, back-and-forth matching of activity at all levels. Furthermore, it has became evident that neurons in the central nervous system have a rich diversity of electrical properties based on ionic conductances that endow them with autorhythmic oscillatory properties. This entire cooperative activity takes a certain time to start and to culminate. Such oscillations/resonances can be seen as timing sensorimotor coordination (among other possible functional roles).[19]

In the case at hand, the rhythm is closely linked to the reciprocal connections and reverberations between the thalamus and the visual cortex. In fact, there is good evidence that the activity of a neuron in the thalamus and the cortex of mammals has a unitary time course of about 100 milliseconds following a burst of presynaptic input.[20] Furthermore, it is generally accepted that the alpha rhythm is the result of synchronized thalamocortical reverberations and synchronously firing neuronal groups.[21] These are but a few indications of the basis of a temporal frame. We will come back to examine visual perceptual events on the basis of self-organizing network operations in more detail in the next chapter.

It should be remarked that the critical period of about 0.15 seconds seems to be the minimum amount of time it takes for a describable and recognizable percept to arise. Beyond this minimum, of course, the unitary nature of a more complex conceptualization can last much longer—up to about 0.5 seconds. This limit can be revealed in the components of the cortical activity known as event-related potentials. The basic idea is, again, to use a stimulus that is time locked and to have a subject wear a set of electrodes so that a large number of samples from its surface electrical activity can be collected. These event-related potentials (ERPs) are notoriously noisy, as can be expected from a remote sensing of a large body of neurons. But recent methods using algorithms that learn to recognize significant correlation have begun to give images of these "shadows of thought."[22]

Figure 4.6a shows, for example, a montage of fifteen electrodes over the entire head of a subject. In this study the task was to estimate the distance a target should be moved to estimate a displayed arrow's trajectory. The "move" task required pressure on a button under the right finger with a force proportional to that distance. In contrast, in the "no move" task the arrow pointed directly at the target, and no pressing was required. Thus although the gross stimulus conditions were comparable, the spatial judgments and response differed between the two cases. Figure 4.6b displays the ERP for the two tasks. It is evident that they differ only in the 300–500 msec range, not before or after. Furthermore, as figure 4.6c shows, the regions of the brain's mass activity in different moments and different tasks are like moving clouds of electrical activity that appear to shift and subside—an electrical shadow of the momentariness of experience.

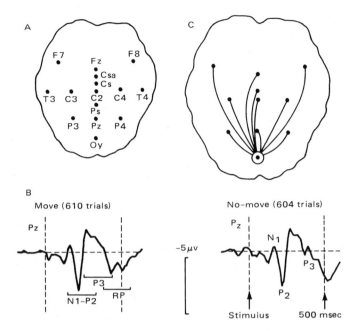

Figure 4.6
(a) Montage of 15 electrodes over a subject's head to extract event related potentials when confronted with a simple visuo-motor task. (b) One example of such ERP from the parietal derivation, showing a sequence of electrical events over 0.5 seconds, and differing between the two tasks only in the later 300–500 msec portion. (c) The overall electrical pattern moves and changes over this temporal frame like a "shadow of thought." Here solid lines indicate strong correlation with the electrode encircled in the move task. High correlation in the no-move task displays a different pattern (not shown). From Gevins et al., Shadows of thought.

This neuropsychological perspective is interesting for our purposes because the parsing of experience naturally corresponds to the aggregates of the mindfulness/awareness practitioner. In fact, the phenomenon of parsing is not evident at first glance for either the neuropsychologist or the practitioner. But it can be revealed through a disciplined method of examining experience, such as mindfulness/awareness.

It is an interesting question, from the standpoint of mindfulness/awareness practice, whether the aggregates express a direct observation of components arising sequentially (whether there is a sequence of development implied in listing them individually), or whether they arise simultaneously from moment to moment (the listing is an inferred decomposition). This issue provides a classical example of how descriptions might change as a function of one's habits of attention and observation, perhaps as a function of the contextual purpose of the description (who is being taught about the aggregates and for what reason). The descriptions of some authors do at times seem to indicate that the aggregates are sequential,[23] but other descriptions (in particular the more classical texts less concerned with the question) are not very explicit about the issue at all;[24] this makes perfect sense given the function of the description of the aggregates in Buddhist discourse.

Even when one does take as an object of inquiry whether the aggregates are sequential or simultaneous, for most people the aggregates appear phenomenologically to arise too rapidly for them to tell. In consonance with neurophysiological observations of the brief timing of a unit of experience, the aggregates seem to arise as a package. For example, even from an information-processing point of view in contemporary cognitive psychology, form and discernment would appear to specify each other. Form can be seen as the arising of something distinct from a background (a figure from a background), but discernment is not the simple registering of the distinction: it is an active (that is, top-down) process of conceptualization that enables even simple distinctions of form to be discerned. Neither form nor discernment is simply given beforehand: as we have seen, we frame our perceptions as intentional items.

On the other hand, the neurophysiological observations indicate (as shown, for example, in figure 4.6) that the initial stages of perceptual organization (at least in these laboratory conditions and for simple visuomotor patterns) precede the more cognitively related electrical correlates by some 100–200 milliseconds. This time difference might just be too fast for detailed attention except when training in attention has stabilized sufficiently to notice the difference. Even so, it is quite remarkable that such fine points of observation could be made, presented, and repeatedly validated by practitioners centuries apart, in terms that make the comparison with neuropsychological evidence quite possible and intriguing.

Furthermore, what is available to an experienced meditator is not necessarily available to a beginner. In particular, this example of the analysis of the aggregates highlights the process of change that one's awareness/attention undergoes in the open-ended stance proposed by mindfulness/awareness. As we outlined in chapter 2, the foundation of mindfulness/awareness practice is the cultivation of mindfulness through a relaxed focusing on the arising of every moment of experience, whether during sitting periods (the "laboratory" situation of mindfulness/awareness) or in daily life. By paying attention over and over again to the details of our embodied situation, awareness of what happens becomes more and more spontaneous. What at the beginning are simply mere flickers of a thought or an emotion become sharper and more apparent in the details of their arising. Through further development, the attention paid to mental movements is sufficiently subtle and quick that mindfulness actually has to be dropped as a distinct attitude. At this point, mindfulness is either sponteneously present or it is not. Then as this inseparability between awareness and mental movement stabilizes further, observations of the fine progression of the aggregates (whether sequential or simultaneous) from moment to moment become possible.

This progression of attention has received even further and more detailed consideration in the Buddhist tradition, but we have presented enough of its basic development for our purposes here. We can now bring this chapter to a close by returning to the theme with which we began: the nature of the ego-self.

The Aggregates without a Self

It might appear that in our search for a self in the aggregates we have come out empty handed. Everything that we tried to grasp seemed to slip through our fingers, leaving us with the sense that there is nothing to hold on to. At this point, it is important to pause and again remind ourselves of just what it was that we were unable to find.

We did not fail to find the physical body, though we had to admit that its designation as *my body* depends very much on how we choose to look at things. Nor did we fail to locate our feelings or sensations, and we also found our various perceptions. We found dispositions, volitions, motivations—in short, all those things that make up our personality and emotional sense of self. We also found all the various forms in which we can be aware—awareness of seeing and hearing, smelling, tasting, touching, even awareness of our own thought processes. So the only thing we didn't find was a truly existing self or ego. But notice that we did find experience. Indeed, we entered the very eye of the storm of experience, we just simply could discern there no self, no "I."

Why then do we feel empty handed? We feel this way because we tried to grasp something that was never there in the first place. This grasping goes on all the time; it is exactly the deep-rooted emotional response that conditions all of our behavior and shapes all of the situations in which we live. It is for this reason that the five aggregates are glossed as the "aggregates of grasping" (*upadanaskandha*). We— that is, our personality, which is largely dispositional formations— cling to the aggregates as if they were the self when, in fact, they are empty (*sunya*) of a self. And yet despite this emptiness of ego-self, the aggregates are full of experience. How is this possible?

The progressive development of insight enhances the experience of calm mindfulness and expands the space within which all experiential arisings occur. As this practice develops, one's immediate attitude (not simply one's after-the-fact reflections) becomes more and more focused on the awareness that these experiences—thoughts, dispositions, perceptions, feelings, and sensations—cannot be pinned down. Our habitual clinging to them is itself only another feeling, another dispositon of our mind.

This arising and subsiding, emergence and decay, is just that emptiness of self in the aggregates of experience. In other words, the very fact that the aggregates are full of experience is the same as the fact that they are empty of self. If there were a solid, really existing self hidden in or behind the aggregates, its unchangeableness would prevent any experience from occurring; its static nature would make the constant arising and subsiding of experience come to a screeching halt. (It is not surprising, therefore, that techniques of meditation that presuppose the existence of such a self proceed by closing off the senses and denying the world of experience.) But that circle of arising and decay of experience turns continuously, and it can do so only because it is empty of a self.

In this chapter we have seen not only that cognition and experience do not appear to have a truly existing self but also that the habitual belief in such an ego-self, the continual grasping to such a self, is the basis of the origin and continuation of human suffering and habitual patterns. In our culture, science has contributed to the awakening of this sense of the lack of a fixed self but has only described it from afar. Science has shown us that a fixed self is not necessary for mind but has not provided any way of dealing with the basic fact that this no-longer-needed self is precisely the ego-self that everyone clings to and holds most dear. By remaining at the level of description, science has yet to awaken to the idea that the experience of mind, not merely without some impersonal, hypothetical, and theoretically constructed self but without ego-self, can be profoundly transformative.

Perhaps it is not fair to ask more of science. To borrow the words of Merleau-Ponty, the strength of science may lie precisely in the fact that it gives up living among things, preferring to manipulate them instead.[25] But if this preference expresses the strength of science, it also indicates its weakness. By renouncing a life amid the things of experience, the scientist is able to remain relatively unaffected by her discoveries.[26] This situation has, perhaps, been tolerable for the past three hundred years, but it is fast becoming intolerable in our modern era of cognitive science.

If science is to continue to maintain its position of de facto authority in a responsible and enlightened manner, then it must enlarge its horizon to include mindful, open-ended analyses of experience, such as the one evoked here. Cognitivism, at least at the moment, does not seem to be capable of such a step, given its narrow conception of cognition as the computation of symbols after the fashion of deductive logic. It would do well to remember, then, that cognitivism did not emerge ready made, like Athena from the head of Zeus. Only a few of its exponents are sensitive to its roots in its earlier years and to the decisions that were subsequently made about which avenues of research to explore. These earlier years, however, have once more become a source of inspiration to a new and controversial approach to cognition in which the self-organizing qualities of biological aggregates play a central role. This approach sheds new light on all of the themes we have touched so far and takes us into part III of our exploration.

III
Varieties of Emergence

5

Emergent Properties and Connectionism

Self-Organization: The Roots of an Alternative

We now embark on the second stage of our exploration of the dialogue between cognitive science and the examination of human experience through the tradition of mindfulness/awareness meditation. In the first stage we saw how the notion of the cognitive agent as a bundle of representations plays a central role in both present-day cognitivism and in the initial stages of the mindful, open-ended examination of experience. In this second stage the dominant theme shifts to the notion of *emergent* properties. This key notion has a complex history, which provides the entry point for our presentation.

Alternatives to the dominant approach of symbol manipulation in cognitive science were already proposed and widely discussed during the early, formative years of cybernetics. At the Macy Conferences,[1] for example, extensive discussion occurred concerning the point that in actual brains there seem to be no rules, no central logical processor, nor does information appear to be stored in precise addresses. Rather, brains can be seen to operate on the basis of massive interconnections in a distributed form, so that the actual connections among ensembles of neurons change as a result of experience. In brief, these ensembles present us with a self-organizing capacity that is nowhere to be found in the paradigm for symbol manipulation. In 1958 Frank Rosenblatt built the "Perceptron," a simple device with some capacity for recognition, purely on the basis of the changes of connectivity among neuronlike components;[2] similarly, W. R. Ashby did the first study of the dynamics of very large systems with random interconnections, showing that they exhibit coherent global behaviors.[3]

The standard history would have it that these alternative views were literally wiped out of the intellectual scene in favor of the computational ideas discussed in chapter 3. It was only in the late 1970s that an explosive rekindling of these ideas took place—after twenty-five years of dominance of the cognitivist orthodoxy (what Daniel Dennett has amusingly termed "High Church Computationalism").[4] Certainly one of the contributing factors in this renewed interest was the parallel rediscovery of self-organizational ideas in physics and nonlinear mathematics, as well as the easy access to fast computers.

The recent motivation to take a second look into self-organization was based on two widely acknowledged deficiencies of cognitivism. The first is that symbolic information processing is based on *sequential* rules, applied one at a time. This "von Neumann bottleneck" is a dramatic limitation when the task at hand requires large numbers of sequential operations (such as image analysis or weather forecasting). A continued search for *parallel* processing algorithms has met with little success because the entire computational orthodoxy seems to run precisely counter to it.

A second important limitation is that symbolic processing is localized: the loss or malfunction of any part of the symbols or rules of the system results in a serious malfunction. In contrast, a *distributed* operation is highly desirable, so that there is at least a relative equipotentiality and immunity to mutilations.

The culmination of experience in the first two decades of the cognitivist dominance can best be expressed by noting a conviction that grew gradually among the community of researchers: it is necessary to invert the expert and the child in the scale of performances. The first attempts were directed at solving the most general problems, such as natural language translation or the problem of devising a "general problem solver." These attempts, which tried to match the intelligence of a person who is a highly trained expert, were seen as tackling the interesting, hard issues. As the attempts became more modest and local, it became apparent that the deeper and more fundamental kind of intelligence is that of a baby who can acquire language from dispersed daily utterances and can constitute meaningful objects from what seems to be a sea of lights. Cognitivist architectures had moved too far from biological inspirations; one does not wish to reduce the cognitive to the biological, but the most ordinary tasks are done faster when performed even by tiny insects than is possible when they are attempted with a computational strategy of the type proposed in the cognitivist orthodoxy. Similarly, the resiliency of the brain to resist damage, or the flexibility of biological cognition to adjust to new environments without compromising all of its competence, is taken for granted by neurobiologists but is nowhere to be seen in the computational paradigm.

The Connectionist Strategy

In this alternative orientation in cognitive science, then, the brain has once more become the main source of metaphors and ideas. Theories and models no longer begin with abstract symbolic descriptions but with a whole army of neurallike, simple, unintelligent components, which, when appropriately connected, have interesting global properties. These global properties embody and express the cognitive capacities being sought.

The entire approach depends, then, on introducing the appropriate connections, which is usually done through a rule for the gradual change of connections starting from a fairly arbitrary initial state. The most thoroughly explored learning rule is "Hebb's Rule." In 1949 Donald Hebb suggested that learning could be based in changes in the brain that stem from the degree of correlated activity between neurons: if two neurons tend to be active together, their connection is strengthened; otherwise it is diminished. Therefore, the system's connectivity becomes inseparable from its history of transformation and related to the kind of task defined for the system. Since the real action happens at the level of the connections, the name connectionism (often called neoconnectionism) has been proposed for this direction of research.[5]

One of the important factors contributing to the explosive interest in this approach today was the introduction of some effective methods of following the changes that can occur in these networks. Great attention has been given to the introduction of statistical measures that provide the system with a global energy function that permits one to follow how the system arrives into convergent states.[6]

Let us consider an example. Take a total number (say N) of simple neuronlike elements and connect them reciprocally. Next present this system with a succession of patterns by treating some of its nodes as sensory ends (a retina if you wish). After each presentation let the system reorganize itself by rearranging its connections following a Hebbian principle, that is, by increasing the links between those neurons that happen to be active together for the item presented. The presentation of an entire list of patterns constitutes the system's learning phase.

After the learning phase, when the system is presented again with one of these patterns, it recognizes it, in the sense that it falls into a unique global state or internal configuration that is said to represent the learned item. This recognition is possible provided the number of patterns presented is not larger than a fraction of the total number of participating neurons (about 0.15 N). Furthermore, the system performs a correct recognition even if the pattern is presented with added noise or the system is partially mutilated.[7]

Emergence and Self-Organization

This example is but one of a whole class of neural network or connectionist models, which we shall discuss further. But first we need to broaden the discussion to understand what is at stake in studying these networks. The strategy, as we said, is to build a cognitive system not by starting with symbols and rules but by starting with simple components that would dynamically connect to each other in dense ways. In this approach, each component operates only in its local environment, so that there is no external agent that, as it were, turns the system's axle. But because of the system's network constitution, there is a global cooperation that spontaneously emerges when the states of all participating "neurons" reach a mutually satisfactory state. In such a system, then, there is no need for a central processing unit to guide the entire operation.[8] This passage from local rules to global coherence is the heart of what used to be called self-organization during the cybernetic years.[9] Today people prefer to speak of emergent or global properties, network dynamics, nonlinear networks, complex systems, or even synergetics.

There is no unified formal theory of emergent properties. It is clear, however, that emergent properties have been found across all domains—vortices and lasers, chemical oscillations, genetic networks, developmental patterns, population genetics, immune networks, ecology, and geophysics. What all these diverse phenomena have in common is that in each case a network gives rise to new properties, which researchers try to understand in all their generality.[10] One of the most useful ways of capturing the emergent properties that these various systems have in common is through the notion of an "attractor" in dynamical systems theory. Since this idea will be of importance for the rest of our discussion, let us pause to consider it through an example.[11]

Consider a *cellular automata*, a simple unit that receives inputs from two immediate neighbors and communicates its internal state to the same immediate neighbors. Assume that the cell or unit can be in only two states (0 or 1, active or inactive) and that the rule governing the change in each automata is simply a (Boolean) function of two arguments (such as "and" or "exclusive or"). Since we can choose such a function for each one of the two states of the cellular automata, the operation of each unit is completely specified by a pair of Boolean functions.

Instead of working with a complex network, we simply connect a string of such elementary units into a circular array, so that there is no input and output from the entire ring, only internal actions. For the purpose of display, however, it is easier to cut this ring open and to present it linearly, with the cells in the 1 state indicated by a black square and those in the opposite state indicated by a blank space. Accordingly, in the display in figure 5.1, the cellular position runs from left to right (with the last cell linked to the first one, according to the chosen ring architecture).

This ring of cellular automata acquires a dynamics by starting at some random state and letting each cell reach an updated state at each (discrete) moment of time in a synchronous fashion (i.e., all of the cells reach their respective states together). In the display, we represent the initial instant at the topmost row and successive instants of time going downward. Thus the successive states of the same cell can be read as a column, and the simultaneous states of all cells can be read as a row. In all the simulations presented in figure 5.2, the ring was composed of eighty cells, and its initial starting state was chosen at random.

It is remarkable to observe that even this simple, almost minimal network has rich self-organizing capacities. A thorough examination of its capacities has been conducted recently by S. Wolfram.[12] We will not recapitulate his work here. It is sufficient for our purposes to note that dynamically these rings fall into four major classes or attractors, as illustrated in figure 5.2. A first class exhibits a simple attractor, which leads all cells to become homogenously active or inactive. For a second, more interesting class of rings the rules give rise to spatial periodicities, that is, some cells remain active while others do not. For

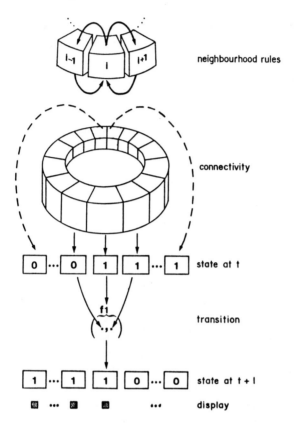

neighbourhood rules

connectivity

state at t

transition

state at t + 1

display

Figure 5.1
Constructing a simple cellular automaton.

a third class the rules give rise to spatiotemporal cycles of length two or longer. These last two classes correspond to cyclic attractors. Finally, for a few rules the dynamics seem to give rise to chaotic attractors, where one does not detect any regularities in space or time.

The basic point we are illustrating here is that the emergence of global patterns or configurations in systems of interacting elements is neither an oddity of isolated cases nor unique to neural systems. In fact, it seems difficult for any densely connected aggregate to escape emergent properties; thus theories of such properties are a natural link for different levels of descriptions in natural and cognitive phenomena. With this larger view of self-organization in mind, let us return now to neural networks and connectionism.

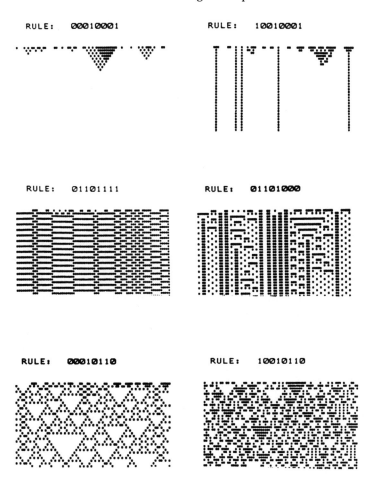

Figure 5.2
Emergent cooperative patterns (or "attractors") in cellular automata.

Connectionism Today

Connectionist theories provide, with amazing grace, working models for a number of interesting cognitive capacities, such as rapid recognition, associative memory, and categorical generalization. The current enthusiasm for this orientation is justified on several counts. First, cognitivist AI and neuroscience had few convincing results to account for (or reconstruct) the kinds of cognitive processes introduced above. Second, connectionist models are much closer to biological systems; thus one can work with a degree of integration between AI and neuroscience that was hitherto unthinkable. Third, in experimental psychology connectionist models facilitate a return to a behaviorist orientation, which circumvents theorizing in terms of high-level, commonsense, mentalistic constructs (a style of theory that had been legitimated by cognitivism but about which psychology remained ambivalent). Finally, the models are general enough to be applied, with little modification, to various domains, such as vision or speech recognition.

There is a variety of examples of emergent neural states for tasks that require no learning, such as eye movements or ballistic limb movements. Obviously, most of the cognitive tasks one wishes to understand involve experience-dependent transformations, hence the interest in learning rules such as Hebb's, which we introduced in our first example. Such rules provide a neural network not just with emergent configurations (as was the case even for our simple ring automaton) but with the capacity to synthesize new configurations according to experience.

We are not going to review here this developing field of research into plastic neural networks and their applications to the study of the brain and artificial intelligence.[13] It is sufficient for our purposes to point out that there are two major classes of learning methods currently being explored. The first one, illustrated by Hebb's rule and inspired by brain mechanisms, is learning by *correlation*: the system is presented with a whole series of examples and is molded by it for future encounters. The second alternative is learning by *copying*, that is, by having a model that acts as an active instructor. This strategy is, in fact, the one proposed early on by Rosenblatt in his Perceptron. In its modern version it is known as "backpropagation." In this technique, changes in the neuronal connections inside the network (called "hidden units") are assigned so as to minimize the difference between the network's response and what is expected of it.[14] Here learning resembles someone trying to imitate an instructor. NetTalk, a celebrated recent example of this method, is a grapheme-phoneme conversion machine that works by being shown a few pages of an English text in its learning phase. As a result, NetTalk can read aloud a new text in what many listeners consider deficient but comprehensible English.[15]

Neuronal Emergences

Recent work has produced some detailed evidence that emergent properties are fundamental to the operation of the brain itself. This point is hardly surprising if one looks at the details of the brain's anatomy. In fact, since the time of Sherrington and Pavlov the understanding of global distributed properties has been an El Dorado of neuroscience, one that is difficult to reach. The reasons for these difficulties have been both technical and conceptual. They have been technical because it is not easy to know what myriad neurons dispersed over the brain are simultaneously doing. Only recently have some of the methods become truly effective.[16] But the difficulties have also been conceptual, for neuroscientists had a strong preference during the 60s and 70s for looking at the brain through cognitivist glasses. Thus information-processing metaphors based on the belief that the brain can be described as a von Neumann computer were more in vogue than emergent network descriptions.

Information-processing metaphors are, however, of limited use. For example, although neurons in the visual cortex do have distinct responses to specific features of the visual stimuli, these responses occur only in an anesthetized animal with a highly simplified internal and external environment. When more normal sensory surroundings are allowed and the animal is studied awake and behaving, it has become increasingly clear that stereotyped neuronal responses become highly context sensitive. There are, for example, distinct effects produced by bodily tilt or auditory stimulation.[17] Furthermore, the neuronal response characteristics depend directly on neurons localized far from their receptive fields.[18] Even a change in posture, while preserving the same identical sensorial stimulation, alters the neuronal responses in the primary visual cortex, demonstrating that even the seemingly remote motorium is in resonance with the sensorium.[19]

A symbolic, stage-by-stage description for a system with this type of constitution seems to go against the grain.

It has, therefore, become increasingly clear to neuroscientists that one needs to study neurons as members of large ensembles that are constantly disappearing and arising through their cooperative inter-actions and in which every neuron has multiple and changing re-sponses in a context-dependent manner. A rule for the constitution of the brain is that if a region (nucleus, layer) *A* connects to *B*, then *B* connects reciprocally back to *A*. This law of reciprocity has only two or three minor exceptions. The brain is thus a highly cooperative system: the dense interconnections among its components entail that eventually everything going on will be a function of what all the components are doing.

This kind of cooperativeness holds both locally and globally: it functions within subsystems of the brain and at the level of the connections among those subsystems. One can take the entire brain and divide it into subsections, depending on the kinds of cells and areas, such as the thalamus, hypocampus, cortical gyri, etc. These subsections are made up of complex networks of cells, but they also relate to each other in a network fashion. As a result the entire system acquires an internal coherence in intricate patterns, even if we cannot say exactly how this occurs. For example, if one artificially mobilizes the reticular system, an organism will change behaviorally from, say, being awake to being asleep. This change does not indicate, however, that the reticular system is the controller of wakefulness. That system is, rather, a form of architecture in the brain that permits certain internal coherences to arise. But when these coherences arise, they are not simply due to any particular system. The reticular system is necessary but not sufficient for certain coherent states, such as wake-fulness and sleep. It is the animal that is asleep or awake, not the reticular neurons. In fact, there are many levels of resolution at which such neuronal emergences can be studied, from the level of cellular properties to entire brain regions, each level of detail requiring a different methodology.[20]

Consider what happens in visual perception in its peripheral stages. The first diagram in figure 5.3 displays the visual pathways of the brain. The optic nerve connects from the eyes to a region in the thalamus called the lateral geniculate nucleus (LGN) and from there to the visual cortex. The standard information-processing de-scription (still found in textbooks and popular accounts) is that infor-

a

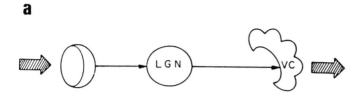

b

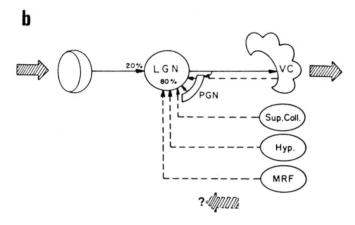

Figure 5.3
Connections in the visual pathway of mammals at the thalamic level.

mation enters through the eyes and is relayed sequentially through the thalamus to the cortex where "further processing" is carried out. But if one looks closely at the way the whole system is put together, one finds little to support this view of sequentiality. The second diagram in figure 5.3 depicts the way the LGN is embedded in the brain network. It is evident that 80 percent of what any LGN cell listens to comes not from the retina but from the dense inter-connectedness of other regions of the brain. Furthermore, one can see that there are more fibers coming from the cortex down to the LGN than there are going in the reverse direction. To look at the visual pathways as constituting a sequential processer seems entirely arbi-trary; one could just as easily see the sequence moving in the reverse direction.

Thus even at the most peripheral end of the visual system, the influences that the brain receives from the eye are met by more activity that flows out from the cortex. The encounter of these two ensembles of neuronal activity is one moment in the emergence of a new coherent configuration, depending on a sort of resonance or active match-mismatch between the sensory activity and the internal setting at the primary cortex.[21] The primary visual cortex is, however, but one of the partners in this particular neuronal local circuit at the LGN level. Other partners, such as the reticular formation, the fibers coming from the superior colliculus, or the corollary discharge of neurons that control eye movements, play an equally active role.[22] Thus the behavior of the whole system resembles a cocktail party conversation much more than a chain of command.

What we have described for the LGN and vision is, of course, a uniform principle throughout the brain. Vision is useful as a case study since the details are better known than for most other nuclei and cortical areas. An individual neuron participates in many such global patterns and bears little significance when taken individually. In this sense, the basic mechanism of recognition of a visual object or a visual attribute could be said to be the emergence of a global state among *resonating neuronal ensembles*.

In fact, Stephen Grossberg has pioneered a detailed analysis of such adaptive resonant neuronal networks;[23] the skeleton of one known as ART (from *adaptive resonance theory*) is shown in figure 5.4. These models are interesting because they match the overall architecture in the visual pathways that we have just outlined, while at the same time they are mathematically precise, thus permitting simulations and artificial implementation. ART is capable of self-organizing, self-sta-bilizing, and self-scaling a recognition "code" (a set of stabilized internal configurations) in response to arbitrary sequences of arbi-trarily many input patterns. The core of ART is two succesive stages (labeled F_1 and F_2 in figure 5.4 and reminiscent of the LGN and visual cortex) that respond to activation patterns in short-term memory (STM). This bottom-up stream meets a bottom-down stream through the activation of long-term memory (LTM) traces. The rest of ART modulates STM and LTM processes, such as grain control and wave resetting. Carpenter and Grossberg find that during the self-or-ganizing phase "attentional" mechanisms are critical for learning; these mechanisms appear when there is mismatch between bottom-up and top-down patterns. These resonant networks have been

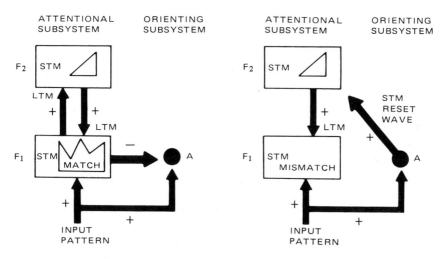

Figure 5.4
The ART model for visual processing through attentional-orienting subsystems. See text for more details. From Carpenter and Grossberg, A massively parallel architecture for a self-organizing neural pattern recognition machine.

shown to be capable of rapidly learning to categorize various streams of input, such as letters into classes, without a predefined list. All the rules in ART describe emergent properties of parallel network interactions.

At this point we would like to return to the topic of emergent biological processes and the five aggregates discussed in the previous chapter. We raised the issue there of whether the aggregates arise sequentially or simultaneously. Within the traditional Buddhist texts, this issue rarely arises, largely because the aggregates do not constitute an information-processing theory; they function rather as a psychological and phenomenological description of ego-mind (of ego-oriented experience) and as a set of categories to be used in firsthand examination of that experience of ego-mind. For us, however, the issue is worth pursuing, since concern with the parsing of experience is one of the more remarkable points of convergence between cognitive science and the mindfulness/awareness tradition. To take a sequential view of the aggregates seems similar to taking a sequential view of brain activity. Form would have to come first through some preattentive segmentation at the retinal and geniculate level, then sensations and perceptions would arise at the reticular and collicular input, whereas concepts and consciousness would be added at different stages of "higher" brain centers, in areas such as V4, MT, or the inferotemporal cortex. If, however, perceptual activity cannot be so simply analyzed into a straightforward sequence, then it becomes difficult to separate the "low" level of form from the "higher" levels of, say, sensations and discernments. The arising of form always involves some predisposition on the part of our structure. If we take the notion of a heap or pile (*skandha*) as a metaphor for the emergent configurations of a neural network, we will be led to think of the aggregates as resonant patterns in one moment of emergence. Such resonant patterns do take time to arise, since they involve many cycles of back-and-forth activity among all participating local networks. In the last chapter we discussed in some detail how this momentary arising of patterns is perceptually and electrically observable in a temporal frame. Furthermore, we also discussed how, following a certain degree of proficiency in the capacity to observe such arising, even the finer temporal details are discernible. The "chunkiness" of such transitory configurations seems to be an inevitable consequence of the emergent properties of a network such as the brain.

It is possible, then, to see the notion of a heap or pile as a metaphor for what we would now call a self-organizing process. The aggregates would arise as one moment of emergence, as in a resonating network where strictly speaking there is no all-or-none separation between simultaneous (since the emergent pattern itself arises as a whole) and sequential (since for the pattern to arise there must be a back-and-forth activity between participating components). Of course, as we said above, the aggregates do not constitute an information-processing theory. Nonetheless, the neuropsychological approach that we have just adumbrated seems compatible with the direct observations based on mindfulness/awareness meditation, thus making all the more remarkable the fact that this tradition has continued to verify the parsing of experience into coherent moments of emergence.

Exeunt the Symbols

This alternative orientation—connectionist, emergent, self-organizational, associationist, network dynamical—is young and diverse. Most of those who would enlist themselves as members hold widely divergent views on what cognitive science is and on its future.

Keeping this disclaimer in mind, we can now present answers to the questions we previously posed to cognitivism from this perspective:

Question 1: What is cognition?

Answer: The emergence of global states in a network of simple components.

Question 2: How does it work?

Answer: Through local rules for individual operation and rules for changes in the connectivity among the elements.

Question 3: How do I know when a cognitive system is functioning adequately?

Answer: When the emergent properties (and resulting structure) can be seen to correspond to a specific cognitive capacity—a successful solution to a required task.

One of the most interesting aspects of this alternative approach in cognitive science is that symbols, in their conventional sense, play no role. In the connectionist approach, symbolic computations are replaced by numerical operations—for example, the differential equations that govern a dynamical system. These operations are more fine grained than those performed using symbols; in other words, a single, discrete symbolic computation would, in a connectionist model, be performed as a result of a large number of numerical operations that govern a network of simple units. In such a system, the meaningful items are not symbols; they are complex patterns of activity among the numerous units that make up the network.

This nonsymbolic approach involves a radical departure from the basic cognitivist assumption that there must be a distinct symbolic level in the explanation of cognition. Cognitivism introduced symbols as a way of bridging the need for a semantic or representational level with the constraint that this level be ultimately physical. Symbols are both meaningful and physical, and a computer is a device that respects the meaning of the symbols while operating only on their physical form. This separation between form and meaning was the masterstroke that created the cognitivist approach—indeed, it was the same one that had created modern logic. But this fundamental move also implies a weakness in addressing cognitive phenomena at a deeper level: How do the symbols acquire their meaning?

In situations where the universe of possible items to be represented is constrained and clear-cut (for example, when a computer is programmed or when an experiment is conducted with a set of predefined visual stimuli), the assignment of meaning is clear. Each discrete physical or functional item is made to correspond to an external item (its referential meaning), a mapping operation that the observer easily provides. Remove these constraints, and the form of the symbols is all that is left, and meaning becomes a ghost, as it would if we were to contemplate the bit patterns in a computer whose operating manual had been lost.

In the connectionist approach, however, meaning is not located in particular symbols; it is a function of the global state of the system and is linked to the overall performance in some domain, such as recognition or learning. Since this global state emerges from a network of units that are more fine grained than symbols, some researchers refer to connectionism as the "subsymbolic paradigm."[24] They argue that the formal principles of cognition lie in this subsymbolic domain, a domain above but closer to the biological than to the symbolic level of cognitivism. At the subsymbolic level, cognitive descriptions are built out of the constituents of what at a higher level would be discrete symbols. Meaning, however, does not reside in these constituents per se; it resides in complex patterns of activity that emerge from the interactions of many such constituents.

Linking Symbols and Emergence

This difference between subsymbolic and symbolic brings us back to our question about the relation between various levels of explanation in the study of cognition. How might subsymbolic emergence and symbolic computation be related?

The most obvious answer is that these two views should be seen as complementary bottom-up and top-down approaches or that they could be pragmatically joined in some mixed mode or simply used at different levels or stages. A typical example of this move would be to describe early vision in connectionist terms, up to, say, the primary visual cortex. Then, at the level of the inferotemporal cortex, the description would be based on symbolic programs. The conceptual status of such a synthesis, however, is far from clear, and concrete examples are still lacking.

In our view, the most interesting relation between subsymbolic emergence and symbolic computation is one of *inclusion*, in which we see symbols as a higher-level description of properties that are ultimately embedded in an underlying distributed system. The case of the so-called genetic code is paradigmatic, and we may use it here for the sake of a concrete example.

For many years biologists considered protein sequences as being instructions coded in the DNA. It is clear, however, that DNA triplets are capable of predictably specifying an aminoacid in a protein if and only if they are embedded in the cell's metabolism, that is in the thousands of enzymatic regulations in a complex chemical network. It is only because of the emergent regularities of such a network as a whole that we can bracket out this metabolic background and thus treat triplets as codes for aminoacids. In other words, the symbolic description is possible at another level. It is clearly possible to treat such symbolic regularities in their own right, but their status and interpretation is quite different from when we simply take them at face value, as if they were independent of the substratum from which they emerge.[25]

The example of genetic information can be transposed directly to the cognitive networks with which neuroscientists and connectionists work. In fact, some researchers have recently expressed this point of view explicitly.[26] In Paul Smolensky's harmony theory, for example, fragmentary "atoms" of knowledge about electrical circuits are linked by distributed statistical algorithms and so yield a model of intuitive reasoning in this domain. The competence of this whole system can be described as doing inferences based on symbolic rules, but the performance sits at a different level and is never achieved by reference to a symbolic interpreter.

How is this inclusive view different from the cognitivist conception of levels of explanation? The difference is actually rather subtle and is mostly a matter of a shift in perspective. The basic point, agreed to by all, is that to formulate explanatory generalizations we need the right kind of descriptive vocabulary or taxonomy. Cognitivism, as we have seen, is founded on the hypothesis that this taxonomy consists of symbols. This symbolic level constrains the kinds of behaviors that are possible for a cognitive system and so is thought to have an independent, explanatory status. In the inclusive view, the need for a symbolic level is acknowledged, but the possibility is left open that this level is only approximate. In other words, symbols are not taken at face value; they are seen as approximate macrolevel descriptions of operations whose governing principles reside at a subsymbolic level.

Among the many issues that change given this possible synthesis, two in particular are worth noting. First, the question of the origin of a symbol and its meaning (why does ATT code for alanine?) can be approached more clearly. Second, any symbolic level becomes highly dependent on the underlying network's properties and peculiarities, as well as bound to its history. A purely procedural account of cognition, independent of its history and the way cognition is embodied, is therefore seriously questioned.

The cognitivists' reply will no doubt be that such a mixed or inclusive mode is fine if one is concerned only with lower-level processes, such as those found in genetic coding. But when one turns to higher-level processes, such as the ability to parse sentences or make inferences, an independent symbolic level will be required. In the case of highly recursive structures, such as human language, it will be argued that the symbolic level is not approximate at all; it is the only precise description available for forms of representation that are productive and systematic.[27]

There is much to be said for this line of argument. The point to be made in reply, though, is that it unjustifiably limits the domain of cognition to very high level processes. For example, Jerry Fodor and Zenon Pylyshyn write in a recent article, "It would not be unreasonable to describe Classical cognitive science [cognitivism] as an extended attempt to apply the methods of proof theory to the modeling of thought (and similarly, of whatever other mental processes are plausibly viewed as involving inferences; predominantly learning and perception). The point is not that logical proofs per se are so important in human thought, but that the way of dealing with them provides a clue as to how to deal with knowledge-dependent processes in general."[28] Despite this last qualification, however, their argument later in the article seems to require that deductive logic be the very paradigm of human thought and hence, presumably, of cognition in general.

We simply see no reason to give in to this narrow conception of cognition. There are many classes of systems, such as the neural networks described in this chapter, whose behavior should be seen as cognitive, and yet their abilities do not encompass these highly systematic and productive features. In fact, it is even possible to argue

that there are nonneural networks that display cognitive properties—
immune systems, for example.[29] When we widen our perspective to
include such forms of cognitive behavior, symbolic computation
might come to be regarded as only a narrow, highly specialized form
of cognition. Although it might be possible to treat this specialized
form as having a high degree of autonomy (by ignoring the larger
system in which it is embedded), the study of cognition would nonetheless include systems consisting of many networks of cognitive
processes, each perhaps with its own distinct cognitive domain.

Cognitivism, perhaps in its desire to establish itself as a mature
research program, has resisted such a perspective. The emergence
view, however, both in its early phase of the study of self-organizing
systems and in its present connectionist form, is open to encompassing a greater variety of cognitive domains. An inclusive or mixed
mode seems, therefore, a natural strategy to pursue. A fruitful link
between a less orthodox cognitivism and the emergence view, where
symbolic regularities emerge from parallel distributed processes, is a
concrete possibility, especially in AI with its predominantly engineering, pragmatic orientation. This complementary endeavor will
undoubtedly produce visible results and might well become the dominant trend for many years to come in cognitive science.[30]

We will not discuss these questions further, for they remain open
and will be decided largely by future research. We wish to raise them
simply in the context of our central question: the dialogue between
cognitive science and human experience.

6
Selfless Minds

Societies of Mind

We have now seen in some detail that brains are highly cooperative systems. Nonetheless, they are not uniformly structured networks, for they consist of many networks that are themselves connected in various ways. As we have already sketched for the case of the visual system, the entire system resembles a patchwork of subnetworks assembled by a complex process of tinkering, rather than a system that results from some clean, unified design. This kind of architecture suggests that instead of looking for grand, unified models for all network behaviors, one should study networks whose abilities are restricted to specific cognitive activities and then look for ways to connect the networks.

This view of cognitive architecture has begun to be taken seriously by cognitive scientists in various ways. In this chapter we will see how it also provides a natural entry point for the next stage of the dialogue between cognitive science and the mindfulness/awareness approach to human experience. To make the discussion clear, we will explore this next stage on the basis of Marvin Minsky's and Seymour Papert's recent proposal to study the mind as a society, for this proposal takes the patchwork architecture of cognition as a central element.[1]

Minsky and Papert present a view in which minds consist of many "agents" whose abilities are quite circumscribed: each agent taken individually operates only in a microworld of small-scale or "toy" problems. The problems must be of a small scale because they become unmanageable for a single network when they are scaled up.[2] This last point has not been obvious to cognitive scientists. It is to a large extent a result of the many years of frustration in AI with attempts to find global solutions (for example, in the form of a General Problem

Solver) and of the relative success in finding solutions to more local tasks—solutions that cannot, however, be extended beyond specific domains. The task, then, is to organize the agents who operate in these specific domains into effective larger systems or "agencies," and these agencies in turn into higher-level systems. In doing so, mind emerges as a kind of society.

It is important to remember here that, although inspired by a closer look at the brain, this model is of the mind. In other words, it is not a model of neural networks or societies; it is a model of the cognitive architecture that abstracts from neurological detail. Agents and agencies are not, therefore, entities or material processes; they are abstract processes or functions. The reader is no doubt familiar with this theme of various levels by now, but the point bears emphasizing, especially since Minsky and Papert sometimes write as if they were talking about cognition at the level of the brain.[3]

The model of the mind as a society of numerous agents is intended to encompass a multiplicity of approaches to the study of cognition, ranging from distributed, self-organizing networks to the classical, cognitivist conception of localized, serial symbolic processing. The society of mind purports to be, then, something of a middle way in present cognitive science. This middle way challenges a homogenous model of the mind, whether in the form of distributed networks at one extreme or symbolic processers at the other extreme.

This move is particularly apparent when Minsky and Papert argue that there are virtues not only to distribution but to insulation, that is to mechanisms that keep various processes apart.[4] The agents within an agency may be connected in the form of a distributed network, but if the agencies were themselves connected in the same way, they would, in effect, constitute one large network whose functions were uniformly distributed. Such uniformity, however, would restrict the ability to combine the operations of individual agencies in a productive way. The more distributed these operations are, the harder it is to have many of them active at the same time without interfering with one another. These problems do not arise, however, if there are mechanisms to keep various agencies insulated from each other. These agencies would still interact, but through more limited connections, such as those typical of sequential, symbolic processing.

The details of such a view are, of course, debatable. But the overall picture of mind not as a unified, homogenous entity, nor even as a collection of entities, but rather as a disunified, heterogenous collection of networks of processes seems not only attractive but also strongly resonant with the experience accumulated in all the fields of cognitive science. Such a society can obviously be considered at more than one level. What counts as an agency, that is, as a collection of agents, could, if we change our focus, be considered as merely one agent in a larger agency. And conversely, what counts as an agent could, if we resolve our focus in greater detail, be seen to be an agency made up of many agents. In the same way, what counts as a society will depend too on our chosen level of focus.

Let us take an example. Minsky begins his *Society of Mind* with the example of an agent whose specialty is building towers out of toy blocks. But to build a tower, one needs to start the tower, add new blocks, and decide when to finish. So this agent—Builder—requires the help of the sub-agents Begin, Add, and Finish, and these sub-agents require still more agents, such as Find and Pick up. The activities of all these agents combine to accomplish the task of building a tower. If we want to think of Builder as a single agent (a homunculus, maybe even with a will, who performs actions), then Builder is whatever it is that switches on all these agents. From the emergent point of view, however, all of these agents combine to produce Builder as an agency that constructs toy towers.

Minsky's and Papert's society of mind is not, of course, concerned with the analysis of direct experience. But Minsky draws on a delightfully wide range of human experience, from playing with children's blocks to being an individual who is aware and can introspect. In many ways, Minsky's work is an extended reflection on cognitive science and human experience, one that is committed to the "subpersonal," but does not wish to lose sight for too long of the personal and experiential. At certain points, Minsky even senses the kinship between some of his ideas and those of the Buddhist tradition, for he begins six of his pages with quotations from the Buddha.[5]

Minsky does not follow the lead that his own citations suggest, however. He argues instead that although there is no room for a truly existing self in cognitive science, we cannot give up our conviction in such a self. At the very end of *The Society of Mind*, science and human experience simply come apart. And since we cannot choose between the two, we are ultimately left with a condition of schizophrenia, in which we are "condemned" (by our constitution) to believe in something we know not to be true (our personal selves).

Let us emphasize that this kind of consequence is not peculiar to Minsky. Indeed, as we saw in our discussion of Jackendoff, cognitivism forces us to separate cognition as representation from cognition as consciousness and in so doing inevitably leads us to the view that, in Jackendoff's words, "consciousness is not good for anything." Thus rather than building a genuine bridge between the computational and the phenomenological mind, Jackendoff simply reduces the latter to a mere "projection" of the former. And yet, as Jackendoff also notes, "Consciousness seems too important to one's life—too much fun—to conceive of it as useless."[6] Thus once again science and human experience simply come apart.

It is only by enlarging the horizon of cognitive science to include an open-ended analysis of human experience that we will be able to avoid this predicament. We will return to consider this impasse in its Minskian form in greater detail. At this point, however, we will turn to a discussion of ideas of society and properties of emergence in two disciplines that examine experience from perspectives other than cognitive science: we will discuss psychoanalysis briefly and the mindfulness/awareness meditation tradition at greater length.

The Society of Object Relations

Within psychoanalysis, a new school, so different from Freudian theory that it has been called a paradigm shift, has emerged.[7] This is *object relations theory*. Freud already anticipated this theory in an embryonic form. For Freud, the superego results from the "internalization" of parental morality as an internalized parental figure. Freud also discussed particular psychological states, such as the mourning process, in terms of relations between the self and such an internalized parent. Object relations theory has extended this idea to encompass all of psychological development and to act as an explanatory framework for adult functioning. In object relations theory, for example in the work of Melanie Klein,[8] the basic mental developmental process is the internalizing of a rich array of persons in various aspects. Fairbairn goes so far as to reconceptualize the concept of motivation into object relations terms; for Fairbairn the basic motivating drive of the human is not the pleasure principle but the need to form relationships.[9] Horowitz joins object relations theory to cognitive science by describing internalized object relations as interpersonal schemas.[10] These schemas and subschemas act very much as Minskian agents.

The convergence between psychoanalysis, in the form of object relations theory, and the concept of mind as a society in artificial intelligence is striking; Turkle suggests that this convergence may be of benefit to both.[11] Object relations theory has been much criticized for reifying interdependent, fluid mental *processes* into an image of independent, static mental *structures*.[12] In the society of mind portrayal of the emergence of agency from agents, however—as in our previous example, Builder—it becomes quite apparent how one can structure such a conceptual system—how one can incorporate aspects of the disunity of mind to which object relations theory points—without reification.

Psychoanalysis is not just theory but a practice. Troubled patients who see an object relations therapist learn to explore their minds, behavior, and emotions in terms of object relations—they come to see their reactions in terms of internalized agents. Does this, we wonder, lead them to question their basic sense of self altogether? This surely happens in some instances between a gifted therapist and a committed patient. But more generally it is unlikely to happen in the present cultural context in Britain and North America since psychoanalysis has been co-opted by psychiatry to an important degree.[13] Thus more often than not it is seen as medicine rather than as a means to gain knowledge about the nature of mind. A successful object relations analysis, like any other analysis, is designed to make the patient better—more functional, with improved object relations, and with greater emotional comfort; it is not designed to lead him to question, "Isn't it odd that I am so zealously pursuing *my* object relations and *my* comfort when all I am is a set of object relations schemas? What is going on?" In more general terms, it is apparent that object relations analysis, like other contemplative traditions, has discovered the contradiction between the lack of a self that analysis discovers and our ongoing sense of self. It is not, however, apparent that psychoanalysis in the form of object relations theory has faced, or even fully acknowledged, this contradiction. Rather, object relations theory appears to accept the basic motivation (the basic grasping) of the ongoing sense of self at face value and employs analytic discoveries about the disunity of the self to cater to the demands of the ongoing sense of self. Because object relations psychoanalysis has not systematically addressed this basic contradiction—the lack of a unitary self in experience versus the ongoing sense of self-grasping—the open-ended quality that is possible in analysis, though present in all psychoanalysis and particularly in object relations therapy, is limited. Lacanian analysis in Europe may be one exception, and it may have gained some of its power and notoriety because of this quality.[14] A fuller discussion of this fascinating bridge between psychoanalysis and modern cognitive science—and eventually with the meditation tradition—is, however, beyond the scope of this book. We therefore turn once again to mindfulness/awareness and the expositions of the Abhidharma.

Codependent Arising

How is it, if we have no self, that there is coherence in our lives? How is it, if we have no self, that we continue to think, feel, and act as though we had a self—endlessly seeking to enhance and defend that nonfindable, nonexperienced self? How and why do the momentary arisings of the elements of experience, the five aggregates and mental factors, follow one another temporally to constitute recurrent patterns?

The Buddha was said to have discovered on the eve of his enlightenment not only the momentariness of the arising of the aggregates but also the entire edifice of causality—the circular structure of habitual patterns, the binding chain, each link of which conditions and is conditioned by each of the others—that constitutes the pattern of human life as a never-ending circular quest to anchor experience in a fixed and permanent self. This insight came to be named with the Sanskrit word *pratityasamutpada*, which literally means "dependence (*pratitya*) upon conditions that are variously originated (*samutpada*)." We will use the term *codependent arising*, since that gloss best expresses the idea, familiar in the context of societies of mind, of transitory yet recurrent, emergent properties of aggregate elements.[15]

This circle is also called the Wheel of Life and the Wheel of Karma. Karma is a topic with a long history, both pre- and post-Buddhist, on which an immense amount of scholarship has been focused.[16] The word *karma* has also found its way into contemporary English vocabulary where it is generally used as a synonym for *fate* or *predestination*. This is definitely not the meaning of karma within Buddhism. Karma constitutes a description of psychological causality—of how habits form and continue over time. The portrait of the Wheel of Life is intended to show how it is that karmic causality actually works. The emphasis on causality is central to the tradition of mindfulness/awareness and as such is quite compatible with our modern scientific sensibility; in the case of mindfulness/awareness, however, the concern is with a causal analysis of direct experience, not with causality as an external form of lawfulness. The concern is also pragmatic: How can the understanding of causality be used to break the chains of conditioning mind (an idea quite contrary to the popular notion of karma as predestination) and foster mindfulness and insight?

There are twelve links (called *nidanas*) in the circular chain (the patterning situation as shown in figure 6.1). The circle is an analytic structure that can be used to describe events of any duration from a single moment to a lifetime or, in the Buddhist view, to many lifetimes. Metaphorically, we could say that these motifs have a fractal character: the same patterns seem to appear even when we change the scale of observation by orders of magnitude. Descriptions of the twelve interdependent links follow.

1 Ignorance
Ignorance is the ground of all karmic causal action. It means being ignorant of, not knowing, the truth(s) about the nature of mind and reality. In the material we have discussed so far, this means being ignorant—personally experientially ignorant—of the lack of ego-self. It also means the confusions—the mistaken views and emotions of believing in a self—that come from that ignorance. Hence it could also be rendered as bewilderment. (In later formulations, it came to include other truths about which a sentient being could be ignorant.)

2 Volitional Action
Out of ignorance, one acts on the basis of a self. That is to say, in the selfless state there are no self-oriented intentions. Because of ignorance of the lack of ego-self, the urge toward habitual, repetitive actions based on a self arises. Ignorance and volitional action are the ground, the prior conditions, sometimes called the past conditions, that give rise to the next eight links (the third through the tenth). If this analytic scheme is being used to talk about the links arising in time, then these eight are said to constitute the present situation.

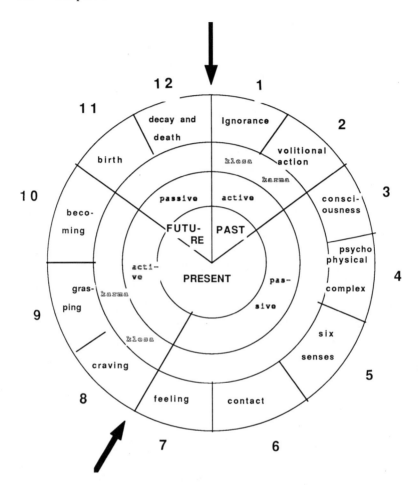

Figure 6.1
Codependent arising as the Wheel of Life.

3 Consciousness

Consciousness refers to sentience in general, the dualistic state we talked about as the fifth aggregate. It may mean the beginning of consciousness in the life of any sentient being or the first moment of consciousness in any given situation. Remember that consciousness is not the only mode of knowing; one is born into a moment or a lifetime of consciousness, rather than wisdom, because of volitional actions that were based on ignorance. If we are speaking of the arising of a particular moment of consciousness, its precise form (which of the six sense bases it arises upon, whether it is pleasant, unpleasant, etc.) is conditioned by the seeds laid down by the volitional action(s) of the previous link.

4 The Psychophysical Complex

Consciousness requires a body and mind together. Moments of consciousness in a given situation can gravitate toward one or the other end of the psychophysical complex: perhaps the consciousness is primarily sensory; perhaps it is primarily mental.

5 The Six Senses

A body and mind mean that one has the six senses. Even brief situations, for example, eating a piece of fruit—involve moments of each of the six sense consciousnesses: one sees, hears, tastes, smells, touches, and one thinks.

6 Contact

Having the six senses means that each sense is able to contact its sense field, its appropriate object. Any moment of consciousness involves contact between the sense and its object (contact is an omnipresent mental factor—see appendix B); without contact, there is no sense experience.

7 Feeling

Feeling—pleasurable, displeasurable, or neutral—arises from contact. All experience has a feeling tone (feeling is also an omnipresent factor). Feeling has, as its basis, one of the six senses. At the point of feeling, one is actually struck by the world—in phenomenological language, one could say that we find ourselves *thrown* into the world.

8 Craving

Craving arises from feeling. Although there are innumerable specific kinds of craving (84,000 in one system), the basic form of craving is desire for what is pleasurable and aversion for what is displeasurable. Craving is a fundamental, automatic reaction.

Craving is an extremely important juncture in this chain of causality. Up to this point, the links have rolled off automatically on the basis of past conditioning. At this point, however, the aware person can do something about the situation: he can interrupt the chain or he can let it go on to the next link (grasping). The handling of craving is what determines the possibilities for perpetuation or change.

It is a traditional exercise to contemplate the chain of codependent arising in both directions, backward as well as forward. Because such an exercise communicates well the codependent emergent quality of this causal analysis, we will show what happens when we go backward in our reasoning from the point of craving: craving for pleasure requires that there be sense feelings; to have feelings, there must be contact with the objects of the senses; to contact the sense objects, there must be the six sense faculties; for the six sense faculties to exist, the entire psychophysical organism is required; for there to be a psychophysical organism, there must be sentience.

9 Grasping

Craving usually results immediately in grasping and clinging. Grasping refers not only to grasping after what one does not have and desires but also to aversion for what one has and desires to be rid of.

10 Becoming

Grasping automatically sets off the reaction toward becoming, toward the formation of a new situation in the future. New tendencies and suppositions are formed as a result of the cumulative effect of the previous seven motifs, which themselves were set into motion by volitional action based on ignorance. Becoming initiates the formation of new patterns that carry over into future situations.

11 Birth

In birth, a new situation, as well as a new mode of being in that situation, is finally born. It is usually at this point only that one senses the causal chain and wants to do something about it. It is at this point, perhaps, that Western philosophers talk about *akrasia* (weakness of the will). The irony is that in normal life, the point at which one wakes up to a situation is past the point where one can do anything about it. Birth into a new situation, even an agreeable one, always has an edge of uncertainty.

12 Decay and Death

Wherever there is birth, there is death; in any process of arising, dissolution is inevitable. Moments die, situations die, and lives end. Even more obvious than the uneasiness of birth is the suffering (and lamentation, as is said) experienced when situations or bodies grow old, decay, and die. In this circular chain of causality, death is the causal link to the next cycle of the chain. The death of one moment of experience is, within the Buddhist analysis of causality, actually a causal precondition for the arising of the next moment. If there is still ignorance and confusion, the wheel will continue turning endlessly in the same fashion.

The circle of conditioned human existence is called *samsara*, which is visualized as a perpetually spinning wheel of existence driven by a relentless causation and pervaded by unsatisfactoriness. There are many vivid traditional images for *samsara*: a ship lost at sea in a raging storm, a deer trapped in a hunter's net, animals racing before a blazing forest fire. According to one traditional story, the Buddha on the eve of his enlightenment worked through the twelve links of the chain seeking a way that the chain could be broken. Nothing could be done about the past; one cannot go back and remove past ignorance and volitional actions. And since one is alive and has a psychophysical organism, the six sense fields and their contact with objects are inevitable. Inevitable also are the feeling states to which the senses give rise and the craving that results. But must craving lead to grasping?

It is at this point, some traditions say, that the Buddha formulated the technique of mindfulness. By precise, disciplined mindfulness to every moment, one can interrupt the chain of automatic conditioning—one can *not* automatically go from craving to grasping and all the rest. Interruption of habitual patterns results in further mindfulness, eventually allowing the practitioner to relax into more open possibilities in awareness and to develop insight into the arising and subsiding of experienced phenomena. That is why mindfulness is the foundational gesture of all the Buddhist traditions.

At this point, we might return briefly to our theoretical formulation. We asked how there could be coherence in our lives over time if there were no self. In the language of societies of mind, the answer lies in the concept of emergence. Just as any agency emerges from the action of individual agents, so the repetitious patterns of habitual actions emerge from the joint action of the twelve links. And just as the existence of the action of each agent is definable only in relation to the actions of all the others, so the operation of each of the links in the chain of codependent arising is dependent on all of the other links. As in any agency, there is no such thing as a habitual pattern per se except in the operation of the twelve agent motifs, nor is there such a thing as the motifs except in relation to the operation of the entire cyclic system.

The historical formation of various patterns and trends in our lives is what Buddhists usually mean by *karma*. It is this accumulation that gives continuity to the sense of ego-self, so evident in everyday, unreflective life. The main motivating and sustaining factor in this process is the omnipresent mental factor of *intention* (see appendix B). Intention—in the form of volitional action—leaves traces, as it were, of its tendencies on the rest of the factors from moment to moment, resulting in the historical accumulation of habits, tendencies, and responses, some wholesome and others unwholesome. When the term *karma* is used loosely, it refers to these accumulations and their effects. Strictly speaking, though, karma is the very process of intention (volitional action) itself, the main condition in the accumulation of conditioned human experience.

In many fields of science, we are familiar with the idea that coherence and development over time need not involve any underlying substance. In evolutionary changes in the history of life, patterns of animal populations give rise to new individuals on the basis of the past (most tangibly expressed in the nuclear genetics of the population) and on the basis of current actions (mating behavior leading to descendence and genetic recombinations). The tracks and furrows of this process are the species and subspecies. But in the logic of Darwin's account of evolution and the Buddhist analysis of experience into codependent arising, we are concerned with the processual transformation of the past into the future through the intermediary of transitional forms that in themselves have no permanent substance.

The agent motifs in the chain of conditioned origination are fairly complex processes. Each of these may be thought of as composed of subagents, or more accurately as themselves agencies composed of agents. In the mindfulness/awareness tradition, of course, the logic is focused upon immediate experience. Is there an experiential—or pragmatic—justification for increasing the layers of agency in the society of causality?

Basic Element Analysis

We have already seen how a moment of consciousness is analyzed into subject, object, and mental factors that bind them together. This schematization was present in the earliest Abhidharma but was greatly elaborated in a technique called basic element (*dharma*) analysis,[17] which reached its peak of eloquence in the *Abhidharmakosa* of Vasubandhu.[18] (It is from this work that we have taken the classification of mental factors presented in appendix B.)

The term for basic element in Sanskrit is *dharma*. Its most general meaning in a psychological context is "phenomenon"—not in the Kantian sense where phenomena are opposed to noumena but simply in the ordinary sense of something that occurs, arises, or is found in experience. In its more technical sense, it refers to an ultimate particular, particle, or element that is reached in an analytic examination. In basic element analysis, moments of experience (the dharmas) were considered analytically irreducible units; they were, in fact, called ultimate realities, whereas the coherences of daily life that were composed of these elements—a person, a house—were called conventional realities.

This idea that experience, or what the phenomenologist would call the life-world, can be analyzed into a more fundamental set of constituents was also a central element in Husserl's phenomenological project. This project broke down because it was, among other things, purely abstract and theoretical. Basic element analysis, on the other hand, was much more successful because it was generated from an open-ended, embodied reflection: it arose as a way of codifying and interpreting the results of the mindfulness/awareness examination of experience. Therefore, even when basic element analysis received certain kinds of devastating criticism from philosophers such as Nagarjuna, it could nonetheless survive as a valuable practice, though seen in a different light.

On a more theoretical level, philosophers might recognize some parallels between basic element analysis and the analytic, rationalist tradition in the West as exemplified by Leibniz, Frege, Russell, and the early Wittgenstein. In both traditions there is a concern with analyzing complex aggregates of societies—whether these be things in the world, linguistic or logical descriptions, mental representations, or direct experience—into their simple and ultimate constituents. Minsky, for example, upholds this analytic tradition when he writes that his "agents of the mind could be the long-sought 'particles' that . . . theories [of mind] need."[19] Such reductionism is almost always accompanied by realism: one adopts a realist stance toward whatever one claims as one's privileged basis, one's ultimate ground.

Here, however, we come upon an interesting difference between Western rationalism and the rationalism embodied in the Abhidharma. In the latter, the designation of basic elements as ultimate reality, we are told, was not an assertion that the basic elements were ontological entities in the sense of being substantially existent.[20] Surely this is an interesting case study—we have here a philosophical system, a reductive system, in which reductive basic elements are postulated as ultimate realities but in which those ultimate realities are not given ontological status in the usual sense. How can that be? Emergents, of course, do not have the status of ontological entities (substances). Might we have a system here in which the basic elements are themselves emergents?

This question is all the more interesting because basic element analysis was not simply an abstract, theoretical exercise. It had both a descriptive and a pragmatic motivation. The concern of the meditator is to break the wheel of conditioned origination and become aware, wise, and free. She is told that she can actually experientially catch herself (within this emergent society of the wheel of the twelve links) at the moment of craving and can begin to undo her conditioning. Will a basic element analysis provide clarity that will help in this task?

We may remember that in basic element analysis each element, each moment of consciousness, consists of the consciousness itself (called, in this system, the primary mind) and its mental factors. The (momentary) mental factors are what bind the (momentary) object (which is, of course, always in one of the six sense fields). The specific quality of each moment of consciousness and its karmic effects on future moments depend upon which mental factors are present.

The relationship between consciousness and the mental factors seems remarkably similar to the relation between Minskian agencies and agents. The contemporary Tibetan scholar Geshe Rabten puts it thus: "The term 'primary mind' denotes the totality of a sensory or mental state composed of a variety of mental factors. A primary mind is like a hand whereas the mental factors are like the individual fingers, the palm, and so forth. The character of a primary mind is thus determined by its constituent mental factors."[21] A hand is an agency of which the fingers, palm, etc., are agents; it is also an agent of the body. These are different levels of description; neither agent nor agency would exist without the other. Like the hand, we could call the primary mind an emergent.

We would do well to look once again at the five omnipresent mental factors: contact, feeling, discernment, intention, and attention.

1 Contact

Contact is a form of rapport between the senses and their objects, a matching of sensitivity between a sense and an object in the sense field. It is a relational property involving three terms: one of the six senses, a material or mental object, and the consciousness based upon these two. There is evidence to suggest that this sensitivity was conceived as a dynamic process giving rise to emergence: the evidence is that contact, as a process, is described as being both a cause and an effect. As a cause, contact is the coming together of three distinct items—a sense, an object, and the potential for awareness. As an effect, contact is that which results from this process of coming together—a condition of harmony or rapport among the three items. This rapport is not the property of either a sense, an object, or an awareness per se. It is a property of the processes by which they interact, in other words, an emergent property. Because of one's conditioning, one thinks that contact—sense organ, sense field, and sense consciousness—implies a self; in this analysis it may be seen in a neutral, "scientific" light as an emergence.

This conception of contact strikes us as quite remarkable. It could be applied almost word-for-word to our discussion of vision as a unitary phenomenon. In a culture that did not have access to scientific notions of circular causality, feedback/feedforward, and emergent properties, nor to logical formalisms for handling self-reference, the only recourse for expressing an emergent may have been to say that a process is both cause and effect. Early Buddhism developed the idea of an emergent both at the (relatively) global level of codependent origination and the (relatively) local level of contact; this development was of central importance to the analysis of the arising of experience without a self. This suggests that our current formulations of emer-

gence are not simply logical tricks soon to be replaced by some other
way of conceptualizing phenomena; rather, our modern forms may
be the rediscovery of a basic aspect of human experience.

2 Feeling

We have already discussed feeling as the second aggregate and the
seventh link in the circle of codependent arising. Normally feelings
lead instantly to reactions that perpetuate karmic conditioning. Bare
feelings, however, are neutral; it is one's response that is, in the
language of mental factor analysis, either wholesome or unwholesome. Normally we never actually experience our feelings because
the mind jumps so quickly to the reaction. Even a neutral feeling
(often even more threatening to the sense of self than a displeasurable
feeling because a neutral feeling seems less self-relevant) leads quickly
to boredom and to the finding of any possible physical or mental
occupation. Meditators often report that they discover for the first
time, in mindfulness practice, what it is like actually to experience a
feeling.

3 Discernment

Perception (discernment)/impulse was discussed as the third aggregate. It normally arises inseparably with feeling. Through mindfulness, however, the meditator may recognize impulses of passion,
aggression, and ignoring for what they are—impulses that need not
automatically lead to action. In terms of mental factor analysis, one
may thus be able to choose wholesome rather than unwholesome
actions. (Eventually, when sufficient freedom from habitual patterns
has been obtained, perception/discernments can—according to some
later formulations—automatically give rise not to self-based impulses
of passion, aggression, and ignoring but to impulses of wisdom and
compassionate action.)

4 Intention

Intention is an extremely important process, which functions to
arouse and sustain the activities of consciousness (with its mental
factors) from moment to moment. Intention is the manner in which
the tendency to volitional action (the second link) manifests itself in
the mind at any given moment. There are no volitional actions without intention. Thus, karma is sometimes said to be the process of
intention itself—that which leaves traces on which future habits will

be based. Normally we act so rapidly and compulsively that we do not see intentions. Some schools of mindfulness training encourage meditators to spend periods of time in which they slow down activities so that they may become aware of the intentions that precede even very trivial volitional actions such as changing position when one becomes uncomfortable. Awareness of intention is thus a direct aid to cutting the chain of conditioned orgination at the craving link.

5 Attention

Attention, the final factor of the five omnipresent mental factors, arises in interaction with intention. Intention directs consciousness and the other mental factors toward some general area, at which point attention moves them toward specific features. (Remember the interaction of agents in Minsky's description of the agency Builder.) Attention focuses and holds consciousness on some object. When accompanied by apperception, attention serves as the basis for the object-ascertaining factors (see appendix B) of recollection and mindfulness, as well as the positive mental factor of alertness.

These five factors, when joined with various of the object-ascertaining and variable factors (listed in appendix B), produce the character of each moment of consciousness. The mental factors present at a given moment interact with each other such that the quality of each factor as well as the resultant consciousness is an emergent.

Ego-self, then, is the historical pattern among moment-to-moment emergent formations. To make use of a scientific metaphor, we could say that such traces (karma) are one's experiential ontogeny (including but not restricted to learning). Here ontogeny is understood not as a series of transitions from one state to another but as a process of becoming that is conditioned by past structures, while maintaining structural integrity from moment to moment. On an even larger scale, karma also expresses phylogeny, for it conditions experience through the accumulated and collective history of our species.

The precise nature of the lists and definitions of mental factors should not be taken too compulsively. Different schools produced different lists of factors. Different schools also disagreed (and disagree to this day) about how important it is for practitioners to study such lists (they were traditionally burned in Zen), about the stage of development at which the individual should study the Abhidharma in general and such lists in particular (given that he should study them at all) and about whether and how such lists should be used in meditative contemplation. All schools of mindfulness/awareness meditation, however, agree that intense mindfulness of what arises from moment to moment in the mind is necessary if one is to start to undo karmic conditioning.

We have achieved two main goals by this analysis: First, we have seen how both a single moment of consciousness and the causal coherence of moments of consciousness over time can be formulated in the language of emergence without the postulation of a self or any other ontological entity. Second, we have seen how such formulations can be both experientially descriptive and pragmatically oriented. This latter point bears further discussion since the notion of pragmatics may take an unfamiliar cast in a system that aims to undercut volitional (egocentric) action.

Mindfulness and Freedom

We have been speaking throughout of a mindful, open-ended analysis of experience, an analysis that includes changes in the mind of the analyzers as they proceed in the analysis. Through mindfulness, the mindfulness/awareness practitioners can begin to interrupt automatic patterns of conditioned behavior (specifically, they can let go of automatic grasping when craving arises). This, in turn, leads to an increase in the ability to be mindful and an eventual expansion of the field of attention into awareness that begins to penetrate the root ignorance. This awareness leads to further insight into the nature of experience, which fosters further desire and ability to give up the whole cycle of blind, habitual patterns based on ignorance and egocentric volitional action.

People often worry that were they to loosen their hold on craving and grasping, their desire would go away, and they would become numb and catatonic. In fact, exactly the reverse is the case. It is the mindless, the unaware, state of mind that is numb—swathed in a thick cocoon of wandering thoughts, prejudgments, and solipsistic ruminations. As mindfulness grows, appreciation for the components of experience grows. The point of mindfulness/awareness is not to disengage the mind from the phenomenal world; it is to enable the mind to be fully present in the world. The goal is not to avoid action but to be fully present in one's actions, so that one's behavior becomes progressively more responsive and aware.

In modern society, freedom is generally thought of as the ability to do whatever one wants. The view of codependent origination is radically different. (One contemporary Buddhist teacher even titled a book *The Myth of Freedom*.[22]) Doing whatever one wants out of a sense of ego (volitional action), according to this system, is the least free of actions; it is chained to the past by cycles of conditioning, and it results in further enslavement to habitual patterns in the future. To be progressively more free is to be sensitive to the conditions and genuine possibilities of some present situation and to be able to act in an open manner that is not conditioned by grasping and egoistic volitions. This openness and sensitivity encompasses not only one's own immediate sphere of perceptions; it also enables one to appreciate others and to develop compassionate insight into their predicaments. The repeated glimpses reported by practitioners of this openness and genuineness in human life explain the vitality of the mindfulness/awareness tradition. It also illustrates how a rich theoretical tradition can be naturally interwoven with human concerns.

Selfless Minds; Divided Agents

From a contemporary standpoint, then, Abhidharma appears as the study of the emergent formation of direct experience without the ground of an ego-self. It is remarkable how well the overall logical form of some Abhidharma formulations fits that of contemporary scientific concern with emergent properties and societies of mind. (Or perhaps we should state it the other way round.) These latter contemporary scientific concerns have, however, been pursued independently of any disciplined analysis and direct examination of human experience. Since the reader may still be skeptical that science and human experience are inseparable partners, we will now turn to consider in more detail what happens when this partnership is one-sided. What happens when the insight that mind is free of self is generated from within the very heart of science and yet is not connected to the rest of human experience?

We have seen how a view of selfless minds begins to take form with the cognitivist separation of consciousness and intentionality. We then saw how cognition can be studied as an emergent phenomenon in self-organizing, distributed networks. In this chapter, we have seen the usefulness of a mixed, "society" mode of description for cognitive processes and human experience. Of what use, then, is the idea of a central agent or self?

Most working cognitive scientists, and even some cognitivist philosophers, are content to ignore this question. One of the virtues of both Minsky's *Society of Mind* and Jackendoff's *Consciousness and the Computational Mind* is that each recognizes this question quite early on and takes it as a central theme. Minsky in particular distinguishes between the lowercase *self*, which refers "in a general sense to an entire person," and the uppercase *Self*, which refers to "that more mysterious sense of personal identity." He then asks, "Is this concept of a Self of any real use at all?" And he answers, "It is indeed—provided that we think of it not as a centralized and all-powerful entity, but as a society of ideas that include both our images of what the mind is and our ideals about what it ought to be."[23]

The distinctions that Minsky draws in these remarks are suggestive, especially in the context of our discussion. They are close to the Buddhist distinction between the coherent pattern of dependently originated habits that we recognize as a person and the ego-self that a person may believe she has and constantly grasps after but which does not actually exist. That is, the word *self* is a convenient way of referring to a series of mental and bodily events and formations, that have a degree of causal coherence and integrity through time. And the capitalized *Self* does exemplify our sense that hidden in these transitory formations is a real, unchanging essence that is the source of our identity and that we must protect. But as we have seen, this latter conviction may be unfounded and, as Minsky insightfully notes, can actually be harmful.

But equally interesting are the ways in which Minsky's distinctions—or those of other cognitive scientists concerned with the same issue, such as Jackendoff—do not match those of the Buddhist tradition. We believe that the lack of fit is ultimately rooted in two related issues. First, contemporary cognitive science does not distinguish between the idea or representation of a Self and the actual basis of that representation, which is an individual's grasping after an ego-self. Cognitive science has challenged the idea that there is a real thing to which the fomer applies, but it has not even thought to consider the latter. Second, cognitive science does not yet take seriously its own findings of the lack of a Self.

Both of these stem from the lack of a disciplined method for examination and inclusion of human experience in cognitive science. The major result of this lack is the issue that has been with us since the beginning: cognitive science offers us a purely theoretical discovery, which remains remote from actual human experience, of mind without self.

For example Minsky, on the same page from which the previous quotations were taken, writes that "perhaps it's *because* there are no persons in our heads to make us do the things we want—nor even ones to make us *want to want*—that we construct the myth that *we're* inside ourselves." This remark confuses two features of mind without self that we have repeatedly seen to be distinct: one is the lack of an ego-self and the other is grasping for an ego-self. We construct the belief or inner discourse that there is an ego-self not because the mind is ultimately empty of such a self but because the everyday conditioned mind is full of grasping. Or to make the point in the vocabulary of mindfulness/awareness, the belief is rooted in the accumulated tendencies that from moment to moment give rise to the unwholesome mental factors that reinforce grasping and craving. It is not the lack of an ego-self per se that is the source of this ongoing belief and private internal conversation; it is the emotional response to that lack. Since we habitually assume that there is an ego-self, our immediate response is to feel a loss when we cannot inferentially find the object of our convictions. We feel as if we have lost something precious and familiar, and so we immediately try to fill that loss with the belief in a self. But how can we lose something that we (that is, our temporary, emergent "wes") never had? And if we never had an ego-self in the first place, what is the point of continually trying to maintain one by telling ourselves we're inside ourselves? If it is to ourselves that we are talking in this conversation, why should we need to tell ourselves all of this in the first place?

This feeling of loss, though somewhat natural when one's investigation is still at an inferential stage, is heightened and prolonged when the discovery of the lack of self remains purely theoretical. In the tradition of a mindful, open-ended examination of experience, the initial conceptual realization of mind without self is deepened to the point where it is realized in a direct, personal way. The realization shifts from being merely inferential to being direct experience through a journey where the actual practice of mindfulness/awareness plays a central role. And as a form of direct experience, generations of meditators attest that the lack of an ego-self does not continue to be experienced as a loss that needs to be supplemented by a new belief or inner dialogue. On the contrary, it is the beginning of a feeling of freedom from fixed beliefs, for it makes apparent precisely the openness and space in which a transformation of what the subject itself is, or could be, becomes possible.

Minsky suggests, however, that we embrace the idea of Self because "so much of what our minds do is hidden from the parts of us that are involved with verbal consciousness."[24] Similarly, Jackendoff suggests that "awareness reflects a curious amalgam of the effects on the mind of both thought and the real world, while leaving totally opaque the means by which these effects come about."[25] There are two problems with this position. In the first place, the hypothesized mental processes of which we are unaware are just that—processes hypothesized by the cognitivist information-processing model of the mind. It is this model that requires a host of subpersonal hidden processes and activities, not our experiences of the mind itself. But surely it is not these ever-changing phantoms of cognitive science that we can blame for our belief that we personally have an ego-self; to think so would be a confusion of levels of discourse. In the second place, even if we did have many mental activities at the subpersonal level inherently hidden from awareness, how would that explain our belief in an ego-self? A glance at the complexity of Jackendoff's and Minsky's models of the mind suggests that were a mind actually to have all of these mechanisms, awareness of them would not necessarily even be desirable. Lack of awareness is not in itself a problem. What is a problem is the lack of discrimination and mindfulness of the habitual tendency to grasp, of which we can become aware. This type of mindfulness can be developed with great precision due to the fundamentally discontinuous—and hence unsolid—nature of our experience. (We have seen how some of this discontinuity and lack of solidity is quite consonant with modern cognitive science, and we are now even able to observe some of it from a neurophysiological standpoint.) The cultivation of such precision is possible not just in formal periods of practice but in our everyday lives. An entire tradition with numerous cultural variants and accessible methods testifies to the possibility and actuality of this human journey of investigation and experience.

As we can see from our discussion of both Minsky and Jackendoff, cognitive science basically ignores this possibility. This indifferent attitude generates two significant problems. First, by means of this ignoring, cognitive science denies itself the investigation of an entire domain of human experience. Even though the "plasticity" of experience, especially in its perceptual forms, has become something of a topic of debate among philosophers and cognitive scientists,[26] no one is investigating the ways in which conscious awareness can be transformed as a result of practices such as mindfulness/awareness. In the mindfulness/awareness tradition, in contrast, the possibility of such transformation is the cornerstone of the entire study of mind.[27]

The second problem is the one we have evoked from the very beginning of this book: science becomes remote from human experience and, in the case of cognitive science, generates a divided stance in which we are led to affirm consequences that we appear to be constitutionally incapable of accepting. Explicit attempts to heal this gap are broached only by a few, such as Gordon Globus, who asks the question, What is a neural network that it may be capable of supporting a *Dasein*, an embodied existence?[28] or Sherry Turkle, who has explored a possible bridge between cognitive science and psychoanalysis.[29] And yet, to the extent that research in cognitive science requires more and more that we revise our naive idea of what a cognizing subject is (its lack of solidity, its divided dynamics, and its generation from unconscious processes), the need for a bridge between cognitive science and an open-ended pragmatic approach to human experience will become only more inevitable. Indeed, cognitive science will be able to resist the need for such a bridge only by adopting an attitude that is inconsistent with its own theories and discoveries.

The deep problem, then, with the merely theoretical discovery of mind without self in as powerful and technical a context as late-twentieth-century science is that it is almost impossible to avoid embracing some form of nihilism. If science continues to manipulate things without embracing a progresssive appreciation of how we live among those things, then the discovery of mind without self will have no life outside the laboratory, despite the fact that the mind in that laboratory is the very same mind without self. This mind discovers its own lack of a personal ground—a deep and remarkable discovery—and yet has no means to embody that realization. Without such embodiment, we have little choice but to deny the self altogether, without giving up for one moment our habitual craving for what has just been denied us.

By *nihilism* we mean to refer precisely to Nietzsche's definition: "*Radical nihilism* is the conviction of an absolute untenability of existence when it comes to the highest values that one recognizes."[30] In other words, the nihilistic predicament is the situation in which we know that our most cherished values are untenable, and yet we seem incapable of giving them up.

This nihilistic predicament emerges quite clearly in both Jackendoff's and Minsky's books. As we mentioned, Jackendoff claims, on the one hand, that "consciousness is not good for anything," and then, on the other hand, that consciousness is "too important for one's life—too much fun—to conceive of it as useless." Thus for Jackendoff belief in the causal efficacy of consciousness is untenable, and yet he—like the rest of us—is incapable of giving it up.

A similar predicament emerges at the end of Minsky's book. On the last pages of his *Society of Mind*, Minsky examines the notion of free will, which he calls "the myth of the third alternative" between determinism and chance. Science tells us that all processes are determined or depend in part on chance. There is no room, therefore, for some mysterious third possibility called a "free will," by which Minsky means "an Ego, Self, or Final Center of Control, from which we choose what we shall do at every fork in the road of time."

What, then, is Minsky's response to this predicament? The final paragraph of his second-to-last page is worth quoting in full:

> No matter that the physical world provides no room for freedom of the will: that concept is essential to our model of the mental realm. Too much of our psychology is based on it for us to ever give it up. We're virtually forced to maintain that belief, even though we know it's false—except, of course when we're inspired to find the flaws in *all* our beliefs, whatever may be the consequence to cheerfulness and mental peace.

At the moment, it is the feeling tone of Minsky's dilemma that concerns us. Although he ends *The Society of Mind* a page later with the more upbeat thought that "whenever anything goes wrong there are always other realms of thought," the quotation on free will is actually his final vision of the relation between science and human experience. As with Jackendoff, science and human experience come apart, and there is no way to put them together again. Such a situation exemplifies perfectly Nietzsche's hundred-year-old diagnosis of our cultural predicament. (The remark of Nietzsche's we quoted is dated 1887.) We are forced—condemned—to believe in something we know can't be true.

We are going to such great lengths to discuss both Minsky's and Jackendoff's work because each clearly presents, in its own way, the predicament we all face. Indeed, Minsky and Jackendoff have done us the great service of not shying away from the situation, as do other scientists and philosophers who imagine that there are secret recesses within the brain that hide an existing self[31] or who suppose that probability and uncertainty at the quantum level provide a home for free will.[32]

Nevertheless, the issues as discussed by Minsky and Jackendoff are rather starkly met. Both are saying that there is an unbridgeable contradiction between cognitive science and human experience. Cognitive science tells us that we do not have a Self that is efficacious and free. We cannot, however, give up such a belief—we are "virtually forced" to maintain it. The mindfulness/awareness tradition, on the other hand, says that we are most certainly *not* forced to maintain it. This tradition offers a fourth alternative, a vision of freedom of action that is radically different from our usual conceptions of freedom.

Let us be clear that this is not an issue in the philosophy of free will. (We are resisting, with great effort, the urge to launch into a discussion of physical versus structural determinism, prediction, and many other philosophical reactions to Minsky's and Jackendoff's claims.) What is at issue is that there is a tradition the very heart of which is to examine such issues in experience. Virtually the entire Buddhist path has to do with going beyond emotional grasping to ego. Meditative techniques, traditions of study and contemplation, social action, and the organization of entire communities have been harnessed toward this end. Histories, psychologies, and sociologies have been (and can be) written about it. As we have described several times, human beings do transform themselves (and they certainly do believe that they can transform themselves) progressively in this way. The result, in this world view, is that real freedom comes not from the decisions of an ego-self's "will" but from action without any Self whatsoever.

What cognitive science is saying about selfless minds is important for human experience. Cognitive science speaks with authority in modern society. Yet there is the danger that cognitive scientists will follow Hume's example: having brilliantly formulated the discovery of selfless minds, a discovery of fundamental relevance to the human situation, but conceiving of no way to bring that discovery together with everyday experience, they will have no recourse but to shrug and go off to any modern equivalent of backgammon. We have been attempting to offer instead a bridge back to human experience.

Minding the World

We have spent the first three parts of this book looking for the self, but even when we could not find it, we never doubted the stability of the world. How could we, when it seemed to provide the setting for all of our examinations? And yet when, having discovered the groundlessness of the self, we turn toward the world, we are no longer sure we can find it. Or perhaps we should say that once we let go of a fixed self, we no longer know how to look for the world. We define the world, after all, as that which is not-self, that which is different from the self, but how can we do this when we no longer have a self as a reference point?

Once more, we seem to be losing our grip on something familiar. Indeed, at this point most people will probably become quite nervous and see the specters of solipsism, subjectivism, and idealism lurking on the horizon, even though we already know that we cannot find a self to serve as the anchor point for such literally self-centered views. We are, perhaps, more attached to the idea that the world has a fixed and ultimate ground than we are to the idea of a personal self. We need, then, to pause and become fully aware of this anxiety that lies underneath the varieties of cognitive and emergent realism. This task takes us to the next step of our journey.

IV

Steps to a Middle Way

7

The Cartesian Anxiety

A Sense of Dissatisfaction

Why should it be threatening to question the idea that the world has pregiven properties that we represent? Why do we become nervous when we call into question the idea that there is some way that the world is "out there," independent of our cognition, and that cognition is a re-presentation of that independent world?

Our spontaneous and unreflective common sense would deny that these questions are scientific, perhaps by thinking, "How else *could* the mind and the world be related?" The realist in us claims that our questions are simply "philosophical"—a polite way of making them seem interesting, yet also irrelevant. It is true that they are partly philosophical, but we can also rephrase them as questions in cognitive science. What actually is the scientific basis for the idea that the mind is some kind of information-processing device that responds selectively to pregiven features of the environment? Why do we assume that cognitive science cannot call into question these notions of representation and information processing not just philosophically but in its day-to-day research?

To think that we cannot raise such issues is a blindness in contemporary common sense, deeply entrenched in our Western tradition and recently reinforced by cognitivism. Thus even when the very ideas of representation and information processing change considerably, as they do in the study of connectionist networks, self-organization, and emergent properties, some form of the realist assumption remains. In cognitivism, the realism is at least explicit and defended; in the emergence approach, however, it often becomes simply tacit and unquestioned. This unreflective stance is one of the greatest dangers facing the field of cognitive science; it limits the range of theories and ideas and so prevents a broader vision and future for the field.

A growing number of researchers in all areas of cognitive science have expressed dissatisfaction with the varieties of cognitive realism. This dissatisfaction derives from a deeper source than the search for alternatives to symbol processing or even mixed "society of mind" theories: it is a dissatisfaction with the very notion of a representational system. This notion obscures many essential dimensions of cognition not just in human experience but when we try to explain cognition scientifically. These dimensions include the understanding of perception and language, as well as the study of evolution and life itself.

Our discussion so far has focused on linking the two poles of science and human experience. Part IV will continue this task, but by developing a nonrepresentationist alternative from within the heart of cognitive science. We now need to pause and reflect on the scientific and philosophical roots of the very idea of representation. We are thinking not merely of the current notions in cognitive science of computation and information processing but of the entire philosophical tendency to view the mind as a "mirror of nature."[1]

Representation Revisited

In the discussion of cognitivism we distinguished between two senses of representation, which we now need to recall. On the one hand, there is the relatively uncontroversial notion of representation as construal: cognition always consists in construing or representing the world a certain way. On the other hand, there is the much stronger notion that this feature of cognition is to be explained by the hypothesis that a system acts on the basis of internal representations. Since it might seem that these two ideas amount to the same thing, we need to refine our distinction somewhat.

We can begin by noting a relatively weak and uncontroversial sense of representation. This sense is purely semantic: It refers to anything that can be interpreted as being about something. This is the sense of representation as construal, since nothing is about something else without construing it as being some way. A map, for example, is about some geographical area; it represents certain features of the terrain and so construes that terrain as being a certain way. Similarly, words on a page represent sentences in a language, which may in turn represent or be about still other things. This sense of representation can be made even more precise. If, for example, our concern happens to be with languages in a more formal setting, we can say that the statements of a language represent their conditions of satisfaction. For example, the statement "snow is white"—taken literally—is satisfied if snow is white; the statement "pick up your shoes"—again, taken literally—is satisfied if the shoes are picked up by the person being addressed.[2]

This sense of representation is weak because it need not carry any strong epistemological or ontological commitments. Thus it is perfectly acceptable to speak of a map representing the terrain without worrying about such things as how maps get their meaning. It is also perfectly acceptable to think of a statement as representing some set of conditions without making further assumptions about whether language as a whole works this way or whether there really are facts in the world separate from language that can then be re-presented by the sentences of the language. Or we can even talk about experiential representations, such as the image I have of my brother, without making any further assumptions about how this image arose in the first place. In other words, this weak sense of representation is pragmatic; we use it all the time without worry.

The obviousness of such an idea, however, is quickly transformed into a much stronger sense of representation that does carry quite heavy ontological and epistemological commitments. This strong sense arises when we generalize on the basis of the weaker idea to construct a full-fledged theory of how perception, language, or cognition in general must work. The ontological and epistemological commitments are basically twofold: We assume that the world is pregiven, that its features can be specified prior to any cognitive activity. Then to explain the relation between this cognitive activity and a pregiven world, we hypothesize the existence of mental representations inside the cognitive system (whether these be images, symbols, or subsymbolic patterns of activity distributed across a network does not matter for the moment). We then have a full-fledged theory that says (1) the world is pregiven; (2) our cognition is of this world—even if only to a partial extent, and (3) the way in which we cognize this pregiven world is to represent its features and then act on the basis of these representations.

We must, then, return to our earlier metaphor, the idea of a cognitive agent that is parachuted into a pregiven world. This agent will survive only to the extent that it is endowed with a map and learns to act on the basis of this map. In the cognitivist version of this story, the map is an innately specified system of representations—sometimes called a "language of thought"—whereas learning to employ this map is the task of ontogeny.

Many cognitive scientists will object that we have presented a caricature. Are we not presupposing a static conception of representation, one that overlooks the rich detail of the inner structure of a cognitive system and unjustifiably construes a representation as merely a mirror? Is it not well known, for example, that visual perception is considered to be a result of mapping the physical patterns of energy that stimulate the retina into representations of the visual scene, which are then used to make inferences and eventually to produce a perceptual judgment? Perception is seen as an active process of hypothesis formation, not as the simple mirroring of a pregiven environment.

This objection, though somewhat fair, misses the point. Our point is not to caricature a sophisticated research program but simply to render explicit some tacit epistemological assumptions in as clear a fashion as possible. Thus although everyone agrees that representation is a complex process, it is nonetheless conceived to be one of recovering or reconstructing extrinsic, independent environmental features. Thus in vision research, for example, one speaks of "recovering shape from shading" or "color from brightness." Here the latter features are considered to be extrinsic properties of the environment that provide the information needed to recover "higher-order" properties of the visual scene, such as shape and color. The basic idea of a world with pregiven features remains.[3]

The complaint that we have presented a caricature would, however, be justified were we not to acknowledge the subtlety and sophistication of cognitive realism in relation to the classical opposition between realism and idealism in philosophy. In the hands of cognitive realism, the notion of representation does undergo something of a mutation. The power of this mutation is that it seems to offer a way out of the classical opposition between realism and idealism.

This opposition is based in the traditional notion of representation as a "veil of ideas" that stands between us and the world. On the one hand, the realist naturally thinks that there is a distinction between our ideas or concepts and that which they represent, namely, the world. The ultimate court of appeal for judging the validity of our representations is this independent world. Of course, each of our representations must cohere with many others, but the point of such internal features is to increase the probability that globally our representations will have some measure of correspondence or degree of fit with an outer and independent world.

The idealist, on the other hand, quickly points out that we have no access to such an independent world except through our representations. We cannot stand outside of ourselves to behold the degree of fit that our representations might have with the world. In fact, we simply have no idea of what the outside world is except that it is the presumed object of our representations. Taking this point to the extreme, the idealist argues that the very idea of a world independent of representations is itself only another of our representations—a second-order or metarepresentation. Our sense of an outer ground thus slips away, and we are left grasping for our internal representations, as if these could provide a sure and stable reference point.

At first sight, contemporary cognitive science seems to offer a way out of this traditional philosophical impasse. Largely because of cognitive science, philosophical discussion has shifted from concern with a priori representations (representations that might provide some noncontingent foundation for our knowledge of the world) to concern with a posteriori representations (representations whose contents are ultimately derived from causal interactions with the environment). This naturalized conception of representation does not invite the skeptical questions that motivate traditional epistemology. In fact, to shift one's concern to organism-environment relations in this way is largely to abandon the task of traditional a priori epistemology in favor of the naturalized projects of psychology and cognitive science.[4] By taking up such a naturalized stance, cognitive science avoids the antinomies that lurk in transcendental or metaphysical realism, without embracing the solipsism or subjectivism that constantly threatens idealism. The cognitive scientist is thus able to remain a staunch realist about the empirical world while making the details of mind and cognition the subject of his investigations.

Cognitive science thus seems to provide a way of talking about representation without being burdened by the traditional philosophical image of the mind as a mirror of nature. But this appearance is misleading. It is true, as Richard Rorty remarks, that there is no way to raise the traditional skeptical questions of epistemology in cognitive science. Global skepticism about the possibility of cognition or knowledge is simply not to the point in the practice of science. But it does not follow, as Rorty seems to think, that the current naturalized conception of representation has nothing to do with the traditional image of the mind as a mirror of nature.[5] On the contrary, a crucial feature of this image remains alive in contemporary cognitive science—the idea of a world or environment with extrinsic, pregiven features that are recovered through a process of representation. In some ways cognitivism is the strongest statement yet of the representational view of the mind inaugurated by Descartes and Locke. Indeed, Jerry Fodor, one of cognitivism's leading and most eloquent exponents, goes so far as to say that the *only* respect in which cognitivism is a major advance over eighteenth- and nineteenth-century representationism is in its use of the computer as a model of mind.[6]

As we have seen, however, cognitivism is only one variety of cognitive realism. In both the emergence and society of mind approaches (and in the schools of basic elements analysis for the experiential pole of our investigation), the notion of representation becomes more and more problematical. We did not explicitly question this notion in our discussion of the varieties of cognitive realism, but if we look back on our journey, we can see that we have slowly drifted away from the idea of mind as an input-output device that processes information. The role of the environment has quietly moved from being the preeminent reference point to receding more and more into the background, while the idea of mind as an emergent and autonomous network of relationships has gained a central place. It is time, then, to raise the question, What is it about such networks, if anything, that is representational?

To make this question somewhat more accessible, consider once again Minsky's discussion toward the end of *Society of Mind*. There he writes, "Whenever we speak about a mind, we're speaking of the processes that carry our brains from state to state . . . concerns about minds are really concerns with relationships between states—and this has virtually nothing to do with the natures of the states themselves."[7] How, then, are we to understand these relationships? What is it about them that makes them mindlike?

The answer that is usually given to this question is, of course, that these relationships must be seen as embodying or supporting representations of the environment. Notice, however, that if we claim that the function of these processes is to represent an independent environment, then we are committed to construing these processes as belonging to the class of systems that are driven from the outside, that are defined in terms of external mechanisms of control (a *hetero-*

nomous system). Thus we will consider information to be a prespecified quantity, one that exists independently in the world and can act as the input to a cognitive system. This input provides the initial premises upon which the system computes a behavior—the output. But how are we to specify inputs and outputs for highly cooperative, self-organizing systems such as brains? There is, of course, a back-and-forth flow of energy, but where does information end and behavior begin? Minsky puts his finger on the problem, and his remarks are worth quoting at length:

> Why are processes so hard to classify? In earlier times, we could usually judge machines and processes by how they transformed raw materials into finished products. But it makes no sense to speak of brains as though they manufacture thoughts the way factories make cars. The difference is that brains use *processes that change themselves*—and this means we cannot separate such processes from the products they produce. In particular, brains make memories, which change the ways we'll subsequently think. *The principal activities of brains are making changes in themselves.* Because the whole idea of self-modifying processes is new to our experience, we cannot yet trust our commonsense judgement about such matters.[8]

What is remarkable about this passage is the absence of any notion of representation. Minsky does not say that the principal activity of brains is to represent the external world; he says that it is to make continuous self-modifications. What has happened to the notion of representation?

In fact, an important and pervasive shift is beginning to take place in cognitive science under the very influence of its own research. This shift requires that we move away from the idea of the world as independent and extrinsic to the idea of a world as inseparable from the structure of these processes of self-modification. This change in stance does not express a mere philosophical preference; it reflects the necessity of understanding cognitive systems not on the basis of their input and output relationships but by their *operational closure*.[9] A system that has operational closure is one in which the results of its processes are those processes themselves. The notion of operational closure is thus a way of specifying classes of processes that, in their very operation, turn back upon themselves to form autonomous networks. Such networks do not fall into the class of systems defined by external mechanisms of control (heteronomy) but rather into the class of systems defined by internal mechanisms of self-organization (autonomy).[10] The key point is that such systems do not operate by representation. Instead of *representing* an independent world, they *enact* a world as a domain of distinctions that is inseparable from the structure embodied by the cognitive system.

We wish to evoke the point that when we begin to take such a conception of mind seriously, we must call into question the idea that the world is pregiven and that cognition is representation. In cognitive science, this means that we must call into question the idea that information exists ready-made in the world and that it is extracted by a cognitive system, as the cognitivist notion of an *informavore* vividly implies.

But before we go any further, we need to ask ourselves why the idea of a world with pregiven features or ready-made information seems so unquestionable. Why are we unable to imagine giving up this idea without falling into some sort of subjectivism, idealism, or cognitive nihilism? What is the source of this apparent dilemma? We must examine directly the feeling that arises when we sense that we can no longer trust the world as a fixed and stable reference point.

The Cartesian Anxiety

The nervousness that we feel is rooted in what, following Richard Bernstein, we can call "the Cartesian anxiety."[11] We mean "anxiety" in a loosely Freudian sense, and we call it "Cartesian" simply because Descartes articulated it rigorously and dramatically in his *Meditations*. The anxiety is best put as a dilemma: either we have a fixed and stable foundation for knowledge, a point where knowledge starts, is grounded, and rests, or we cannot escape some sort of darkness, chaos, and confusion. Either there is an absolute ground or foundation, or everything falls apart.

There is a marvelous passage from Kant's *Critique of Pure Reason* that conveys the power of the Cartesian anxiety. Throughout the *Critique* Kant builds the edifice of his theory of knowledge by arguing that we have a priori or given, innate categories, which are the foundations of knowledge. Toward the end of his discussion of the "Transcendental Analytic" he writes,

> We have now not merely explored the territory of pure understanding [the a priori categories] and carefully surveyed every part of it, but have also measured its extent and assigned to

everything in it its rightful place. This domain is an island, enclosed by nature itself with unalterable limits. It is the land of truth—an enchanting name!—surrounded by a wide and stormy ocean, the native home of illusion, where many a fog bank and many a swiftly melting iceberg give the deceptive appearance of farther shores, deluding the adventurous seafarer ever anew with empty hopes, and engaging him in enterprises which he can never abandon and yet is unable to carry to completion.[12]

Here we have the two extremes, the either-or of the Cartesian anxiety: There is the enchanting land of truth where everything is clear and ultimately grounded. But beyond that small island there is the wide and stormy ocean of darkness and confusion, the native home of illusion.

This feeling of anxiety arises from the craving for an absolute ground. When this craving cannot be satisfied, the only other possibility seems to be nihilism or anarchy. The search for a ground can take many forms, but given the basic logic of representationism, the tendency is to search either for an outer ground in the world or an inner ground in the mind. By treating mind and world as opposed subjective and objective poles, the Cartesian anxiety oscillates endlessly between the two in search of a ground.

It is important to realize that this opposition between subject and object is not given and ready-made; it is an idea that belongs to the human history of mind and nature that we mentioned in chapter 1. For example, prior to Descartes, the term idea was used only for the contents of the mind of God; Descartes was one of the first to take this term and apply it to the workings of the human mind.[13] This linguistic and conceptual shift is just one aspect of what Richard Rorty describes as the "invention of the mind as a mirror of nature," an invention that was the result of patching together heterogenous images, conceptions, and linguistic usages.[14]

These Cartesian roots become quite obvious when we have reason to doubt the appropriateness of this metaphor of mirroring. As we set out in search of other ways of thinking, the Cartesian anxiety arises to dog us at every step. Yet our contemporary situation is also unique, for we have become increasingly skeptical about the possiblity of discerning any ultimate ground. Thus when the anxiety arises today, we seem unable to avoid the turn toward nihilism, for we have not learned to let go of the forms of thinking, behavior, and experience that lead us to desire a ground.

We saw in our previous discussion that cognitive science is not immune from this nihilistic tendency. For example, the link between nihilism and the Cartesian anxiety can be seen very clearly in *The Society of Mind* when Minsky confronts our inability to find a fully independent world. As he notes, the world is not an object, event, or process inside the world.[15] Indeed the world is more like a background—a setting of and field for all of our experience, but one that cannot be found apart from our structure, behavior, and cognition. For this reason, what we say about the world tells us as much about ourselves as it does about the world.

Minsky's response to this realization is a mixed one, in a way that is similar to his response to the lack of a Self. He writes, "Whatever you purport to say about a thing, you're only expressing your own beliefs. Yet even that gloomy thought suggests an insight. Even if our models of the world cannot yield good answers about the world as a whole, and even though their other answers are frequently wrong, they can tell us something about ourselves."[16] On the one hand, Minsky uses the impossibility of finding a fully independent and pregiven world as an opportunity for developing insight into ourselves. But on the other hand, this insight is based in a feeling of gloominess about our situation. Why should this be?

We have been portraying these ideas through the words of Minsky because he is an outstanding modern cognitive scientist and has actually taken the time to articulate his ideas clearly. But he is not alone. When pressed to discuss this issue, many people would accept that we do not really have knowledge of the world; we have knowledge only of our representations of the world. Yet we seem condemned by our consitution to treat these representations as if they were the world, for our everyday experience feels as if it were of a given and immediate world.

Such a situation does indeed seem gloomy. But notice that such gloominess would make sense only if there were a pregiven, independent world—an outer ground—but one that we could never know. Given such a situation, we would have no choice but to fall back on our inner representations and treat them as if they provided a stable ground.

This mood of gloominess arises, then, from the Cartesian anxiety and its ideal of the mind as a mirror of nature. According to this ideal, knowledge should be of an independent, pregiven world, and this knowledge should be attained in the precision of a representation. When this ideal cannot be satisfied, we fall back upon ourselves in search of an inner ground. This oscillation is apparent in Minsky's remark that whatever one purports to say is only an expression of one's beliefs. To say that what one thinks is a only a matter of subjective representation is precisely to fall back upon the idea of an inner ground, a solitary Cartesian ego that is walled in by the privacy of its representations. This particular turn is all the more ironic, since Minsky does not believe that there exists a self that could serve as an inner ground in the first place. In the end, then, Minsky's entanglement in the Cartesian anxiety requires not only that we believe in a self that we know cannot be found but also that we believe in a world to which we have no access. And once again, the logic of such a predicament leads inevitably to a condition of nihilism.

Steps to a Middle Way

We have already seen in our exploration of human experience through the practice of mindfulness/awareness that our grasping after an inner ground is the essence of ego-self and is the source of continuous frustration. We can now begin to appreciate that this grasping after an inner ground is itself a moment in a larger pattern of grasping that includes our clinging to an outer ground in the form of the idea of a pregiven and independent world. In other words, our grasping after a ground, whether inner or outer, is the deep source of frustration and anxiety.

This realization lies at the heart of the theory and practice of the *Madhyamika* or "middle way" school of the Buddhist tradition. Whether one tries to find an ultimate ground inside or outside the mind, the basic motivation and pattern of thinking is the same, namely, the tendency to grasp. In Madhyamika, this habitual tendency is considered to be the root of the two extremes of "absolutism" and "nihilism." At first, the grasping mind leads one to search for an absolute ground—for anything, whether inner or outer, that might by virtue of its "own-being" be the support and foundation for everything else. Then faced with its inability to find any such ultimate ground, the grasping mind recoils and clings to the absence of a ground by treating everything else as illusion.

There are, then, two fundamental respects in which the philosophical analysis of Madhyamika is directly relevant to our predicament.

First, it explicitly recognizes that the search for an ultimate ground—what today we would call the *project of foundationalism*—is not limited to the notion of the subject and its basis in what we have called *ego-self*; it also includes our belief in a pregiven or ready-made world. This point, realized in India centuries ago and elaborated in the diverse cultural settings of Tibet, China, Japan, and Southeast Asia, has only begun to be appreciated in Western philosophy in the past one hundred years or so. Indeed, most of Western philosophy has been concerned with the issue of where an ultimate ground is to be found, not with calling into question or becoming mindful of this very tendency to cling to a ground.

Second, Madhyamika explicitly recognizes the link between absolutism and nihilism. Our ethnocentric narratives tell us that concern with nihilism—in its precise Nietzschean sense—is a Western phenomenon due, among other things, to the collapse of theism in the nineteenth century and the rise of modernism. The presence of a deep concern with nihilism in Indian philosophy from even pre-Buddhist times should challenge such an ethnocentric assumption.

Within the tradition of mindfulness/awareness meditation, the motivation has been to develop a direct and stable insight into absolutism and nihilism as forms of grasping that result from the attempt to find a stable ego-self and so limit our lived world to the experience of suffering and frustration. By progressively learning to let go of these tendencies to grasp, one can begin to appreciate that all phenomena are free of any absolute ground and that such "groundlessness" (sunyata) is the very fabric of dependent coorigination.

We could make a somewhat similar point phenomenologically by saying that groundlessness is the very condition for the richly textured and interdependent world of human experience. We expressed this point in our very first chapter by saying that all of our activities depend on a background that can never be pinned down with any sense of ultimate solidity and finality. Groundlessness, then, is to be found not in some far off, philosophically abstruse analysis but in everyday experience. Indeed, groundlessness is revealed in cognition as "common sense," that is, in knowing how to negotiate our way through a world that is not fixed and pregiven but that is continually shaped by the types of actions in which we engage.

Cognitive science has resisted this view, preferring to see any form of experience as at best "folk psychology," that is, as a rudimentary form of explanation that can be disciplined by representational theories of mind. Thus the usual tendency is to continue to treat cognition as problem solving in some pregiven task domain. The greatest ability of living cognition, however, consists in being able to pose, within broad constraints, the relevant issues that need to be addressed at each moment. These issues and concerns are not pregiven but are *enacted* from a background of action, where what counts as relevant is contextually determined by our common sense.

8

Enaction: Embodied Cognition

Recovering Common Sense

The tacit assumption behind the varieties of cognitive realism (cognitivism, emergence, and the society of mind) has been that the world can be divided into regions of discrete elements and tasks. Cognition consists in problem solving, which must, if it is to be successful, respect the elements, properties, and relations within these pregiven regions.

This approach to cognition as problem solving works to some degree for task domains in which it is relatively easy to specify all possible states. Consider for example the game of chess. It is relatively easy to define the constitutents of the "space of chess": there are positions on the board, rules for movements, turns that are taken, and so on. The limits of this space are clearly defined; in fact, it is an almost crystalline world. It is not surprising, then, that chess playing by computer is an advanced art.

For less circumscribed or well-defined task domains, however, this approach has proved to be considerably less productive. Consider, for example, a mobile robot that is supposed to drive a car within a city. One can still single out in this "driving space" discrete items, such as wheels and windows, red lights, and other cars. But unlike the world of chessplaying, movement among objects is not a space that can be said to end neatly at some point. Should the robot pay attention to pedestrians or not? Should it take weather conditions into account? Or the country in which the city is located and its unique driving customs? Such a list of questions could go on forever. The driving world does not end at some point; it has the structure of ever-receding levels of detail that blend into a nonspecific background. Indeed, successfully directed movement such as driving depends upon acquired motor skills and the continuous use of common sense or background know-how.

Such commonsense knowledge is difficult, perhaps impossible, to package into explicit, propositional knowledge—"knowledge *that*" in the philosopher's jargon—since it is largely a matter of readiness to hand or "knowledge *how*" based on the accumulation of experience in a vast number of cases. Recent examinations of how skills are acquired appear to confirm this point.[1] Furthermore, when we enlarge the task domains from artificial microworlds to the world at large, it is not clear that we can even specify what is to count as an object independent of the type of action that is being performed. The individuation of objects, properties, and events appears to vary according to the task at hand.[2]

These points are not new to the field of cognitive science, although their full import has only begun to be appreciated. Indeed, it is fair to say that by the 1970s, after two decades of humblingly slow progress, it dawned on many workers in cognitive science that even the simplest cognitive action requires a seemingly infinite amount of knowledge, which we take for granted (it is so obvious as to be invisible) but which must be spoon-fed to the computer. The early cognitivist hope for a general problem solver had to be abandoned in favor of programs that would run in local knowledge domains, where small-scale problems could be solved and where the programmer could put into the machine as much of her background knowledge as was necessary. Similarly, the current connectionist strategy depends either on restricting the space of possible attractors by means of assumptions about the known properties of the world, which are incorporated as additional constraints for regularization,[3] or, in more recent models, on using backpropagation methods where learning resembles the imitation of an external model. Thus in both cognitivism and connectionism, the unmanageable ambiguity of background common sense is left largely at the periphery of the inquiry, with the hope that it will somehow eventually be clarified.[4]

If, however, our lived world does not have predefined boundaries, then it seems unrealistic to expect to capture commonsense understanding in the form of a representation—where *representation* is understood in its strong sense as the re-presentation of a pregiven world.[5] Indeed, if we wish to recover common sense, then we must invert the representationist attitude by treating context-dependent know-how not as a residual artifact that can be progressively eliminated by the discovery of more sophisticated rules but as, in fact, the very essence of *creative* cognition.

This attitude toward common sense has begun to affect the field of cognitive science, especially in artificial intelligence. We should note, however, that the philosophical source for this attitude is to be found largely in recent Continental philosophy, especially in the school of philosophical hermeneutics, which is based in the early work of Martin Heidegger and his student Hans Gadamer.[6] The term *hermeneutics* originally referred to the discipline of interpreting ancient texts, but it has been extended to denote the entire phenomenon of interpretation, understood as the *enactment* or *bringing forth* of meaning from a background of understanding. In general, Continental philosophers, even when they explicitly contest many of the assumptions underlying hermeneutics, have continued to produce detailed discussions that show how knowledge depends on being in a world that is inseparable from our bodies, our language, and our social history—in short, from our *embodiment*.[7]

Although several cognitive scientists have recently turned to these discussions for inspiration, the spontaneous philosophy of cognitive science continues to resist such a nonobjectivist orientation. The varieties of cognitive realism are in particular strongly tied to analytic philosophy, which tends to view folk psychology as a tacit theory in need of either reduction or replacement.[8] Indeed, it is fair to say that analytic philosophy in general resists this notion of cognition as embodied understanding. Thus as Mark Johnson notes in a recent work,

> The idea that understanding is an event in which one has a world, or, more properly, a series of ongoing related meaning events in which one's world stands forth, has long been recognized on the Continent, especially in the work of Heidegger and Gadamer. But Anglo-American analytic philosophy has steadfastly resisted this orientation in favor of meaning as a fixed relation between words and the world. It has been mistakenly assumed that only a viewpoint that transcends human embodiment, cultural embeddedness, imaginative understanding, and location within historically evolving traditions can guarantee the possibility of objectivity.[9]

The central insight of this nonobjectivist orientation is the view that knowledge is the result of an ongoing interpretation that emerges from our capacities of understanding. These capacities are rooted in the structures of our biological embodiment but are lived and experienced within a domain of consensual action and cultural history.

They enable us to make sense of our world; or in more phenomenological language, they are the structures by which we exist in the
manner of "having a world." To quote Johnson once more,

> Meaning includes patterns of embodied experience and pre-
> conceptual structures of our sensibility (i.e., our mode of per-
> ception, or orienting ourselves, and of interacting with other
> objects, events, or persons). These embodied patterns do not
> remain private or peculiar to the person who experiences them.
> Our community helps us interpret and codify many of our felt
> patterns. They become shared cultural modes of experience and
> help to determine the nature of our meaningful, coherent under-
> standing of our "world."[10]

Although these themes are derived from Continental philosophy,
most of the Continental discussions have proceeded without taking
into consideration scientific research on cognition—the major exception being the early work of Merleau-Ponty. The challenge posed by
cognitive science to the Continental discussions, then, is to link the
study of human experience as culturally embodied with the study of
human cognition in neuroscience, linguistics, and cognitive psychology. In contrast, the challenge posed to cognitive science is to
question one of the more entrenched assumptions of our scientific
heritage—that the world is independent of the knower. If we are
forced to admit that cognition cannot be properly understood without
common sense, and that common sense is none other than our bodily
and social history, then the inevitable conclusion is that knower and
known, mind and world, stand in relation to each other through
mutual specification or dependent coorigination.

If this critique is valid, then scientific progress in understanding
cognition will not be forthcoming unless we start from a different
basis from the idea of a pregiven world that exists "out there" and is
internally recovered in a representation. In recent years, a few researchers within cognitive science have taken this critique from the
philosophical level into the laboratory and into specific work in AI.
These researchers have put forth concrete proposals that involve a
more radical departure from cognitivism than is found in the emergence approach, and yet they incorporate the ideas and methods
developed within this context.

Self-Organization Revisited

In the previous chapter, we discussed how cognitive science has slowly drifted away from the idea of mind as an input-output device that processes information toward the idea of mind as an emergent and autonomous network. We intend to make this idea more tangible by providing a concrete example of what we mean by an autonomous system.

Our example is based on the simple cellular automata, which we introduced to exemplify how systems exhibit emergent properties when endowed with network architectures. In the previous account these cellular automata were completely decoupled entities, and so their emergent states were not constrained by a history of coupling with an appropriate world. By enriching our account to include this dimension of *structural coupling*, we can begin to appreciate the capacity of a complex system to enact a world.[11]

There are many forms of coupling that we could provide for our rings. Let us suppose, though, that we simply drop the ring into a milieu of random 0s and 1s, much like a cell that is plunged into a chemical milieu. Imagine further that when one of the cells of this automata encounters one of these two alternatives (0s and 1s), the state of the cell is replaced by the perturbation that it encountered (see figure 8.1). For the sake of brevity, let us give the name *Bittorio* to this particular ring of cellular automata having this form of structural coupling with the chosen milieu.

In figure 8.2, the arrow to the left indicates the moment where one perturbation reaches one particular cell at one particular instant. The dynamics that follow indicate the ensuing change (or lack of it), that is, the way in which Bittorio compensates for this perturbation. If Bittorio's rule belongs to the first or fourth class (a simple or a chaotic attractor), then the consequence of the perturbation is simply invisible: Bittorio either goes back to its previous homogenous state, or it remains in a randomlike state.

It follows that only the second and third classes of rules can provide us with dynamics capable of producing interesting consequences for the kind of structural coupling we have chosen for Bittorio. As figure 8.2 shows, for Bittorios with these rules a single perturbation induces a change from one to another spatiotemporal configuration. Both of these configurations are stable and distinguishable.

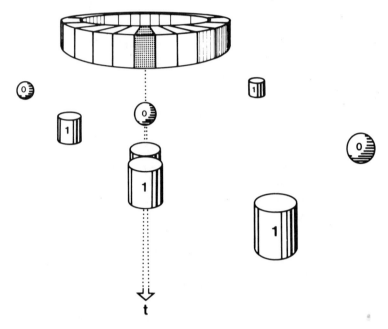

Figure 8.1
Cellular automata Bittorio in a random soup of 1s and 0s.

The case of Bittorio of rule 10010000, illustrated in figure 8.3, is worth commenting on in more detail. As can be seen, the encounter with just one perturbation changes the spatial periodicities from one to another stable configuration. But a second perturbation at the same cell undoes the previous change. Hence any odd sequence of perturbations at the same locus will lead to a change in state configuration for Bittorio, whereas any even sequence of perturbations will be invisible since it leaves Bittorio unchanged. Thus of all the innumerable sequences of possible perturbations, this Bittorio picks up or singles out from the milieu a very specific subset, namely, finite odd sequences, since only these sequences induce a repeatable change in Bittorio's configuration. In other words, given its rule and given its form of structural coupling, this Bittorio becomes an "odd sequence recognizer."

Another example of such emergent significations is shown in figure 8.4 for Bittorio of rule 01101110. Here a sequence of two perturbations is the only trigger capable of leading to a change in the state configuration of Bittorio. This is readily seen in figure 8.4 where we have

RULE: Ø1111ØØØ

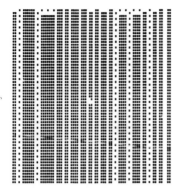

RULE: 111ØØ11Ø

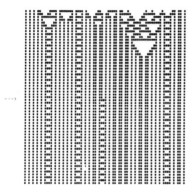

RULE: Ø11Ø1ØØØ

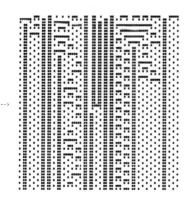

Figure 8.2
Bittorio's life history showing changes in this history depending on the perturbations it encounters.

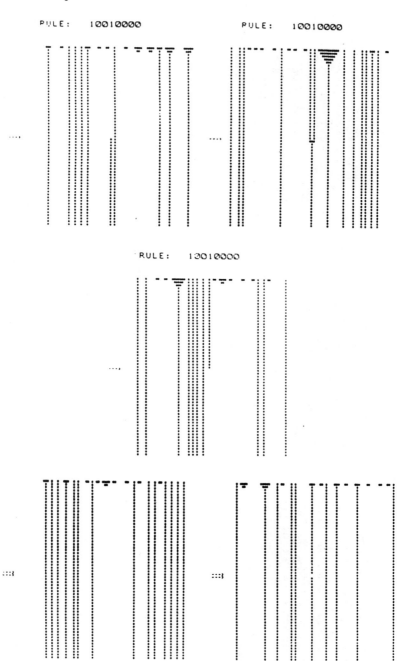

Figure 8.3
A Bittorio of rule 10010000, choosing only odd sequences of perturbations.

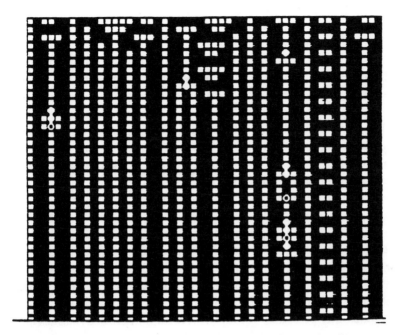

Figure 8.4
A Bittorio responsive to a sequence of double perturbations.

superimposed several encounters at different cellular loci to facilitate comparison. Anything other than double perturbations in one location leaves this Bittorio unchanged.

Other explorations with simultaneous perturbations and more complex forms of structural coupling reveal more rich and interesting behaviors for these Boolean cellular automata. The above examples, however, are enough for the purposes of illustration here.

We wish to emphasize that in these two specific cases (figures 8.3 and 8.4) we have not provided Bittorio with a program to distinguish "odd sequences" or "two successive perturbations." Instead we have specified, on the one hand, a form of closure for the system (the network's internal dynamical emergences) and, on the other hand, the way in which this system will couple with a given milieu (replacement of the state of each cell with the perturbation it encounters in a milieu of random 0s and 1s). The result, however, is that over time this coupling selects or enacts from a world of randomness a domain of distinctions ("odd sequences" or "two successive perturbations") that has relevance for the structure of the system. In other words, on the basis of its autonomy the system selects or enacts a domain of significance.

We use these words *significance* and *relevance* advisedly, for they imply that there is some kind of interpretation involved in the encounters. In the case of Bittorio, this interpretation is obviously a far cry from the kinds of interpretation that depend on experience. Nevertheless, we can say that a minimal kind of interpretation is involved, where *interpretation* is understood widely to mean the enactment of a domain of distinctions out of a background. Thus Bittorio, on the basis of its autonomy (closure), performs an interpretation in the sense that it selects or brings forth a domain of significance out of the background of its random milieu.

The distinctions that Bittorio selects, such as odd sequences, indicate the regularities with which Bittorio covaries. These regularities constitute what we could call Bittorio's world. It should be apparent that this world is not pregiven and then recovered through a representation. We did not design Bittorio to be an odd sequence recognizer; we simply provided Bittorio with certain internal dynamics and then dropped it into a random milieu. Nevertheless, given the history of coupling between the internal dynamics and the milieu, *odd sequence* becomes a significant distinction for Bittorio. For this reason, we describe Bittorio's world as enacted through a history of structural coupling.

Bittorio provides, then, a paradigm for how closure and coupling suffice to bring forth a world of relevance for a system. Of course, this paradigm is rather simple. Our intention, however, is not to provide a model of any specific phenomenon, and we certainly do not intend to suggest that such a simple form of closure and coupling is sufficient for a system to experience a world. Rather, our intention is simply to provide a *minimal* example of how an autonomous system brings forth significance from a background. It is the simplicity of the example that enables us to follow in detail the entire process by which a kind of distinction is enacted.

Despite the simplicity of the example, we should not underestimate the moral it suggests. Since we can already recognize the emergence of a minimal kind of significance with just the simple form of autonomy (closure) and coupling given to Bittorio, imagine the rich and complex kinds of significance that would be brought forth by living cells or complex cellular networks, such as the brain and the immune system. Though far more complex and intricate, these systems nonetheless share with Bittorio the properties of being autonomous (having operational closure) and being structurally coupled.[12]

Such autonomous systems stand in sharp contrast to systems whose coupling with the environment is specified through input/output relations. The digital computer is the most familiar example of this latter kind of system. Here the meaning of a given keyboard sequence is always assigned by the designer. Living systems, however, are far from being in this category. Under very restricted circumstances we can speak as if we could specify the operation of a cell or an organism through input/ouput relations. In general, though, the meaning of this or that interaction for a living system is not prescribed from outside but is the result of the organization and history of the system itself. Let us now turn, then, to consider some actual living examples.

Color as a Study Case

Perhaps the best example, one which we intend to explore in some depth here, is color perception. We have two reasons for choosing to focus on color. First, the study of color provides a microcosm of cognitive science, for each discipline in figure 1.1—neuroscience, psychology, artificial intelligence, linguistics, and philosophy—has made important contributions to our understanding of color. Indeed, other disciplines, such as genetics and anthropology, have contributed as well. Second, color has immediate perceptual and cognitive significance in human experience. For these two reasons, color provides a paradigmatic domain in which our twin concerns of science and human experience naturally intersect.

For ease of exposition our discussion of color will proceed through several stages. We will first discuss how colors themselves appear—what could be called the structure of color appearance. We will then discuss color as a perceived attribute of things in the world. Finally, we will consider color as an experiential category. Let us emphasize that these stages are not found separately in experience; our experience is simultaneously shaped by all three. Theories of color do, however, tend to take as their point of departure one or the other of these three aspects. Thus our stages, though expository, are not arbitrary.

Color Appearance

Let us begin, then, not with the visual system or with colored objects but simply with color itself. There are two important features of the structure of color appearance. First, all of the colors that we see can be described as some combination of six basic colors: red, green, yellow, blue, black, and white. For example, orange is a combination of red and yellow; turquoise is a combination of blue and green; violet and indigo are combinations of red and blue, etc. Second, the appearance of color varies along three dimensions, those of hue, saturation, and brightness. *Hue* refers to the degree of redness, greenness, yellowness, or blueness of a given color. Red, green, yellow, and blue are the four fundamental or psychologically unique hues, which combine to form complex or psychologically binary hues. For example, red and yellow combine to form reddish-yellows and yellowish-reds (oranges), whereas blue and red combine to form blueish-reds and reddish-blues (purples). For each unique hue, there is another unique hue with which it cannot coexist to form a binary hue. Thus red cannot coexist with green, and yellow cannot coexist with blue. Red and green are therefore known as *opponent* hues, as are blue and yellow. It should be noted that not every color need be of a certain hue. White and black, as well as the intermediate shades of gray, are colors, but they have no hue. They are therefore known as achromatic colors—colors that have zero hue—whereas colors with hue are called chromatic. The chromatic colors can also differ in the strength or *saturation* of their hue. Saturated colors have a greater degree of hue, whereas desaturated colors are closer to gray. *Brightness* is the final dimension of color appearance. Along this dimension, colors vary from dazzling at one end to dim or barely visible at the other end.

Why does color have this structure? Why, for example, are hues organized into pairs that are mutually exclusive or opponent? The model of color vision that takes as its point of departure the structure of color appearance, and so attempts to answer these questions, is known as the *opponent-process theory*. This theory owes its origin to the research of the nineteenth-century physiologist Ewald Hering but was proposed in its modern form by Leo Hurvich and Dorothea Jameson in 1957.[13] According to this theory, there are three color "channels" in the visual system: one channel is achromatic and signals differences in brightness; the other two are chromatic and signal differences in hue. It should be noted that these channels are specified in psychophysical experiments, not neurophysiological ones. The exact nature of their physiological embodiment is still a matter of debate. Nevertheless, it is accepted that the channels correspond in some way to the complex cross-connections among retinal cells and postretinal neuronal ensembles.

In the retina there are three different but intermingled mosaics of cone cells, whose overlapping photopigment absorption curves peak around 560, 530, and 440 nanometers respectively. These three cone mosaics constitute the so-called long-wave (L), middle-wave (M), and short-wave (S) receptors. Excitatory and inhibitory processes in post-receptoral cells enable the signals from these receptors to be added and/or subtractively compared. In the opponent-process model, the addition of the signals from all three receptors generates the achromatic (brightness) channel. The difference between the signals from the L and M receptors generates the red-green channel, and the difference between the sum of the signals from the L and M receptors and the signals from the S receptors generates the yellow-blue channel. These two chromatic channels are opponent: an increase in red is always gained at the expense of green and vice-versa; an increase in yellow is always gained at the expense of blue and vice-versa.

This opponent-process theory explains the structure of color appearance by showing how it results from the differential responses of the achromatic and chromatic channels. Thus the organization of hues into mutually exclusive or antagonistic pairs reflects an underlying opponent organization. We never experience any color to be a combination of red and green, or yellow and blue, because the chromatic channels cannot simultaneously signal "red" and "green," or "yellow" and "blue." The opponent-process theory also explains why some hues are unique and others are binary. Unique hues result from a signal from one chromatic channel while the other chromatic channel is neutral or balanced. For example, unique green results when the red-green channel signals "green" and the yellow-blue channel is neutral so that it signals neither "yellow" nor "blue." Binary hues, on the other hand, result from the interplay of the two channels with each other. Thus orange results from the red-green channel signaling "red" and the yellow-blue channel signaling "yellow."

Now that we have a basic understanding of how color appearance is generated, let us turn to the second stage in our investigation, color as a perceived attribute of things in the world.

Color as a Perceived Attribute

Since we perceive colors to be spatially located, we might assume that the color we perceive an area to have can be correlated with the light reflected locally from that area. Thus if some area looks whiter than another, it must be because more light is reflected from the area. Or if some area looks green, it must be that the area reflects predominantly middle-wave light. If we fail to see the area as green in such a situation, then our perception must be mistaken; what we see must be an illusion.

If we examine the situation more closely, however, we are in for interesting surprises. If we actually measure the light reflected from the world around us, we will discover that there simply is no one-to-one relationship between light flux at various wavelengths and the colors we perceive areas to have. Suppose, for example, that we perceive some area to be green. Areas that look green typically reflect a high percentage of middle-wave light and a low percentage of long-wave and short-wave light. We might suppose, then, that the area looks green because it reflects more middle-wave light to the eye. This supposition would be true, however, only in the limited case where the area is viewed in isolation, that is, if we exclude everything else from the field of view. But when this area is viewed as part of a complex scene, it will continue to look green even if it reflects more long-wave and short-wave light than middle-wave light. In other words, when the area is viewed as part of a complex scene, the light that it locally reflects is not sufficient to predict its perceived color. Therefore, there simply is no one-to-one correspondence between perceived color and locally reflected light.

This relative independence of perceived color from locally reflected light has been known to vision scientists for quite some time.[14] The independence is manifested in two complementary phenomena. In the first, the perceived colors of things remain relatively constant despite large changes in the illumination. This phenomenon is known as *approximate color constancy*. In the second, two areas that reflect light of the same spectral composition can be seen to have different colors depending on the surroundings in which they are placed. This phenomenon is known as *simultaneous color contrast* or *chromatic induction*.[15]

These two phenomena force us to conclude that we cannot account for our experience of color as an attribute of things in the world by appealing simply to the intensity and wavelength composition of the light reflected from an area. Instead, we need to consider the complex and only partially understood processes of cooperative comparison among multiple neuronal ensembles in the brain, which assign colors to objects according to the emergent, global states they reach given a retinal image.

Consider the following interesting demonstration. We take two identical slide projectors superimposed over a common screen and fit each with identical copies of a slide containing a checkerboard of grays, whites, and blacks. The two slides are superimposed so that they are exactly aligned. We also put a red filter in one of the projectors, so that the overall pattern that results is an array of pinks of different saturations. Let us now turn one slide by 90 degrees. The result is a full, multicolored image, containing small squares that are yellow, blue, and green, as well as red and pink.[16]

The effect of this experiment is quite dramatic: a multicolored image arises where physics would lead us to expect only various shades of pink. This chromatic effect can be described by the white-to-white and red-to-red ratios across the edges of the small squares accomplished by the rotation of one of the slides. How can this happen?

As we mentioned when discussing the opponent-process theory, the light that reaches the eye perturbs three different but intermingled mosaics of cones, which constitute three retinal surfaces: the S, M, and L receptors. These three retinal surfaces are by no means identical or homogenous. For example, the L receptor has a density of cones about five times higher than the S receptor and slightly less than the M receptor. Furthermore, due to the inner connectivity of the retina, local differences of activity in the three receptor surfaces depend on what happens in the rest of the retina. In this manner, internal *relative* values are generated. Abrupt deviations from such reference values in the local levels of activity become the difference that makes a difference: within the boundaries of such deviations a uniform color is perceived.

This description highlights the emergent configurations at the retinal level and so is only partial. There are structures at all levels of the visual pathways that participate in the perception of color. In primates, the participation of subensembles of neurons in color perception has been demonstrated in the thalamus (LGN), primary and extrastriate visual cortex, inferotemporal cortex, and frontal lobes.[17] Most notable is a collection of neurons in the so-called area V4 of the extrastriate cortex where even individual neuronal responses can be roughly associated with the color constancies of a visual field.[18] These neuronal structures constitute a color subnetwork—a sort of perceptual "agent," to use Minsky's terminology. Thus nothing short of a large and distributed neuronal network is involved in our perception of color.

Colors are not, of course, perceived in isolation from other attributes, such as shape, size, texture, motion, and orientation. For example, the artist Kandinsky commented on the relation between color and motion. In one of his essays he wrote, "If two circles are drawn and painted respectively yellow and blue, a brief contemplation will reveal in the yellow a spreading movement out from the center, and a noticeable approach to the spectator. The blue, on the other hand, moves into itself, like a snail retreating into its shell, and draws away from the spectator. The eye feels stung by the first circle while it is absorbed into the second."[19]

The motion that Kandinsky refers to here is obviously not movement in the physical space of the picture. It is, rather, motion in our perceptual space. As Mark Johnson notes in a discussion of this passage from Kandinsky, "The 'movement' refers to structures in our perceptual interaction, in which we form unified images and trace out relations among the various elements in the work."[20]

Recent trends in physiology enable us to understand the bodily basis for these "structures of perceptual interaction." In recent years physiology has moved toward the study of vision as a patchwork of visual modalities, including at least form (shape, size, rigidity), surface properties (color, texture, specular reflectance, transparency), three-dimensional spatial relationships (relative positions, three-dimensional orientation in space, distance), and three-dimensional movement (trajectory, rotation). It has become evident that these different visual modalities are emergent properties of concurrent subnetworks, which have a degree of independence and even anatomical separability but cross-correlate and work together so that at almost every moment a visual percept is coherent.[21] (This kind of architecture is, once again, strongly reminiscent of Minsky's societies of agents.) Figure 8.5 depicts some of the identified anatomical elements of these visual subnetworks. Among the modalities, color seems to be one of the more simple, for color indicators can be obtained solely on the basis of luminance and contrast levels. This simplicity betrays, however, the equally important fact that color is always perceived within a more encompassing visual context. All of the subnetworks work cooperatively; we never see color as an isolated item.

Furthermore, visual perception is in active exchange with other sensory modalities. For example, the associations of color and sound, as well as color and horizontal/vertical perception (involving the sense of orientation and equilibrium), are well known to artists, though less studied by neurobiologists. Beyond these intermodal relations there are, of course, varieties of cognitive expectancies and memories. Such "top-down" dependency is to be expected, for, like those of the LGN and visual cortex, the pathways depicted in figure 8.5 are all bidirectional. Thus, to reiterate one of our central points, the neuronal network does not function as a one-way street from perception to action. Perception and action, sensorium and motorium, are linked together as successively emergent and mutually selecting patterns.

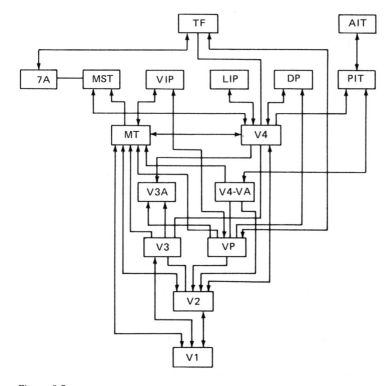

Figure 8.5
Parallel streams in the visual pathway. From DeYoe and Van Essen, Concurrent processing streams in monkey visual cortex.

To bring home this point that color perception partakes of both other visual and sensory modalities, let us consider a much more dramatic example: the complete loss of color perception. In a recent article Oliver Sacks and Robert Wasserman presented an account of a patient who, due to an accident, became completely color-blind.[22] This particular case of so-called acquired cerebral achromatopsia is fascinating because it occurred in an artist known for his especially colorful, abstract paintings. As a result of a car accident, this person—referred to as "Mr. I"—could no longer perceive any colors: he lived in a visual world that resembled black-and-white television.

The participation of color perception in other modalities of experience is evident from Mr. I's descriptions in the weeks following his accident. Because of the absence of color, the overall character of his experience changed dramatically: everything he saw "had a distasteful, 'dirty' look, the whites glaring, yet discolored and off-white, the blacks cavernous—everything wrong, unnatural, stained, and impure."[23] As a result, he found foods disgusting and sexual intercourse impossible. He could no longer visually imagine colors, nor could he dream in color. His appreciation of music was also impaired, for he could no longer experience musical tones by synestheticly transforming them into plays of color. Eventually, Mr. I seemed to forget completely his former world of color. His habits, behavior, and actions changed as he became progressively more of a "night person." In his words, "I love the nighttime. . . . I often wonder about people who work at night. They never see the sunlight. They prefer it. . . . It's a different world: there's a lot of space—you're not hemmed in by streets, people. . . . It's a whole new world. Gradually I am becoming a night person. At one time I felt kindly toward color, very happy about it. In the beginning, I felt very bad, losing it. Now I don't even know it exists—it's not even a phantom."[24]

This description provides rare insight into how our perceived world, which we usually take for granted, is constituted through complex and delicate patterns of sensorimotor activity. Our colored world is brought forth by complex processes of structural coupling. When these processes are altered, some forms of behavior are no longer possible. One's behavior changes as one learns to cope with new conditions and situations. And, as one's actions change, so too does one's sense of the world. If these changes are dramatic enough—as in Mr. I's loss of color—then a different perceived world will be enacted.

The preceding examples have shown us how color as an attribute is intimately involved with other attributes of our perceived world. Our examination so far shows that we will not be able to explain color if we seek to locate it in a world independent of our perceptual capacities. Instead, we must locate color in the perceived or experiential world that is brought forth from our history of structural coupling. Indeed, this point will become even more apparent when we consider color as an experiential category. Before we turn to this third stage in our discussion of color, however, let us pause to consider an objection.

Where Is Color?

Suppose someone, in reply to our discussion, were to demand, "What is the point of all these complex neuronal processes if not to compensate for the changes in illumination and recover some stable feature of objects? Consider, for example, the surface reflectance of an object. This property corresponds to the percentage of incident light at each wavelength that an object reflects. This percentage or ratio describes the way in which an object, by virtue of its physical constitution, alters the ambient light; it is therefore a stable property, one that remains constant through changes in illumination. Why not say, then, that although we must account for color experience by revealing its constitution through emergent patterns of neuronal activity, this experience is nonetheless a result of having to solve the information-processing problem of recovering surface reflectance?"

Recent computational models of color vision seem to support this line of argument. The surface reflectances of objects in our surrounding world, such as bricks, grass, buildings, etc., can be expressed in a rather limited (three-dimensional) set of prototypical functions.[25] Thus it would seem that all the visual system has to do is sample the scene with its three color channels and thereby reconstitute the surface reflectances from the activity in these channels. On the basis of these models, several vision scientists, as well as certain philosophers, have argued not only that the function of color vision is the recovery of surface reflectance but also that color itself is just the property of surface reflectance.[26]

This objectivist proposal gives rise to several considerable problems, which serve to reinforce our point that the colors we see must be located not in a pregiven world but rather in the perceived world brought forth from our structural coupling. Consider first the idea that color is just surface reflectance. We have already seen that colors have certain properties and bear certain relations to each other: color varies along the three dimensions of hue, saturation, and brightness; hues are either unique or binary and are organized into opponent pairs, etc. Now if color is just surface reflectance, we should be able to match these features of color with corresponding features of surface reflectance. But there are no such corresponding features. Surface reflectances can be classified according to whether they reflect more or less light in the short-, middle-, and/or long-wave regions of the spectrum, but they cannot be classified as being unique or binary, nor can they be classified as standing in opponent relations to other reflectances. Nor can these properties of uniqueness, binariness, and opponency be found in the structure of light. For these reasons, the properties that specify what colors are simply have no nonexperiential, physical counterparts.[27]

Second, color is not simply a perceived attribute of surfaces; it is also a perceived attribute of volumes such as the sky. Furthermore, we experience colors as attributes of afterimages and in dreams, memories, and synesthesia. The unity among these phenomena is not to be found in some nonexperiential, physical structure but rather in color as a form of experience that is constituted through emergent patterns of neuronal activity.

Let us now consider the idea that the function of color vision is to represent and thereby recover surface reflectance. The first thing to note about this idea is that it arises not from the biological and ecological investigation of color vision but from the engineering attempt to devise a system that will be able to detect objects by discounting variations in the illumination and recovering the invariant reflectances in a scene. Although this engineering research program is of considerable importance for our understanding of the more abstract principles involved in vision, it should not be allowed to dictate conclusions about the biological and ecological purposes that natural color vision serves. Indeed, attention to these biological and ecological purposes reveals that color vision is concerned as much with properties that change, such as lighting, weather conditions, and time of day, as with properties that remain constant, such as surface reflectance.[28]

Finally, there is a hidden, but much deeper problem with the objectivist view of color vision: the objectivist simply assumes that surface reflectances are to be found in some pregiven world that is independent of our perceptual and cognitive capacities. But how are we to specify what counts as a surface? How are we to specify its edges, boundaries, texture, and orientation, if not in relation to some perceiver for whom these distinctions are relevant?

The objectivist supposition that surface reflectances are pregiven rests on the assumption that since surface reflectance is a physical property, it can be measured and specified in entirely physical terms. But although the reflectance at any point in a scene can be specified in physical terms, what counts as a surface may in fact involve tacit reference to a type of perceiver. This point is obscured in computational models that emphasize the limited dimensions in which so-called naturally occurring reflectances can vary. If we actually examine these models, we will see that the natural reflectances correspond not only to the reflectances of typical objects from our human environment, as opposed to the environments of considerably different visual creatures, but also that these objects have been picked out or specified prior to the actual task of vision. In other words, these models treat the visual system as if it were simply presented with a certain class of prespecified objects whose reflectances must then be recovered.

This approach involves a considerable and artifical simplification of our actual perceptual situation. The visual system is never simply presented with pregiven objects. On the contrary, the determination of what and where an object is, as well as its surface boundaries, texture, and relative orientation (and hence the overall context of color as a perceived attribute), is a complex process that the visual system must continually achieve. This achievement, as we have seen in our discussion of the patchwork architecture of vision, results from a complex cooperative process involving active dialogue among all the visual modalities. Indeed, color vision is actually involved in the cooperative processes by which the visual scene comes to be segmented into a collection of surfaces. In the words of P. Gouras and E. Zrenner, "It is impossible to separate the object sensed from its color because it is the color contrast itself that forms the object."[29] Thus colors and surfaces go together: both depend on our embodied perceptual capacities.

Color as a Category
Our discussion so far has concentrated on the perception of color, considered either on its own terms (color appearance), as it were, or as an attribute of things (surface colors, volume colors, etc.). But our

experience of color is not only perceptual; it is also cognitive: we organize all the various hue/saturation/brightness combinations that we perceive into a limited set of color categories and give names to these categories. As we will now see, color categories provide yet another dramatic illustration of how color is brought forth.

Linguistic Aspects of Color   Consider the numerous names that we have in English for colors: red, yellow, orange, green, blue, purple, violet, indigo, pink, turquoise, aquamarine, mauve, chartreuse, etc. Given these many names, as well as the numerous names in other languages, we might suppose that color categories are ultimately arbitrary, that is, that nothing compels us to categorize colors in one way rather than another. Indeed, this view was at one time dominant within the fields of linguistics and anthropology.[30]

This view was dramatically challenged in 1969 with the publication of a now classic work by Brent Berlin and Paul Kay.[31] In this work, Berlin and Kay specified a set of linguistic criteria for determining which color names in a given language constitute "basic" color terms. These basic color terms name the basic color categories in a given language. Then, in an examination of over ninety languages, Berlin and Kay determined that there are at most eleven basic color categories encoded in any language, though not all languages encode all eleven. These basic categories are red, green, blue, yellow, black, white, gray, orange, purple, brown, and pink. Berlin and Kay also presented speakers of various languages with a standardized array of color chips and asked them to specify both the boundaries and the best examples of the colors to which their basic terms refer. They found that although there was considerable variation among speakers over color category boundaries, individuals virtually always agreed on the best example of a color category. Furthermore, they found that when several languages contained a common basic term, such as a basic term for blue, speakers virtually always agreed on the best example of the color category no matter which language they spoke. Berlin and Kay argued therefore that the basic color categories do not have a uniform structure, for some members of the categories are central and so constitute category "foci." Since these central members are universally agreed upon, Berlin and Kay concluded that "the eleven basic color categories are pan-human perceptual universals."[32]

Although some languages do not encode all eleven basic color categories, we should not suppose that the color domain is impoverished for speakers of these languages. On the contrary, the set of basic color terms in a given language always encompasses the entire color space. For example, the language of the Dani tribe of New Guinea has only two basic color terms. In studies of the Dani, Rosch (then Heider) showed that these two terms, which had previously been translated as "white" and "black," were actually better translated as "white-warm" and "dark-cool," for the former term covered white plus all the warm colors (red, yellow, orange, reddish-purple, pink), whereas the latter covered black plus all the cool colors (blue, green).[33]

Color and Cognition   The studies we have discussed so far have been about color language. There is an entire subfield in psychology, called language and cognition, that considers and disputes the ways in which language and cognition may or may not be related. Prior to Berlin and Kay, a well-known series of experiments had demonstrated that memory for colors (a cognitive variable) was a function of color naming (a linguistic variable).[34] Since naming was assumed to be culturally relative, it was thus argued and widely accepted that cognition had been demonstrated to be culturally relative. But what if both color language and color cognition are functions of some third underlying factor—color physiology, for example? A natural laboratory for testing such questions was provided by the Dani of New Guinea since their language lacked virtually all color vocabulary. In a series of experiments, Rosch found that (1) central members of basic color categories were perceptually more salient, could be learned more rapidly, and were more easily remembered in both short-term and long-term memory than were peripheral colors, even by speakers of Dani who do not have names for the central colors; (2) the structures of the color spaces derived from Dani and English color naming were very different but were quite similar for those derived from Dani and English color memory; and (3) when Dani were taught basic color categories, they found it quite easy to learn categories that were structured in the universal fashion (with central members as central) but extremely difficult to learn categories that were structured in a deviant manner (with peripheral colors as central, where blue-green might be central and blues and greens peripheral).[35] Very similar effects were found in the development of color names in young children in our own culture.[36] All of these results argued strongly that both cognitive and linguistic aspects of color categorization are related to underlying (probably physiological) factors. Thus color categories appear to be a panhuman, species-specific universal.

Our discussion so far would seem to suggest that color categories are entirely determined by emergent patterns of neuronal activity in the human visual system—the color subnetwork that we reviewed above. Thus notice that the focal colors red, green, blue, yellow, black, and white can be mapped directly onto the responses of the three color channels in the opponent-process theory of color vision. But what about focal orange, purple, brown, and pink? More recent research suggests that distinctly cognitive operations are required to generate these focal colors. The cognitive operations appear to be of two kinds: one is universal for our species and the other is culture specific.[37]

In 1978 Paul Kay and Chad McDaniel provided a model of how color categories could be generated from a certain set of neuronal responses plus certain species-specific cognitive processes.[38] The neuronal responses correspond to the red-green, yellow-blue, and black-white responses of neuronal ensembles, such as those found by R. DeValois and G. Jacobs in the LGN of the macaque, a species of monkey that has color vision quite similar to ours.[39] (One could also construct a model using the psychophysical color channels. Indeed, it is perhaps preferable to do so, since the exact neural embodiment of these channels is still disputed.) The cognitive processes correspond to operations that can be modeled by using a branch of mathematics known as fuzzy set theory. Unlike standard set theory, fuzzy set theory operates with sets that admit degrees of membership. Degree of membership in a set is specified by a function that assigns to each member of the set some value between 0 and 1. Thus for color, focal colors have degree of membership 1 in their respective categories, whereas nonfocal colors have degrees of membership between 0 and 1. In Kay and McDaniel's model, the red-green, yellow-blue, and black-white neuronal responses directly determine the basic categories red, green, yellow, blue, black, and white. Orange, purple, brown, and pink, however, are "computed" or "generated" by cognitive operations on these neuronal responses. These cognitive operations correspond to the operation of fuzzy set intersection. Thus orange is the fuzzy intersection of red and yellow, purple of red and blue, pink of white and red, and brown of black and yellow. Since these categories require such cognitive derivations, Kay and McDaniel term them *derived* basic color categories.

Color and Culture   Finally, color categories depend on culture-specific cognitive processes. Thus in another study, Paul Kay and Willett Kempton found that the lexical classification of colors can affect subjective judgments of similarity among colors.[40] For example, English contains terms for both green and blue, whereas Tarahumara (a Uto-Aztecan language of northern Mexico) has a single term that means "green or blue." This linguistic difference appears to be correlated with a difference in subjective judgments of similarity among colors between speakers of the two languages: English speakers tend to exaggerate the perceived distances of colors close to the green-blue boundary, whereas speakers of Tarahumara do not.

Other evidence for culture-specific cognitive processes comes from R. E. MacLaury. He has found that purple is sometimes placed entirely within the cool range (blue-green) and other times on the boundary between the cool range and red and that brown is sometimes placed within the yellow category and other times within black.[41] MacLaury also reports that many Native American languages of the Pacific Northwest encode an otherwise rare "yellow-with-green" basic category.[42]

These examples show that color categorization in its entirety depends upon a tangled hierarchy of perceptual and cognitive processes, some species specific and others culture specific. They also serve to illustrate the point that color categories are not to be found in some pregiven world that is independent of our perceptual and cognitive capacities. The categories red, green, yellow, blue, purple, orange—as well as light/warm, dark/cool, yellow-with-green, etc.— are experiential, consensual, and embodied: they depend upon our biological and cultural history of structural coupling.

We can now appreciate, then, how color provides a paradigm of a cognitive domain that is neither pregiven nor represented but rather experiential and enacted. It is very important to note that just because color is not pregiven does not mean that it does not exhibit universals or that it cannot yield to rigorous analysis by the various branches of science. Since color provides such a paradigm, we will return to it at various points. The time has come, however, to step back and consider some of the lessons this cognitive domain provides for our understanding of perception and cognition in general.

Cognition as Embodied Action

Let us begin, once again, with visual perception. Consider the question, "Which came first, the world or the image?" The answer of most vision research—both cognitivist and connectionist—is unambiguously given by the names of the tasks investigated. Thus researchers speak of "recovering shape from shading," "depth from motion," or "color from varying illuminants." We call this stance the *chicken position:*

> *Chicken position*: The world out there has pregiven properties. These exist prior to the image that is cast on the cognitive system, whose task is to recover them appropriately (whether through symbols or global subsymbolic states).

Notice how very reasonable this position sounds and how difficult it is to imagine that things could be otherwise. We tend to think that the only alternative is the *egg position:*

> *Egg position*: The cognitive system projects its own world, and the apparent reality of this world is merely a reflection of internal laws of the system.

Our discussion of color suggests a middle way between these two chicken and egg extremes. We have seen that colors are not "out there" independent of our perceptual and cognitive capacities. We have also seen that colors are not "in here" independent of our surrounding biological and cultural world. Contrary to the objectivist view, color categories are experiential; contrary to the subjectivist view, color categories belong to our shared biological and cultural world. Thus color as a study case enables us to appreciate the obvious point that chicken and egg, world and perceiver, specify each other.

It is precisely this emphasis on mutual specification that enables us to negotiate a middle path between the Scylla of cognition as the recovery of a pregiven outer world (realism) and the Charybdis of cognition as the projection of a pregiven inner world (idealism). These two extremes both take representation as their central notion: in the first case representation is used to recover what is outer; in the second case it is used to project what is inner. Our intention is to bypass entirely this logical geography of inner versus outer by studying cognition not as recovery or projection but as embodied action.

Let us explain what we mean by this phrase *embodied action*. By using the term *embodied* we mean to highlight two points: first, that cognition depends upon the kinds of experience that come from having a body with various sensorimotor capacities, and second, that these individual sensorimotor capacities are themselves embedded in a more encompassing biological, psychological, and cultural context.[43] By using the term *action* we mean to emphasize once again that sensory and motor processes, perception and action, are fundamentally inseparable in lived cognition. Indeed, the two are not merely contingently linked in individuals; they have also evolved together.

We can now give a preliminary formulation of what we mean by *enaction*. In a nutshell, the enactive approach consists of two points: (1) perception consists in perceptually guided action and (2) cognitive structures emerge from the recurrent sensorimotor patterns that enable action to be perceptually guided. These two statements will perhaps appear somewhat opaque, but their meaning will become more transparent as we proceed.

Let us begin with the notion of perceptually guided action. We have already seen that for the representationist the point of departure for understanding perception is the information-processing problem of recovering pregiven properties of the world. In contrast, the point of departure for the enactive approach is the study of how the perceiver can guide his actions in his local situation. Since these local situations constantly change as a result of the perceiver's activity, the reference point for understanding perception is no longer a pregiven, perceiver-independent world but rather the sensorimotor structure of the perceiver (the way in which the nervous system links sensory and motor surfaces). This structure—the manner in which the perceiver is embodied—rather than some pregiven world determines how the perceiver can act and be modulated by environmental events. Thus the overall concern of an enactive approach to perception is not to determine how some perceiver-independent world is to be recovered; it is, rather, to determine the common principles or lawful linkages between sensory and motor systems that explain how action can be perceptually guided in a perceiver-dependent world.[44]

This approach to perception was in fact among the central insights of the analysis undertaken by Merleau-Ponty in his early work. It is therefore worthwhile to quote one of his more visionary passages in full:

> The organism cannot properly be compared to a keyboard on which the external stimuli would play and in which their proper

form would be delineated for the simple reason that the organism contributes to the constitution of that form. . . . "The properties of the object and the intentions of the subject . . . are not only intermingled; they also constitute a new whole." When the eye and the ear follow an animal in flight, it is impossible to say "which started first" in the exchange of stimuli and responses. Since all the movements of the organism are always conditioned by external influences, one can, if one wishes, readily treat behavior as an effect of the milieu. But in the same way, since all the stimulations which the organism receives have in turn been possible only by its preceding movements which have culminated in exposing the receptor organ to external influences, one could also say that *behavior is the first cause of all the stimulations*.

Thus the form of the excitant is *created by* the organism itself, by its proper manner of offering itself to actions from the outside. Doubtless, in order to be able to subsist, it must encounter a certain number of physical and chemical agents in its surroundings. But it is the organism itself—according to the proper nature of its receptors, the thresholds of its nerve centers and the movements of the organs—*which chooses the stimuli in the physical world to which it will be sensitive*. "The environment (*Umwelt*) emerges from the world through the actualization or the being of the organism—[granted that] an organism can exist only if it succeeds in finding in the world an adequate environment." This would be a keyboard which moves itself in such a way as to offer—and according to variable rhythms—such or such of its keys to the in itself monotonous action of an external hammer [italics added].[45]

In such an approach, then, perception is not simply embedded within and constrained by the surrounding world; it also contributes to the enactment of this surrounding world. Thus as Merleau-Ponty notes, the organism both initiates and is shaped by the environment. Merleau-Ponty clearly recognized, then, that we must see the organism and environment as bound together in reciprocal specification and selection.

Let us now provide a few illustrations of the perceptual guidance of action. In a classic study, Held and Hein raised kittens in the dark and exposed them to light only under controlled conditions.[46] A first group of animals was allowed to move around normally, but each of them was harnessed to a simple carriage and basket that contained a member of the second group of animals. The two groups therefore shared the same visual experience, but the second group was entirely passive. When the animals were released after a few weeks of this treatment, the first group of kittens behaved normally, but those who had been carried around behaved as if they were blind: they bumped into objects and fell over edges. This beautiful study supports the enactive view that objects are not seen by the visual extraction of features but rather by the visual guidance of action.

Lest the reader feel that this example is fine for cats but removed from human experience, consider another case. Bach y Rita has designed a video camera for blind persons that can stimulate multiple points in the skin by electrically activated vibration.[47] Using this technique, images formed with the camera were made to correspond to patterns of skin stimulation, thereby substituting for the visual loss. Patterns projected on to the skin have no "visual" content unless the individual is behaviorally active by directing the video camera using head, hand, or body movements. When the blind person does actively behave in this way, after a few hours of experience a remarkable emergence takes place: the person no longer inteprets the skin sensations as body related but as images projected into the space being explored by the bodily directed "gaze" of the video camera. Thus to experience "real objects out there," the person must actively direct the camera (by head or hand).

Another sensory modality where the relation between perception and action can be seen is olfaction. Over many years of research, Walter Freeman has managed to insert an array of electrodes into the olfactory bulb of a rabbit so that a small portion of the global activity can be measured while the animal behaves freely.[48] He found that there is no clear pattern of global activity in the bulb unless the animal is exposed to one specific odor several times. Furthermore, such emergent patterns of activity seem to be created out of a background of incoherent or chaotic activity into a coherent attractor.[49] As in the case of color, smell is not a passive mapping of external features but a creative form of enacting significance on the basis of the animal's embodied history.

There is in fact growing evidence that this kind of fast dynamics can underlie the configuration of neuronal ensembles. It has been reported in the visual cortex in cats and monkeys linked to visual stimulation; it has been found in radically different neural structures such as the avian brain and even the ganglia of an invertebrate, *Hermissenda*.[50] This universality is important, for it indicates the fundamental nature of this kind of mechanism of sensorimotor coupling and hence enaction. Had this kind of mechanism been a more species-specific process, typical of, say, only the mammalian cortex, it would have been be far less convincing as a working hypothesis.[51]

Let us now turn to the idea that cognitive structures emerge from the kinds of recurrent sensorimotor patterns that enable action to be perceptually guided. The pioneer and giant in this area is Jean Piaget.[52] Piaget laid out a program that he called *genetic epistemology*: he set himself the task of explaining the development of the child from an immature biological organism at birth to a being with abstract reason in adulthood. The child begins with only her sensorimotor system, and Piaget wishes to understand how sensorimotor intelligence evolves into the child's conception of an external world with permanent objects located in space and time and into the child's conception of herself as both an object among other objects and as an internal mind. Within Piaget's system, the newborn infant is neither an objectivist nor an idealist; she has only her own activity, and even the simplest act of recognition of an object can be understood only in terms of her own activity. Out of this, she must construct the entire edifice of the phenomenal world with its laws and logic. This is a clear example in which cognitive structures are shown to emerge from recurrent patterns (in Piaget's language, "circular reactions") of sensorimotor activity.

Piaget, however, as a theorist, never seems to have doubted the existence of a pregiven world and an independent knower with a pregiven logical endpoint for cognitive development. The laws of cognitive development, even at the sensorimotor stage, are an assimilation of and an accommodation to that pregiven world. We thus have an interesting tension in Piaget's work: an objectivist theorist who postulates his subject matter, the child, as an enactive agent, but an enactive agent who evolves inexorably into an objectivist theorist. Piaget's work, already influential in some domains, would bear more attention from non-Piagetians.

One of the most fundamental cognitive activities that all organisms perform is categorization. By this means the uniqueness of each experience is transformed into the more limited set of learned, meaningful categories to which humans and other organisms respond. In the behaviorist era of psychology (which was also the heyday of cultural relativism in anthropology), categories were treated as arbitrary, and categorization tasks were used in psychology only to study the laws of learning.[53] (The sense of arbitrariness also reflects the subjectivist trends in contemporary thought that emphasize the element of interpretation in all experience.) In the enactive view, although mind and world arise together in enaction, their manner of arising in any particular situation is not arbitrary. Consider the object on which you are sitting, and ask yourself what it is. What is its name? If you are sitting on a chair, the chances are that you will have thought *chair* rather than *furniture* or *armchair*. Why? Rosch proposed that there was a basic level of categorization in taxonomies of concrete objects at which biology, culture, and cognitive needs for informativeness and economy all met.[54] In a series of experiments, Rosch et al. found the basic level of categorization to be the most inclusive level at which category members (1) are used, or interacted with, by similar motor actions, (2) have similar perceived shapes and can be imaged, (3) have identifiable humanly meaningful attributes, (4) are categorized by young children, and (5) have linguistic primacy (in several senses).[55]

The basic level of categorization, thus, appears to be the point at which cognition and environment become simultaneously enacted. The object appears to the perceiver as affording certain kinds of interactions, and the perceiver uses the objects with his body and mind in the afforded manner. Form and function, normally investigated as opposing properties, are aspects of the same process, and organisms are highly sensitive to their coordination. And the activities performed by the perceiver/actor with basic-level objects are part of the cultural, consensually validated forms of the life of the community in which the human and the object are situated—they are basic-level activities.

Mark Johnson proposed another very intriguing basic categorization process.[56] Humans, he argues, have very general cognitive structures called *kinesthetic image schemas:* for example, the *container schema*, the *part-whole schema*, and the *source-path-goal schema*. These schemas originate in bodily experience, can be defined in terms of certain structural elements, have a basic logic, and can be metaphorically projected to give structure to a wide variety of cognitive domains. Thus, the container schema's structural elements are "interior, boundary, exterior," its basic logic is "inside or outside," and its metaphorical projection gives structure to our conceptualizations of the visual field (things go in and out of sight), personal relationships (one gets in or out of a relationship), the logic of sets (sets contain their members), and so on.

On the basis of a detailed study of these kinds of examples, Johnson argues that image schemas emerge from certain basic forms of sensorimotor activities and interactions and so provide a preconceptual structure to our experience. He argues that since our conceptual understanding is shaped by experience, we also have image-schematic concepts. These concepts have a basic logic, which imparts structure to the cognitive domains into which they are imaginatively projected. Finally, these projections are not arbitrary but are accomplished through metaphorical and metonymical mapping procedures that are themselves motivated by the structures of bodily experience. Sweetzer provides specific case studies of this process in linguistics. She argues that historical changes of meaning of words in languages can be explained as metaphorical extensions from the concrete and bodily relevant senses of basic-level categories and image schemas to more abstract meanings—for example, "to see" comes to mean "to understand."[57]

Focusing on categorization, Lakoff has written a compendium of the work that various people have done that can be interpreted to challenge an objectivist viewpoint.[58] Recently Lakoff and Johnson have produced a manifesto of what they call an experientialist approach to cognition. This is the central theme of their approach:

> Meaningful conceptual structures arise from two sources: (1) from the structured nature of bodily and social experience and (2) from our innate capacity to imaginatively project from certain well-structured aspects of bodily and interactional experience to abstract conceptual structures. Rational thought is the application of very general cognitive processes—focusing, scanning, superimposition, figure-ground reversal, etc.—to such structures.[59]

This statement would seem consonant with the view of cognition as enaction for which we are arguing.

One provocative possible extension of the view of cognition as enaction is to the domain of cultural knowledge in anthropology. Where is the locus of cultural knowledge such as folktales, names for fishes, jokes—is it in the mind of the individual? In the rules of society? In cultural artifacts? How can we account for the variation found across time and across informants?[60] Great leverage for anthropological theory might be obtained by considering the knowledge to be found in the interface between mind, society, and culture rather than in one or even in all of them. The knowledge does not preexist in any one place or form but is enacted in particular situations—when a folktale is told or a fish named. We leave it to anthropology to explore this possibility.

Heideggerian Psychoanalysis

A view of psychopathology fundamentally different from either the Freudian approach or object relations theory was offered by Karl Jaspers, Ludwig Binswagner, and Merleau-Ponty based on the philosophy of Heidegger.[61] Intended to account for psychological disorders more general, more characterological, than the hysterical and compulsive symptomatology in which Freudian analysis specializes, this account can be dubbed the ontological view to contrast with Freud's representational, cognitivist, epistemological view.[62] In the ontological view, a character disorder can be understood only in terms of a person's entire mode of being in the world. A theme, such as inferiority and dominance, which is usually only one dimension among many used by an individual in defining his world, becomes fixated, through an early experience, such that it becomes the only mode through which the person can experience himself in the world. It becomes like the light by which objects are seen—the light itself cannot be seen as an object—and thus there is no comparison possible with other modes of being in the world.[63] Existential psychoanalysis has extended this type of analysis to pathologies other than character disorders at the same time that it has recharacterized so-called pathologies as existential choices.[64]

The extent to which this phenomenological portrait of pathology lacks any specific methods of its own for treatment is well known, however. The patient might attempt to recall the initial incidents that produced the totalizing of one theme, enact and work through this theme through transference with the therapist, or undergo body work to discover and alleviate the embodied stance of the theme—all, however, are equally characteristic of therapies in which the disorder is conceived in a Freudian, object relations, or other theoretical fashion.

The possibilities for total personal reembodiment inherent in the mindful, open-ended approach to experience that we have been describing may provide the needed framework and tools for implementation of an existential, embodied psychoanalysis. In fact, the relationship between meditation practice, Buddhist teachings, and therapy is a topic of great interest and great controversy among Western mindfulness/awareness practitioners.[65]   Psychological therapy in the Western sense is a historically and culturally unique phenomenon; there is no specific counterpart within traditional Buddhism. Many Western meditators (whether they consider themselves students of Buddhism or not) either are therapists or are considering becoming therapists, and many more have the experience of undergoing therapy. But again, we must remind the reader of our disclaimer concerning what is said in this book about psychoanalysis. An adequate discussion of this ferment would lead us too far afield at this point, but we invite the reader to consider what form a reembodying psychoanalysis might take.

The Retreat into Natural Selection

In preparation for the next chapter, we now wish to take note of a prevalent view within cognitive science, one which constitutes a challenge to the view of cognition that we have presented so far. Consider, then, the following response to our discussion: "I am willing to grant that you have shown that cognition is not simply a matter of representation but depends on our embodied capacities for action. I am also willing to grant that both our perception and categorization of, say, color, are inseparable from our perceptually guided activity and that they are enacted by our history of structural coupling. Nevertheless, this history is not the result of just any pattern of coupling; it is largely the result of biological evolution and its mechanism of natural selection. Therefore our perception and cognition have *survival value*, and so they must provide us with some more or less *optimal fit* to the world. Thus, to use color once more as an example, it is this optimal fit between us and the world that explains why we see the colors we do."

We do not mean to attribute this view to any particular theory within cognitive science. On the contrary, this view can be found virtually anywhere within the field: in vision research, it is common both to the computational theory of Marr and Poggio[66] and to the "direct theory" of J. J. Gibson and his followers.[67] It is prevalent in virtually every aspect of the philosophical project of "naturalized epistemology."[68] It is even voiced by those who insist on an embodied and experientialist approach to cognition.[69] For this reason, this view can be said to constitute the "received view" within cognitive science of the evolutionary basis for cognition. We cannot ignore, then, this retreat into natural selection.

Let us begin, once again, with our now familiar case study of color. The cooperative neuronal operations underlying our perception of color have resulted from the long biological evolution of the primate group. As we have seen, these operations partly determine the basic color categories that are common to all humans. The prevalence of these categories might lead us to suppose that they are optimal in some evolutionary sense, even though they do not reflect some pre-given world.

This conclusion, however, would be considerably unwarranted. We can safely conclude that since our biological lineage has continued, our color categories are *viable* or *effective*. Other species, however, have evolved *different* perceived worlds of color on the basis of different cooperative neuronal operations. Indeed, it is fair to say that the neuronal processes underlying human color perception are rather peculiar to the primate group. Most vertebrates (fishes, amphibians, and birds) have quite different and intricate color vision mechanisms. Insects have evolved radically different constitutions associated with their compound eyes.[70]

One of the most interesting ways to pursue this comparative investigation is through a comparison of the dimensionalities of color vision. Our color vision is *trichromatic*: as we have seen, our visual system comprises three types of photoreceptors cross-connected to three color channels. Therefore, three dimensions are needed to represent our color vision, that is, the kinds of color distinctions that we can make. Trichromacy is certainly not unique to humans; indeed, it would appear that virtually every animal class contains some species with trichromatic vision. More interesting, however, is that some animals are *dichromats*, others are *tetrachromats*, and some may even be *pentachromats*. (Dichromats include squirrels, rabbits, tree shrews, some fishes, possibly cats, and some New World monkeys; tetrachromats include fishes that live close to the surface of the water like goldfish, and diurnal birds like the pigeon and the duck; diurnal birds may even be pentachromats).[71] Whereas two dimensions are needed to represent dichromatic vision, four are needed for tetrachromatic vision (see figure 8.6), and five for pentachromatic vision. Particularly interesting are tetrachromatic (perhaps pentachromatic) birds, for

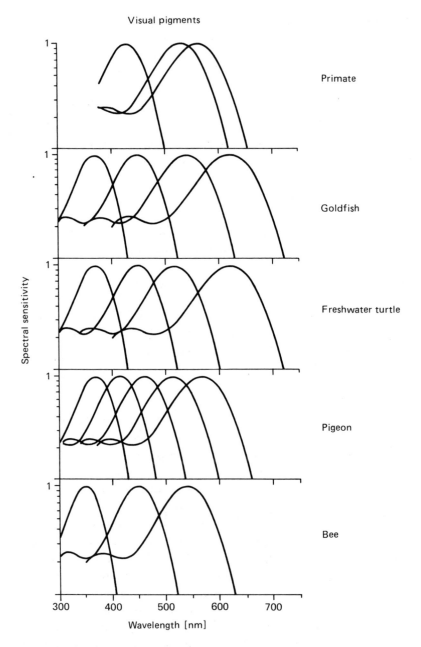

Figure 8.6
Tetrachromatic vs. trichomatic mechanisms are illustrated here on the basis of the different retinal pigments present in various animals.

their underlying neuronal operations appear to differ dramatically from ours.[72]

When people hear of this evidence for tetrachromacy, they respond by asking, "What are the other colors that these animals see?" This question is understandable but naive if it is taken to suggest that tetrachromats are simply better at seeing the colors we see. It must be remembered, though, that a four-dimensional color space is fundamentally different from a three-dimensional one: strictly speaking, the two color spaces are incommensurable, for there is no way to map the kinds of distinctions available in four dimensions into the kinds of distinctions available in three dimensions without remainder. We can, of course, obtain some analogical insights into what such higher dimensional color spaces might be like. We could imagine, for example, that our color space contains an additional temporal dimension. In this analogy, colors would flicker to different degrees in proportion to the fourth dimension. Thus to use the term *pink*, for example, as a designator in such a four-dimensional color space would be insufficient to pick out a single color: one would have to say *rapid-pink*, etc. If it turns out that the color space of diurnal birds is pentachromatic (which is indeed possible), then we are simply at a loss to envision what their color experience could be like.[73]

It should now be apparent, then, that the vastly different histories of structural coupling for birds, fishes, insects, and primates have enacted or brought forth different perceived worlds of color. Therefore, our perceived world of color should not be considered to be the optimal "solution" to some evolutionarily posed "problem." Our perceived world of color is, rather, a result of one possible and viable phylogenic pathway among many others realized in the evolutionary history of living beings.

Again, the response on the behalf of the "received view" of evolution in cognitive science will be, "Very well, let us grant that color as an attribute of our perceived world cannot be explained simply by invoking some optimal fit, since there is such a rich diversity of perceived worlds of color. Thus the diverse neuronal mechanisms underlying color perception are not different solutions to the same evolutionarily posed problem. But all that follows is that our analysis must be made more precise. These various perceived worlds of color reflect various forms of adaptation to diverse ecological niches. Each animal group optimally exploits different regularities of the world. It is still a matter of optimal fit with the world; it is just that each animal group has its own optimal fit."

This response is a still more refined form of the evolutionary argument. Although optimizations are considered to differ according to the species in question, the view remains that perceptual and cognitive tasks involve some form of optimal adaptation to the world. This view represents a sophisticated neorealism, which has the notion of *optimization* as its central explanatory tool. We cannot proceed further, then, without examining more closely this idea in the context of evolutionary explanations. We cannot attempt to summarize the state of the art of evolutionary biology today, but we do need to explore some of its classical foundations and their modern alternatives.

9
Evolutionary Path Making and Natural Drift

Adaptationism: An Idea in Transition

The evolutionary themes that we need to discuss actually run parallel to those we have pursued in our discussion of cognition. We have seen that the notion of representation (in its strong version) is the centerpiece of most contemporary cognitive science. Similarly, the notion of *adaptation* is the centerpiece for much of recent evolutionary biology. Many critiques of this so-called *adaptationist program* have appeared in recent years, however, resulting in a full-scale revision of what was, until quite recently, a uniform view.[1]

The orthodoxy under revision today is the theory of organic evolution in its *neo-Darwinian* formulation. Neo-Darwinism is to modern evolutionary theory what cognitivism is to cognitive science—in more ways than one. Like cognitivism, the neo-Darwinian program is relatively easy to state succinctly.

The heritage from which neo-Darwinism arose was, of course, that of Darwin himself. This heritage can be summarized in three basic points:

1. Evolution occurs as a gradual modification of organisms by descent; that is, there is reproduction with heredity.
2. This hereditary material constantly undergoes diversification (mutation, recombination).
3. There is a central mechanism to explain how these modifications occur: the mechanism of natural selection. This mechanism operates by picking the designs (phenotypes) that cope with the current environment most efficiently.

This classical Darwinism become neo-Darwinism during the 1930s as a result of the so-called modern synthesis between the Darwinian ideas based on zoology, botany, and systematics on the one hand and the rising knowledge in cellular and population genetics on the other.

This synthesis established the basic view that modifications occur by small changes in organismic traits specified by heritable units, the genes. The genetic makeup responsible for the ensemble of traits leads to differential reproduction rates, hence to changes in the genetic makeup of an animal population over generations. Evolution simply is the totality of these genetic changes in interbreeding populations. The pace and tempo of evolution are measured by the changes in the fitness of genes; thus it is possible to give a quantitative basis for the visible adaptation of animals to the environments in which they live. These concepts are, of course, ones with which we are all familiar. But we need to clarify them one step further to do justice to their multiple scientific roles.

Consider the concept of adaptation. The most intuitive sense of adaptation is that it is some form of design or construction that matches optimally (or at least very well) some physical situation. For example, the fins of fishes are well suited for an aquatic environment, whereas the ungulate hoof is well suited for running on the prairies. Although this conception of adaptation is quite popular, most professional evolutionary theorists do not construe adaptation in this way. Instead, adaptation has come to refer specifically to the *process* that is linked to reproduction and survival, that is, to *adapting*. This process is—or so one supposes—what accounts for the apparent degree of adaptational design observed in nature.

To make this idea of adapting do theoretical work, however, we need some way to analyze the adaptedness of organisms. This is where the notion of *fitness* comes in. From the vantage point of adaptedness, the task of evolution consists in finding heritable strategies, sets of interrelated genes that will be more or less capable of contributing to differential reproduction. When a gene changes so as to improve in this task, it improves its fitness. This idea of fitness is often formulated as a measure of *abundance*. It is usually taken as a measure of individual abundance (as a measure of the surplus offspring achieved), but it can also be construed as a measure of population abundance (as the effect of genes on the rate of growth of a population).

It has become increasingly clear, however, that this way of measuring fitness as abundance has a number of conceptual and empirical difficulties. First of all, in most animal groups reproductive success depends on sexual encounters with other individuals. Second, since the effects of any given gene are always intertwined with a multitude of other genes, it is not always possible to differentiate the effects of individual genes. Third, the milieu where the genes are supposed to express themselves is enormously varied and time dependent. Finally, this milieu must be seen in the context of the entire life cycle and ecology of an animal.

Fitness can also be taken as a measure of *persistence.* Here fitness measures the probability of reproductive permanence over time. What is optimized is not the amount of offspring but the probability of extinction. Clearly this approach is more sensitive to long-term effects, and so it is an improvement over the more narrow view of fitness as abundance. By the same token, however, it poses formidable problems at the level of measurement.

Armed with these refinements, the dominant orthodoxy in evolutionary thinking over the last few decades saw evolution as a "field of forces."[2] Selective pressures (the physical metaphor is fitting) act on the genetic variety of a population, producing changes over time according to an optimization of the fitness potential. The adaptationist or neo-Darwinian stance comes from taking this process of natural selection as the main factor in organic evolution. In other words, orthodox evolutionary theory does not deny that there are a number of other factors operating in evolution; it simply downplays their importance and seeks to account for the observed phenomena mainly on the basis of optimizing fitness.

It is precisely this orthodox, neo-Darwinian theory of evolution that is typically invoked or presupposed in discussions of the relation between evolution and cognition and so constitutes the received view of evolution within cognitive science. Our intention in this chapter is to embark upon a critical examination of this orthodox view. It is important to make clear at the outset, however, that our criticisms will not be leveled at the scientific plausibility of the adaptationist program. It seems to us that this research program, like cognitivism, is as plausible as any other scientific enterprise. It cannot be refuted on purely logical grounds or on the basis of a few isolated observations. We must take some time, then, to explore the nature of the serious empirical difficulties that this orthodox theory faces, difficulties that have led evolutionary biologists to enlarge their horizon to encompass alternative accounts and theories.

In the next section we will sketch some of the more important open questions and points of dispute that have motivated the development of these alternative accounts. Taken together, these points will lead us toward a view of evolution that we shall refer to as *natural drift*.[3] Evolution as natural drift is the biological counterpart of cognition as embodied action, and therefore also provides a more embracing theoretical context for the study of cognition as a biological phenomenon.

A Horizon of Multiple Mechanisms

The points of dispute that we need to discuss are various and intermixed, but they all converge upon the same fundamental limitation in the dominant interpretation of natural selection.

Linkage and Pleiotropy

Genes are clearly linked together, and so it is not really possible—not even by some smart trade-off—to treat an organism as merely an array of characters or traits. The fact that the presence of a gene does not result in the manifestation of an isolated trait, except in a few remarkable cases (such as eye color) is known to biologists as *linkage* and *pleiotropy*. Pleiotropic effects are not bizarre properties of a few exceptionally complex traits. Genic interdependence expresses the straightforward fact that the genome is not a linear array of independent genes (manifesting as traits) but a highly interwoven network of multiple reciprocal effects mediated through repressors and derepressors, exons and introns, jumping genes, and even structural proteins. In what other way could one even begin to explain that there is, for example, a genetic link between left-handedness and coeliac disease (an intestinal irritability as a reaction to wheat protein resulting in diarrhea)?[4] This linkage involves just about every known metabolic pathway and organ operation in the body.

Perhaps the most dramatic cases of genomic wholeness (in macroevolution rather than ontogeny) are the drastic discontinuities in how species change over time, known as *punctuated equilibria*.[5] This much-discussed idea has essentially dispensed with the idea of evolutionary gradualism (that evolution occurs through the step-by-step accumulation of selected point mutations). The fossil record does not look incomplete; intermediate forms often simply cannot be imagined. How, for example, could one produce a transition from a species with dorso-ventral asymmetry to one with a mirror type of asymmetry? There are surely no organisms that have all their organs collapsed in the midplane. Transitions must be a matter of global rearrangements involving cooperative effects and genetic exchanges. Such effects can be shown to appear in simple cases even in the absence of any selection.[6]

Pleiotropy provides obvious difficulties for adaptationism. How can a gene be selectively optimized if it has multiple effects, which need not increase fitness in the same manner or even in the same direction? Selection might push to decrease the frequency of a certain gene, but pleiotropy, on the other hand, might push to increase or maintain the gene. The net result is some compromise that cannot be described as simply the result of selective pressures.

As usual in science, such difficulties can be seen either as serious flaws or as details that will be explained later. The confirmed neo-Darwinian acknowledges the existence of genetic interdependence but is confident that more refined techniques of measurement will separate the contribution of pleiotropy from that of natural selection, or that natural selection itself will decouple genes with opposite effects. Nonetheless, the fact remains that classical fitness measures of traits have yet to provide any clear answer to the problem of pleiotropic effects.

There are therefore reasons to ask whether the very program of studying evolution as trait fitness optimization is not fundamentally flawed. Instead, one could seek to study evolution through a theoretical framework that puts a strong emphasis on organisms and societies as integral wholes, rather than as arrays of traits—no matter how many trade-offs one is willing to take into account.[7]

Development
The weakness of favoring an approach whose point of departure is a view of organisms as arrays of independent traits appears with renewed vengeance in considering the role of development in the evolutionary process. The classical approach that is still alive in most textbooks simply jumps from genes and gene frequencies to phenotypes and reproductively able organisms. The developmental stage connecting birth to adulthood is acknowledged but immediately set aside.[8]

Evolutionary biologists, however, have been busy showing on their own terrain how pattern formation and morphogenesis are highly constrained cellular choreographies that drastically delimit the scope of possibilities for change. In the words of a classic text by de Beer, "It has become increasingly clear from researches in embryology that the processes whereby the structures are formed are as important as the structures themselves from the point of view of evolutionary morphology and homology."[9]

Consider, for example, the development of the different segments in the embryo of the fruit fly *Drosophila*, a choice material for developmental studies (see figure 9.1).[10] The egg segments itself successively into committed regions giving rise to dorsal, ventral, etc. By an early stage, the so-called blastoderm, there is a full-fledged epigenetic code for the animal's topography. This code defines a finite set of alternative developmental decisions and a constrained set of transformations among them. For example, antennae and genitalia are quite close in this embryological grammar, a fact that coincides well with the significant number of so-called homeotic mutants that cause transformations in these distant points of the blastoderm. This model can be analyzed further through a distributed mechanism based on morphogenetic gradients, in a manner that resembles the kind of analysis pursued by connectionists. Indeed, the main point is the same: once again, one discovers the importance of emergent properties in a complex network (whether neural, genetic, or cellular). In the same manner, the stripes and patchcoat color of various mammals can be characterized by a constrained set of expected patterns. One example is a "spot" pattern that tends to transform distally to a stripe pattern on narrowing regions such as tails.

The point here is that as embryological landscapes and genetic networks become more familiar, the most powerful explanatory accounts will appeal increasingly to the intrinsic self-organizing prop-

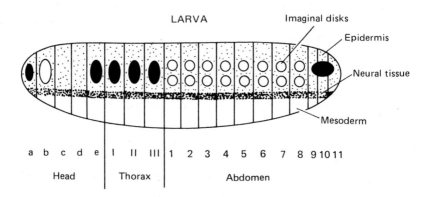

Figure 9.1
Segmentation in the embryo of the fruit fly *Drosophila*.

erties of such networks. These factors are, accordingly, referred to as *intrinsic factors* in evolution. We should note, however, that it is important to avoid the all-too-easy tendency of opposing natural selection as external with developmental constraints as internal, for this inner/outer dichotomy is not at all fruitful in attempting to understand evolution.

Random Genetic Drift

Apart from pleiotropy and development, still another element confounds the basic logic of the adaptationist program. This is the irruption of *randomness*. It is widely recognized by now that there is a significant degree of random *genetic drift* (which is not to be confused with our idea of evolution as natural drift) among the genetic compositions of animal populations. A first source of such randomness is the sheer effect of proximity: if a gene is actively selected, it will bring along—in a "hitchhiking" effect—any others that are close enough. Since position in chromosomes is hardly linked to epigenetic effects, such proximity effects are a considerable source of serendipity.

Second, if a biological population is maintained at a particular finite size, its gene and genotype frequencies will "drift" from generation to generation. Such drift is due to the fact that the genotype frequencies of parents, when filtered through the differential reproductive probabilities, may not be representative of the genotype frequencies of the parents' next generation. The next generation's gene and genotype frequencies may diverge from those of the previous one. Therefore, even if one construes evolution as genotype changes (remember we are attempting to sketch an alternative), then evolution has occurred entirely independent of any selective pressure, due to what a statistician might call a "sampling error." A number of observations have made clear that such drift is far from marginal.[11] Among these is the perplexing observation that about 40 percent of the genome is not expressed and is repetitive. This portion is accordingly known as "junk" DNA. From a classical standpoint, such a massive amount of genetic material is totally inactive and so simply should not be there.

Stasis

Adaptation as a measure of increased progeny in a next generation might have virtually nothing to do with long-range evolutionary permanence or with survival of an organismal lineage. Zoologists are familiar with the widespread *stasis* of some groups—with the fact that groups not only stay around but remain with little changes, even though their environment has from our vantage point changed dramatically.[12]

For example, studies of one of the more familiar groups among vertebrates, the salamanders of the family *Plethodontidae*, suggest that these organisms have persisted with little change for over fifty million years. Despite minor pigmentation and size differences, the species in this group are remarkably uniform, especially in skeletal structure, which is the form best preserved in the fossil record. In contrast, present members display considerable genetic diversity in every parameter measured. All the terrestrial vertebrate genera that cooccurred with *Plethodontidae* sixty million years ago are now extinct. With regard to food sources and predator diversity, the environment has certainly changed dramatically. Yet the morphology of this species has basically remained the same (though clearly the same morphology can accommodate various different behaviors).

Genotypic plasticity, which is at the base of evolutionary stasis, is also evident in the microbial world where constant genetic exchange occurs side by side with an astounding degree of stasis. These and other observations suggest that focusing on persistence, rather than abundance, might be a better way to approach adaptation.

Units of Selection

The adaptationist program has also been criticized for its almost unquestioned assumption that the individual is the only unit of evolution and selection. In contrast, theories that emphasize multiple levels or units of selection working in parallel are entirely plausible and suggest revised interpretations of many phenomena that have puzzled those who assume selection can operate only at the individual level. At one extreme there is the selfish DNA hypothesis, which views genes themselves as the main units of selection.[13] At the other extreme is the Wynne-Edwards notion of group selection invoked to account for the maintenance of altruistic traits.[14] A full list of units looks rather formidable: DNA short sequences, genes, whole gene families, the cell itself, the species genome, the individual, "inclusive" groups of genes that are carried by different individuals, the social group, the actually interbreeding population, the entire species (as a potentially interbreeding group), the ecosystem of actually interacting species, and the global biosphere. Each unit harbors modes of coupling and selection constraints, has unique self-organizing qualities, and so has its own emergent status with respect to other levels of description.[15]

We shall not attempt to summarize this complex debate here—a debate that has proceeded so far by each favored level dismissing the other as nonsensical.[16] Despite these partisan debates, the fact remains that future evolutionary theory will in one way or another include a clear articulation of various units of selection and their relations.

Beyond the Best in Evolution and Cognition

The above points of contention are sufficiently deep and critical to make the adaptationist approach look considerably less compelling. Let us clearly state the crux of the matter: to explain an observed biological regularity as an optimal fit or optimal correspondence with pregiven dimensions of the environment appears less and less tenable on both logical and empirical grounds. As Richard Lewontin said in a recent critique of the classical position, "It is not that these phenomena [developmental constraints, pleiotropy, etc.] are not mentioned, but they are clearly diversions from the big event, the ascent of Mount Fitness by Sir Ron Fisher and his faithful Sherpas."[17] Increasingly, evolutionary biologists have become engaged in a movement away from Mount Fitness toward a larger and as yet incompletely formulated new theory.[18] Our task is to provide an outline from our point of view of some of the main elements of this new emerging orientation.

Evolutionary and cognitive issues coincide along at least two important lines, which are implicitly active in cognitive science today:

1. Evolution is often invoked as an explanation for the kind of cognition that we or other animals presently have. This idea makes reference to the adaptive value of knowledge, and it is usually framed along classical neo-Darwinian lines.

2. Evolution is often used as a source of concepts and metaphors in building cognitive theories. This tendency is clearly visible in the proposal of so-called selective theories of brain function and learning.

In either case, the central issue remains whether evolutionary processes can be understood by the representationist idea that there is a correspondence between organism and environment provided by the optimizing constraints of survival and reproduction. Baldly stated, representationism in cognitive science is the precise homologue of adaptationism in evolutionary theory, for optimality plays the same central role in each domain. It follows that any evidence that weakens the adaptationist viewpoint ipso facto provides difficulties for the representationist approach to cognition.

In chapters 5 and 6 we described how cognitive scientists were relentlessly led by the requirements of their research to the study of subnetworks that act on local scales. These networks interact with each other in tangled webs, forming societies of agents, to use Minsky's language. It should be clear from our list of current problems that evolutionary theorists have reached independently much the same conclusions. The constraints of survival and reproduction are far too weak to provide an account of how structures develop and change. Accordingly, no global optimal fitness scheme apparently suffices to explain evolutionary processes. There are, to be sure, local genetic agents for, say, oxygen consumption or feather growth, which can be measured on some comparative scale where optimality may be sought, but no single scale will do the job for all processes.[19]

The central issue can be put in the form of an analogy.[20] John needs a suit. In an fully symbolic and representationist world, he goes to his tailor who measures him and produces a nice suit according to the exact specifications of his measurements. There is, however, another obvious possibility, one that does not demand so much from the environment. John goes to several department stores and chooses a suit that fits well from among the various ones available. Although these do not suit him exactly, they are good enough, and he chooses the optimal one for fit and taste. Here we have a good selectionist alternative that uses some optimal criteria of fitness. The analogy admits, however, of further refinement. John, like any human being, cannot buy a suit in isolation from the rest of what goes on in his life. In buying a suit, he considers how his looks will affect the response of his boss at work, the response of his girl friend, and he may also be concerned with political and economic factors. Indeed, the very decision to buy a suit is not given from the outset as a problem but is constituted by the global situation of his life. His final choice has the form of satisfying some very loose constraints (e.g., being well dressed) but does not have the form of a fit—and even less so of an optimal fit—to any of these constraints.

With this third step in the analogy we rejoin the types of issues being raised in evolutionary theory, as well as those in cognitive science, that involve the impossibility of simply "scaling up" from local solutions to overall performance. The analogy also moves us closer to the issues that have to be reformulated in a more encompassing evolutionary theory. Let us now retake these issues in biological detail.

Evolution: Ecology and Development in Congruence

Part of the difficulty in moving beyond the adaptationist framework is to determine what to do after we abandon the idea of natural selection as the main explanation, so that every structure, mechanism, trait, or disposition cannot be explained away by its contribution to survival value. The temptation is to say, But then are things there for no reason at all? The task in evolutionary biology is to change the logical geography of the debate by studying the tangled, circular relations of congruence among the items to be explained.

The first step is to switch from a prescriptive logic to a proscriptive one, that is, from the idea that what is not allowed is forbidden to the idea that what is not forbidden is allowed. In the context of evolution this shift means that we remove selection as a prescriptive process that guides and instructs in the task of improving fitness. In contrast, in a proscriptive context natural selection can be seen to operate, but in a modified sense: selection discards what is not compatible with survival and reproduction. Organisms and the population offer variety; natural selection guarantees only that what ensues satisfies the two basic constraints of survival and reproduction.

This proscriptive orientation shifts our attention to the tremendous diversity of biological structures at all levels. Indeed, one of the main points of modern biological thought is the way in which such a tremendous amount of diversity is not just compatible with, but actually woven into, the basic constraint of maintaining a continuous lineage. In fact, all the issues that we have discussed as problems for the adaptationist account become sources of explanation for alternative viewpoints because they highlight the way in which the enormous diversity constantly generated at all levels in the genetic and evolutionary process both shapes and is shaped by the coupling with an environment. We have already seen repeatedly that such emergent properties provide one of the main lessons from research in neuro-

science and the study of self-organizing systems and nonlinear networks. Indeed, neurobiologists, developmental biologists, immunol-
ogists, and linguists all find themselves in the position of trying to
understand how so much profligacy is pruned to provide the sub-
strata for various viable pathways rather than selected along trajectories to match a given external standard.[21]

The second step, then, is to analyze the evolutionary process as
satisficing (taking a suboptimal solution that is satisfactory) rather than
optimizing: here selection operates as a broad survival filter that
admits any structure that has sufficient integrity to persist.[22] Given
this point of view, the focus of analysis is no longer on traits but rather
on organismic patterns via their life history. Another metaphor recently suggested for this post-Darwinian conception of the evolutionary process is evolution as *bricolage*, the putting together of parts
and items in complicated arrays, not because they fulfill some ideal
design but simply because they are possible.[23] Here the evolutionary
problem is no longer how to force a precise trajectory by the requirements of optimal fitness; it is, rather, how to prune the multiplicity
of viable trajectories that exist at any given point.[24]

One of the more interesting consequences of this shift from optimal
selection to viability is that the precision and specificity of morpho-
logical or physiological traits, or of cognitive capacities, are entirely
compatible with their apparent irrelevance to survival. To state this
point in more positive terms, much of what an organism looks like
and is "about" is completely *underdetermined* by the constraints of
survival and reproduction. Thus adaptation (in its classical sense),
problem solving, simplicity in design, assimilation, external "steer-
ing," and many other explanatory notions based on considerations of
parsimony not only fade into the background but must in fact be
completely reassimilated into new kinds of explanatory concepts and
conceptual metaphors.

Let us now explicitly articulate the alternative to the view that we
have been taking such pains to criticize. The view that we call evolution by natural drift can be articulated in four basic points:

1. The unit of evolution (at any level) is a network capable of
a rich repertoire of self-organizing configurations.

2. Under structural coupling with a medium, these configurations generate selection, an ongoing process of satisficing that

triggers (but does not specify) change in the form of viable trajectories.

3. The specific (nonunique) trajectory or mode of change of the unit of selection is the interwoven (nonoptimal) result of multiple levels of subnetworks of selected self-organized repertoires.

4. The opposition between inner and outer causal factors is replaced by a coimplicative relation, since organism and medium mutually specify each other.

We intend this set of articulated mechanisms to replace the adaptationist outline that we presented at the beginning of this chapter and to give content to our announced alternative view. This view of evolution depends on the conjoint applicability of three conditions:

1a. The richness of the self-organizing capacities in biological networks

2a. A mode of structural coupling permitting the satisficing of viable trajectories

3a. The modularity of subnetworks of independent processes that interact with each other by tinkering

These three conditions are obviously not logically interdependent. Thus we can conceive of modular networks that couple with constraints requiring directed selection rather than satisficing. Or we can conceive of rich networks that have histories of satisficing but are not modular and so do not manifest any developmental qualities. It is therefore both interesting and remarkable that living organisms empirically satisfy these three conjoint conditions. This situation is not true of systems in general; nor is it true as a matter of logic. It is true of those kinds of beings that we are, namely, living systems.

Since these ideas entail a change in our scientific views, they are of course subject to resistance. There are basically two points of resistance to the ideas presented here. First, there is resistance on the part of those who still feel close to the classical viewpoint. Here we find a dismissal of the kinds of arguments that we have unfolded in this chapter; they are claimed to be matters of minor detail or far-off clouds on the horizon waiting to be dispelled by more research. Second, there is a more pervasive and subtle form of resistance. Here we find agreement with our claim that evolutionary theory needs to undergo revision, yet a sufficient amount of the old view is retained, so that the revision is not radical but merely cosmetic. In the present case, though (1a) is almost universally accepted in biology and cognitive science, (2a) and (3a) are still minority positions.

The difference for us between a merely partial change and the more thorough revision that we intend turns on how the notion of coupling with an environment is conceptualized. Our claim is that the logic of (1)–(3), when applied consistently, leads us inevitably to (4). Let us consider this issue more closely.

According to traditional wisdom, the environment in which organisms evolve and that they come to know is given, fixed, and unique. Here again we find the idea that organisms are basically parachuted into a pregiven environment. This simplistic view undergoes refinement when we allow for changes in the environment, an allowance that was already empirically familiar to Darwin. Such a moving environment provides the selective pressures that form the backbone of neo-Darwinian evolutionary theory.

In moving toward evolution as natural drift, however, we introduce a further step: we recast selective pressures as broad constraints to be satisfied. The crucial point here is that we do not retain the notion of an independent, pregiven environment but let it fade into the background in favor of so-called intrinsic factors. Instead, we emphasize that the very notion of what an environment is cannot be separated from what organisms are and what they do. This point has been made quite eloquently by Richard Lewontin: "The organism and the environment are not actually separately determined. The environment is not a structure imposed on living beings from the outside but is in fact a creation of those beings. The environment is not an autonomous process but a reflection of the biology of the species. Just as there is no organism without an environment, so there is no environment without an organism."[25]

The key point, then, is that the species brings forth and specifies its own domain of problems to be solved by satisficing; this domain does not exist "out there" in an environment that acts as a landing pad for organisms that somehow drop or parachute into the world. Instead, living beings and their environments stand in relation to each other through *mutual specification* or *codetermination*. Thus what we describe as environmental regularities are not external features that have been internalized, as representationism and adaptationism both assume. Environmental regularities are the result of a conjoint history, a congruence that unfolds from a long history of codetermination. In Lewontin's words, the organism is both the subject and the object of evolution.[26]

We cannot emphasize this point too strongly, for the temptation in the movement toward a nonadaptationist evolutionary view is to retain the organism and environment as separate poles and then to attempt to determine the "proportion" that is played by each—a bit of intrinsic factors plus a bit of external constraints. This mode of breaking down the dynamics of evolution, however, simply will not do, for it forces upon us all the supposedly outdated problems of the innate versus the acquired, nature versus nurture. But as Susan Oyama has so insightfully analyzed, this supposedly dead issue of nature versus nurture will actually refuse to go away unless we learn to see organisms and environments as mutually unfolded and enfolded structures.[27] In Oyama's words,

> Form emerges in successive interaction. Far from being imposed on matter by some agent, it is a function of the reactivity of matter at many hierarchical levels, and of the responsiveness of those interactions to each other. Because mutual selectivity, reactivity, and constraint take place only in actual processes, it is these that orchestrate the activity of different portions of DNA, that make genetic and environmental influences interdependent as genes and gene products are environments to each other, as extraorganismal environment is made internal by psychological or biochemical assimilation, as internal state is externalized through products and behavior that select and organize the surrounding world.[28]

Genes are, then, better conceived as elements that specify what in the environment must be fixed for something to operate as a gene, that is, to be predictably correlated with a result. In every successful reproduction an organism passes on genes as well as an environment in which these genes are embedded. We see features of this environment, such as sunlight or oxygen, as independent of the organism only because our frame of reference is relative. The interconnectedness of the world, however, says otherwise. Once again, the world is not a landing pad into which organisms parachute: nature and nurture stand in relation to each other as product and process.

> What all this means is not that genes and environment are necessary for all characteristics, inherited or acquired (the usual enlightened position), but that there is no intelligible distinction

between inherited (biological, genetically based) and acquired
(environmentally mediated) characteristics . . . Once the distinction between the inherited and the acquired has been eliminated, not only as extremes but even as a continuum, evolution
cannot be said to depend on the distinction. What is required for
evolutionary change is not genetically encoded as opposed to
acquired traits, but functioning developmental systems: ecologi-
cally embedded genomes.[29]

Lewontin and Oyama are exemplary for their understanding of this
crucial point. By and large biologists have not thought through this
point with the rigor and consistency it demands. The reason, of
course, is that if we take this mutual enfoldment view of life and
world seriously, it initially results in a sense of vertigo due to the
collapse of what we had supposed to be sure and stable foundations.
But rather than sweeping this sense of groundlessness under the rug
by once again pitching the internal and the external against each other
(which we already know will not work), we need to delve deeper into
this sense of groundlessness and follow through all of its implications,
philosophically and experientially.

We should also take note of recent theories that approach neural
cognitive mechanisms in selective Darwinian terms.[30] In our terms,
these theories incorporate not just (1a) but also argue in various
degrees for (2a) and (3a). Sometimes these so-called selectionist theories follow through the implications of these points to embrace the
fully coimplicative nature of organism and environment. For example,
Gerald Edelman, a leading exponent of such selectionist theories,
expressed to a reporter in a recent interview, "You and the world are
embedded together."[31] Nevertheless, it is not always clear to what
extent selectionists are willing to let go of the objectivist convictions
that often linger in their writings.

Lessons from Evolution as Natural Drift

In the previous chapter we argued that perception consists in perceptually guided action and that cognitive structures emerge from the
recurrent sensorimotor patterns that enable action to be perceptually
guided. We summarized this view by saying that cognition is not
representation but embodied action and that the world we cognize is
not pregiven but enacted through our history of structural coupling.

We then raised an objection in the form of the view that perceptual and cognitive processes involve various optimal adaptations to the world. It was this objection that prompted our excursion into evolutionary biology in this chapter. What lessons, then, can we draw from this excursion?

Let us return, once again, to our favored example of color. When we last left this cognitive domain, we had seen that there are different, incommensurable "color spaces": some require only two dimensions for their description (dichromacy), some require three (trichromacy), others require four (tetrachromacy), perhaps even five (pentachromacy). Each of these different kinds of color space is enacted or brought forth through a specific history of structural coupling.

One of our motives in this chapter has been to show how such unique histories of coupling can be understood from the vantage point of evolution. To this end, we have provided a critique of the adaptationist view of evolution as a process of (more-or-less) progressive fitness, and we have articulated an alternative view of evolution as natural drift. We claim, then, that these unique histories of coupling, which enact incommensurable kinds of color space, should not be explained as optimal adaptations to different regularities in the world. Instead, they should be explained as the result of different histories of natural drift. Furthermore, since organism and environment cannot be separated but are in fact codetermined in evolution as natural drift, the environmental regularities that we do associate with these various color spaces (for example, surface reflectances) must ultimately be specified in tandem with the perceptually guided activity of the animal.

Let us provide another example from the comparative study of color vision. It is well known that honey bees are trichromats whose spectral sensitivity is shifted toward the ultraviolet.[32] It is also well known that flowers have contrasting reflectance patterns in ultraviolet light. Consider now our "chicken-and-egg" question from the previous chapter: Which came first, the world (ultraviolet reflectance) or the image (ultraviolet sensitive vision)? Most of us would probably answer with little hesitation, The world (ultraviolet reflectance). It is therefore interesting to observe that the colors of flowers appear to have *coevolved* with the ultraviolet sensitive, trichromatic vision of bees.[33]

Why should such coevolution occur? On the one hand, flowers attract pollinators by their food content and so must be both conspicuous and yet different from flowers of other species. On the other hand, bees gather food from flowers and so need to recognize flowers from a distance. These two broad and reciprocal constraints appear to have shaped a history of coupling in which plant features and the sensorimotor capacities of bees coevolved. It is this coupling, then, that is responsible for both the ultraviolet vision of bees and the ultraviolet reflectance patterns of flowers. Such coevolution therefore provides an excellent example of how environmental regularities are not pregiven but are rather enacted or brought forth by a history of coupling. To quote Lewontin once more,

> Our central nervous systems are not fitted to some absolute laws of nature, but to laws of nature operating within a framework created by our own sensuous activity. Our nervous system does not allow us to see the ultraviolet reflections from flowers, but a bee's central nervous system does. And bats "see" what nighthawks do not. We do not further our understanding of evolution by general appeal to "laws of nature" to which all life must bend. Rather, we must ask how, within the general constraints of the laws of nature, organisms have constructed environments that are the conditions for their further evolution and reconstruction of nature into new environments.[34]

This insistence on the codetermination or mutual specification of organism and environment should not be confused with the more commonplace view that different perceiving organisms simply have different perspectives on the world. This view continues to treat the world as pregiven; it simply allows that this pregiven world can be viewed from a variety of vantage points. The point we are making, however, is fundamentally different. We are claiming that organism and environment are mutually enfolded in multiple ways, and so what constitutes the world of a given organism is enacted by that organism's history of structural coupling. Furthermore, such histories of coupling proceed not through optimal adaptation but rather through evolution as natural drift.

The treatment of the world as pregiven and the organism as representing or adapting to it is a dualism. The extreme opposite of dualism is a monism. We are not proposing monism; enaction is specifically designed to be a middle way between dualism and monism. The one example of a virtually monistic system that has been proposed is the "ecological approach" of J. J. Gibson and his followers.[35] It will be instructive to explore the difference between our middle-way emphasis on the codetermination of animal and environment with the Gibsonian approach. Since this point is important, we will conclude this section by taking several paragraphs to clarify the differences.

Gibson's theory has essentially two distinct features. The first is compatible with our approach to perceptually guided action. Gibson claims that in the study of perception the world must be described in a way that shows how it constitutes environments for perceiving animals. In Gibson's view, certain properties are found in the environment that are not found in the physical world per se. The most significant properties consist in what the environment affords for the animal, which Gibson calls *affordances*. Stated in precise terms, affordances consist in the opportunities for interaction that things in the environment possess relative to the sensorimotor capacities of the animal. For example, relative to certain animals, some things, such as trees, are climbable or afford climbing. Thus affordances are distinctly ecological features of the world.

Second, Gibson offers a unique theory of perception to explain how the environment is perceived. He argues that there is sufficient information in the ambient light to specify the environment directly, that is, without the mediation of any kind of representation (symbolic or subsymbolic). In more precise terms, his fundamental hypothesis is that there are invariances in the topology of the ambient light that directly specify properties of the environment, including affordances.

This second element—which actually defines the Gibsonian research program—is not compatible with our approach to perceptually guided action. This point is easy to miss because both approaches deny the representationist view of perception in favor of the idea that perception is perceptually guided action. In Gibson's view, however, perceptually guided action consists in "picking up" or "attending to" invariances in the ambient light that directly specify their environmental source. For Gibson, these optical invariances, as well as the environmental properties they specify, do not depend in any way upon the perceptually guided activity of the animal (though Gibson's followers do relativize them to a given animal niche).[36] Thus Gibson writes, "Invariance comes from reality, not the other way round. Invariance in the ambient optic array over time is not constructed or deduced; it is there to be discovered."[37] Similarly, he claims, "The observer may or may not perceive or attend to the affordance, according to his needs, but the affordance, being invariant is always there to be perceived."[38]

In a nutshell, then, whereas Gibson claims that the environment is independent, we claim that it is enacted (by histories of coupling). Whereas Gibson claims that perception is direct detection, we claim that it is sensorimotor enactment. Thus the resulting research strategies are also fundamentally different: Gibsonians treat perception in largely optical (albeit ecological) terms and so attempt to build up the theory of perception almost entirely from the environment. Our approach, however, proceeds by specifying the sensorimotor patterns that enable action to be perceptually guided, and so we build up the theory of perception from the structural coupling of the animal.

One other point deserves mention. It might be thought that perception as direct detection is compatible with the perceived world as enacted. The idea here would be that since our perceived world is enacted through our history of coupling, it does not need to be re-presented and so can be directly perceived. Some Gibsonians appear to argue for something resembling this idea when they claim that the "mutuality" of animal and environment grounds the notion of direct perception.[39] Their idea is that given a proper account of animal-environment mutuality, we do not need to invoke any kind of representational item (symbolic or subsymbolic) that would mediate or stand between animal and environment; therefore, perception is direct.

We believe that this idea results from the mistaken assumption that animal-environment mutuality is sufficient for direct perception. From the fact, however, that there is a mutuality between animal and environment—or in our terms that the two are structurally coupled— it simply does not follow that the act of perceiving is direct in the Gibsonian sense of "responding" or "resonating" to optical invariants. Of course, this latter Gibsonian claim is a substantive empirical hypothesis and so does not stand or fall on the basis of logical considerations. Nevertheless, our point is that this claim represents only one way of explicating the relation between perceptually guided action and animal-environment mutuality. We disalign ourselves with this explication because we believe it leads to a research strategy in which one attempts to build an ecological theory of perception entirely from the side of the environment. Such an attempt neglects not only the structural unity (autonomy) of the animal but also the codetermination of animal and environment that we have gone to such great lengths to stress.[40]

Defining the Enactive Approach

As we can now appreciate, to situate cognition as embodied action within the context of evolution as natural drift provides a view of cognitive capacities as inextricably linked to histories that are *lived*, much like paths that exist only as they are laid down in walking. Consequently, cognition is no longer seen as problem solving on the basis of representations; instead, cognition in its most encompassing sense consists in the enactment or bringing forth of a world by a viable history of structural coupling.

It should be noted that such histories of coupling are not optimal; they are, rather, simply viable. This difference implies a corresponding difference in what is required of a cognitive system in its structural coupling. If this coupling were to be optimal, the interactions of the system would have to be (more or less) prescribed. For coupling to be viable, however, the perceptually guided action of the system must simply facilitate the continuing integrity of the system (ontogeny) and/or its lineage (phylogeny). Thus once again we have a logic that is proscriptive rather than prescriptive: any action undertaken by the system is permitted as long as it is does not violate the constraint of having to maintain the integrity of the system and/or its lineage.

Yet another way to express this idea would be to say that cognition as embodied action is always about or directed toward something that is missing: on the one hand, there is always a next step for the *system* in its perceptually guided action; and on other hand, the actions of the system are always directed toward *situations* that have yet to become actual. Thus cognition as embodied action both poses the problems and specifies those paths that must be tread or laid down for their solution.

This formulation also provides us with a way of specifying the aboutness or intentionality of cognition as embodied action. It should be recalled that, in general, intentionality has two sides: first, intentionality includes how the system construes the world to be (specified in terms of the semantic content of intentional states); second, intentionality includes how the world satisfies or fails to satisfy this construal (specified in terms of the conditions of satisfaction of intentional states).[41] We would say that the intentionality of cognition as embodied action consists primarily in the directedness of action. Here the two-sidedness of intentionality corresponds to what the system takes its possibilities for action to be and to how the resulting situations fulfill or fail to fulfill these possibilities.[42]

What does this reconceptualization of the intentionality of cognition imply in more pragmatic terms for cognitive science? Consider that there are two domains in which we can describe any cognitive system: on the one hand, we can focus on the structure of the system by describing it as composed of various subsystems, etc., and on the other hand, we can focus on the behavioral interactions of the system by describing it as a unity capable of various forms of coupling. In switching back and forth between these two kinds of description, we—that is, cognitive scientists—must determine both how the environment constrains the system and how these constraints themselves are specified by the sensorimotor structure of the system (recall the quotation from Merleau-Ponty in the previous chapter). In so doing, we are able to explain how regularities—sensorimotor and environmental—emerge from structural coupling. The research task in cognitive science is to make transparent the mechanisms by which such coupling actually unfolds and thereby how specific regularities arise. Many theoretical elements are already in place (emergent properties in network behaviors, natural drift in lineages of reproductive organisms, developmental switches, etc.); many others remain to be specified.

We are now ready to formulate in precise terms the enactive approach in cognitive science. Let us answer, then, the same questions that we addressed to cognitivism and to the emergence program.

> *Question 1*: What is cognition?
> *Answer*: Enaction: A history of structural coupling that brings
>   forth a world.

> *Question 2*: How does it work?
> *Answer*: Through a network consisting of multiple levels of
>   interconnected, sensorimotor subnetworks.

> *Question 3*: How do I know when a cognitive system is
>   functioning adequately?

Answer: When it becomes part of an ongoing existing world (as the young of every species do) or shapes a new one (as happens in evolutionary history).

Much that appears in these answers has hitherto been absent from cognitive science—not just from cognitivism but from present-day, state-of-the-art connectionism. The most significant innovation is that since representations no longer play a central role, the role of the environment as a source of input recedes into the background. It now enters in explanations only on those occasions when systems undergo breakdowns or suffer events that cannot be satisfied by their structures. Accordingly, intelligence shifts from being the capacity to solve a problem to the capacity to enter into a shared world of significance.

At this point, however, the pragmatic reader might be somewhat impatient: "All this fuss about enaction as opposed to representation is fine, but what *real* difference does it make, say, in artificial intelligence and robotics? If something like the enactive approach begins to affect the way engineers build cognitive artifacts, then I'll pay attention."

We take this kind of pragmatic response quite seriously. Indeed, we have stressed from the very first chapter that cognitive science cannot be separated from cognitive technology. Thus we do not offer the enactive approach as a refined, European-flavored position that has no hands-on applications in cognitive science. On the contrary, we claim that without the key notions of the enactive approach, cognitive science will be unable both to account for living cognition and to build truly intelligent, cognitive artifacts. We will now consider how the enactive approach can affect hands-on research in cognitive science, especially robotics and artificial intelligence.

Enactive Cognitive Science

In general, within enactive cognitive science a process akin to evolution as natural drift takes the place of task-oriented design. For example, simulations of prolonged histories of coupling with various evolutionary strategies enable us to discover trends wherein cognitive performances arise.[43] Such a strategy is feasible in all areas of cognitive science—provided that we are willing to relax the constraints of some specific problem-solving performance. This willingness does in fact appear to be increasing in recent research. (Thus consider the development of so-called classifier systems, which are designed to confront an undefined environment that must be shaped into significance.)[44] Our discussion will focus on recent developments in the field of robotics, that is, the attempt to develop mobile and intelligent artifacts, which is increasingly found at the center of AI research.

Like connectionism, the field of robotics has gradually begun to appreciate that much early pioneering work in the cybernetic era was—contrary to the received cognitivist history—on the right track after all. Thus a recent popular book acknowledges the importance of this early work, especially that of Gray Walter and Ross Ashby who built machines that could be autonomous and operate in ordinary human environments.[45] Let us take a closer look at an explicitly formulated research strategy that harkens back to this earlier era but also takes the further step of formulating within robotics research a program akin to our enactive orientation.

The research to which we refer is that of Rodney Brooks in the AI laboratory at MIT.[46] On the first page of his paper, "Intelligence without Representation," Brooks presents his approach:

> In this paper I . . . argue for a different approach to creating Artificial Intelligence:
>
> • We must incrementally build up the capabilities of intelligent systems at each step of the way and thus automatically ensure that the pieces and their interfaces are valid.
> • At each step we should build complete intelligent systems that we let loose in the real world with real sensing and real action. Anything less provides a candidate with which we can delude ourselves.
>
> We have been following this approach and have built a series of autonomous mobile robots. We have reached an unexpected conclusion (C) and have a rather radical hypothesis (H).
>
> C: When we examine very simple level intelligence we find that explicit representations and models of the world simply get in the way. It turns out to be better to use the world as its own model.
> H: Representation is the wrong unit of abstraction in building the bulkiest parts of intelligent systems.
>
> Representation has been the central issue in Artificial Intelligence work over the last 15 years only because it has provided

an interface between otherwise isolated modules and conference papers.

It is interesting to note that in this paper Brooks also traces the origin of what he describes as the "deception of AI" to the tendency in AI for abstraction, for factoring out perception and motor skills. As we have argued here, however, and as Brooks argues for his own reasons, such abstraction misses the essence of intelligence, which resides only in its embodiment.

Brooks's goal is to build "completely autonomous robots, mobile agents that co-exist in the world with humans, and are seen by those humans as intelligent beings in their own right."[47] His key move in working toward this goal is not the usual decomposition of a system by *function* but rather a novel decomposition by *activity* (see figure 9.2). In his words,

> An alternative decomposition makes no distinction between peripheral systems, such as vision, and central systems. Rather the fundamental slicing up of an intelligent system is in the orthogonal direction dividing it into *activity* producing subsystems. Each activity, or behavior, producing system individually connects sensing to action. We refer to an activity producing system as a *layer* [see figures 9.2 and 9.3]. An activity is a pattern of interactions with the world. Another name for our activities might well be *skill* emphasizing that each activity can at least

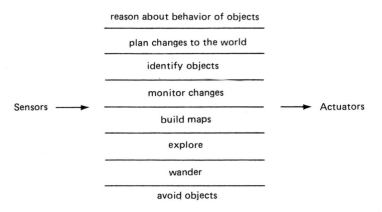

Figure 9.2
Behavior-based decomposition. From Brooks, Achieving artificial intelligence through building robots.

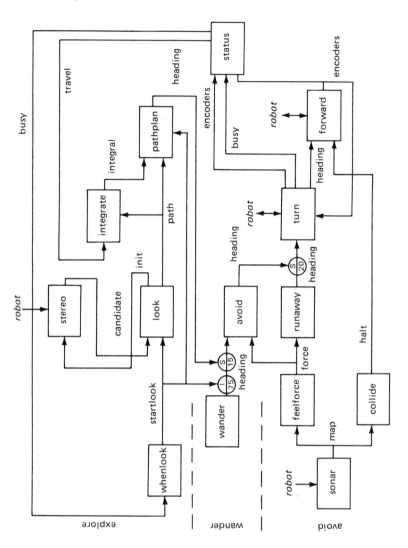

Figure 9.3
Finite state machines are wired together into layers of control. Each layer is built on top of existing layers. Lower levels never rely on the existence of higher-level layers. From Brooks, Intelligence without repre-

post facto be rationalized as pursuing some purpose. We have chosen the word activity however because our layers must decide when to act for themselves, not be some subroutine to be invoked at the beck and call of some other layer. . . .

The idea is to first build a very simple complete autonomous system, and **test it in the real world**. Our favorite example of such a system is a Creature, actually a mobile robot, which avoids hitting things. It senses objects in its immediate vicinity and moves away from them, halting if it senses something in its path. It is still necessary to build this system by decomposing it into parts, but there need be no clear distinction between a "perception subsystem," a "central system" and an "action system." In fact there may well be two independent channels connecting sensing to action (one for initiating motion, and one for emergency halts), so there is no single place where "perception" delivers a representation of the world in the traditional sense.[48]

It is, of course, of the utmost significance that Brooks insists that there are no representations involved in the layers of his Creatures. Instead, each individual layer simply specifies or makes evident those aspects of the Creature's world that are relevant. Equally significant is that his Creatures have no central system. Instead, the layers carry out their activities on their own; the compatibility of the layers gives rise to a sense of purpose only in the eyes of the observers: "Out of the local chaos of their interactions there emerges, in the eye of an observer, a coherent pattern of behavior."[49]

The implementation of this "decomposition by activity" has yielded so far a succession of four mobile robots in which layer is superimposed upon layer, thereby making the autonomous behavior of the Creature more and more interesting (see figure 9.3). These robots are all Creatures in the sense that on power-up they are viable in any world in which they are let loose. Brooks's hope is to reach the level of insect intelligence (a true landmark in Brooks's view) within two years by building a Creature composed of fourteen layers. Thus Brooks's strategy stands in sharp contrast to the classical approach, where robots or other AI artifacts are given specific goals, tasks, or plans.

The pragmatist bent on having immediate results tomorrow might be frustrated with this approach. We, however, are willing to bet with Brooks that in the relatively short term, perhaps a few years, such artifacts will have evolved into generations of sufficiently intelligent Creatures whose efficacy can begin to be exploited. We believe that this fully enactive approach to AI is one of the most promising avenues of research available today, but it needs to be given a chance by appreciating its possibilities in a context that is not limited to concern with short-term applications.

This example of what we are calling enactive AI is distinctively and clearly formulated as such by its proponents (of course, they do not use our term *enactive*). As Brooks himself states, his approach is neither connectionism nor production rules nor hermeneutics. It is motivated by the same good old engineering concerns that gave us both cognitivism and connectionism. It is precisely these engineering concerns that reveal most clearly how the notion of cognition as enaction is being generated by the very logic of research and development in present-day cognitive science. The enactive approach, then, is no mere philosophical preference but the result of forces internal to research in cognitive science, even in the case of those hard-nosed engineers who desire to build truly intelligent and useful machines.

The replacement of task-oriented design by cognitive modeling that is closer to evolution as natural drift also has implications for the relations between the emergence and enactive approaches. Here the issue turns on how we construe what a distributed network can do. If we emphasize how historical processes lead to emergent regularities without fixed and final constraints, then we recover the more open-ended biological condition. On the other hand, if we emphasize how a given network acquires a very specific capacity in a very definite domain (for example, NetTalk), then representations return, and we have the more typical use of connectionist models.

Consider as an example Paul Smolensky's harmony theory. Smolensky's paradigm of subsymbolic computation is generally compatible with the concerns of the enactive program. The remaining point of difference consists in Smolensky's evaluation of his models by reference to an unviolated level of environmental reality. Thus on the one hand, exogenous features in the task domain correspond to pregiven features of the world, and on the other hand, endogenous activity in the network acquires through experience an abstract meaning that optimally encodes environmental regularity. The goal is to find endogenous activity that corresponds to an optimality characterization of the surroundings. The enactive program, on the other hand, would require that we eschew any form of optimal fitness by taking this kind of cognitive system into a situation where endogenous and exogenous features are mutually definitory over a prolonged history that requires only a viable coupling.

The road we take, then, depends strongly on the degree of interest we have in staying close to biological reality, at the expense, perhaps, of short-term engineering applications. It is, of course, always possible to define a fixed domain within which a connectionist system can function, but this approach obscures the deeper issues about the biological embodiment of cognition that are so central to the enactive program. Thus just as connectionism grew out of cognitivism inspired by closer contact with the brain, the enactive program takes a further step in the same direction to encompass the temporality of cognition as lived history, whether seen at the level of the individual (ontogeny), the species (evolution), or social patterns (culture).

In Conclusion

This enactive program, which remains removed from the predominantly objectivist/subjectivist mood of most contemporary science, would have been mere heterodoxy only a few years ago. Today, however, the inner logic of research in cognitive psychology, linguistics, neuroscience, artificial intelligence, evolutionary theory, and immunology seems to incorporate more and more working elements of an enactive orientation. We have developed in some detail the situation in the field of robotics, not because we think such engineering products are the final result of this scientific orientation but rather to make it clear that in any concrete research program even the most pragmatic levels are touched. This is not the place to develop other areas that illustrate the same ideas at work. The debate is now heatedly on its way, and so researchers will no doubt subscribe to various intermediate positions and draw somewhat different epistemological conclusions. Nevertheless, these debates indicate that an enactive program is no longer the property of a few eccentric researchers but rather an alive and diverse research program that continues to grow.

We have now reached the end of our presentation of the enactive approach in cognitive science. We have seen not only that cognition is embodied action, and so inextricably tied to histories that are lived, but also that these lived histories are the result of evolution as natural drift. Thus our human embodiment and the world that is enacted by our history of coupling reflect only one of many possible evolutionary pathways. We are always constrained by the path we have laid down, but there is no ultimate ground to prescribe the steps that we take. It is precisely this lack of an ultimate ground that we have evoked at various points in this book by writing of groundlessness. This groundlessness of laying down a path is the key philosophical issue that remains to be addressed.

V
Worlds without Ground

10

The Middle Way

Evocations of Groundlessness

Our journey has now brought us to the point where we can appreciate that what we took to be solid ground is really more like shifting sand beneath our feet. We began with our common sense as cognitive scientists and found that our cognition emerges from the background of a world that extends beyond us but that cannot be found apart from our embodiment. When we shifted our attention away from this fundamental circularity to follow the movement of cognition alone, we found that we could discern no subjective ground, no permanent and abiding ego-self. When we tried to find the objective ground that we thought must still be present, we found a world enacted by our history of structural coupling. Finally, we saw that these various forms of groundlessness are really one: organism and environment enfold into each other and unfold from one another in the fundamental circularity that is life itself.

Our discussion of enactive cognition points directly toward the heart of our concerns in this chapter and the next. The worlds enacted by various histories of structural coupling are amenable to detailed scientific investigation, yet have no fixed, permanent substrate or foundation and so are ultimately groundless. We must now turn to face directly this groundlessness of which we have had multiple evocations. If our world is groundless, how are we to understand our day-to-day experience within it? Our experience feels given, unshakable, and unchangeable. How could we not experience the world as independent and well grounded? What else could experience of the world mean?

Western science and philosophy have brought us to the point where we are faced with, in the words of the philosopher Hilary Putnam, "the impossibility of imagining what credible 'foundations' might look like,"[1] but they have not provided any way for us to develop direct and personal insight into the groundlessness of our own experience. Philosophers may think that this task is unnecessary, but this is largely because Western philosophy has been more concerned with the rational understanding of life and mind than with the relevance of a pragmatic method for transforming human experience.

Indeed, it is largely a given in contemporary philosophical debate that whether the world is mind-dependent or mind-independent makes little difference, if any, to our everyday experience. To think otherwise would be to deny not only "metaphysical realism" but empirical, everyday commonsense realism, which is absurd. But this current philosophical assumption confuses two very different senses that the term *empirical realism* can have. On the one hand, it might mean that our world will continue to be the familiar one of objects and events with various qualities, even if we discover that this world is not pregiven and well grounded. On the other hand, it might mean that we will always experience this familiar world as if it were ultimately grounded, that we are "condemned" to experience the world as if it had a ground, even though we know philosophically and scientifically that it does not. This latter supposition is not innocent, for it imposes an a priori limitation on the possibilities for human development and transformation. It is important to see that we can contest this supposition without calling into question the first sense in which things can be said to be real and independent.

The reason this point is important is that our historical situation requires not only that we give up philosophical foundationalism but that we learn to live in a world without foundations. Science alone— that is, science without any bridge to everyday human experience—is incapable of this task. As Hilary Putnam incisively remarks in a recent work, "Science is wonderful at destroying metaphysical answers, but incapable of providing substitute ones. Science takes away foundations without providing a replacement. Whether we want to be there or not, science has put us in the position of having to live without foundations. It was shocking when Nietzsche said this, but today it is commonplace; *our* historical position—and no end to it is in sight— is that of having to philosophize without 'foundations'."[2]

Although it is true that our historical situation is unique, we should not draw the conclusion that we stand alone in the attempt to learn to live without foundations. To interpret our situation in this way would immediately prevent us from recognizing that other traditions have, in their own ways, addressed this very issue of the lack of foundations. In fact, the problematic of groundlessness is the focal point of the Madhyamika tradition. With one or two exceptions, Western philosophers have yet to draw on the resources of this tradition. Indeed, one often gets the impression that Western philosophers are not simply unfamiliar with Madhyamika but that they suppose a priori that our situation is so unique that no other philosophical tradition could be relevant. Richard Rorty, for example, after thoroughly criticizing the project of foundationalism in his *Philosophy and the Mirror of Nature*, offers in its place a conception of "edifying philosophy" whose guiding ideal is "continuing the conversation of the West."[3] Rorty does not even pause to consider the possibility of there being other traditions of philosophical reflection that might have addressed his very concerns. In fact, it is one such important tradition, the Madhyamika, which has served as the basis for our thought in this book.[4]

Nagarjuna and the Madhyamika Tradition

Hitherto we have spoken of the Buddhist tradition of mindfulness/ awareness as though it were all one unified tradition. And in fact, the teachings of no-self—the five aggregates, some form of mental factor analysis, and karma and the wheel of conditioned origination—are common to all of the major Buddhist traditions. At this point, however, we come to a split. The teaching of emptiness (sunyata), which we are about to explore, according to the Buddhist tradition itself as well as to scholarship, did not become apparent until approximately 500 years after the Buddha's death, at which time the *Prajnaparamita* and other texts that expound this doctrine began to appear. During those 500 years, the Abhidharma tradition had become elaborated into eighteen different schools that debated each other about various subtle points and debated the many non-Buddhist schools within Hinduism and Jainism. Those who adopted the newer teachings called themselves the Great Vehicle (Mahayana) and designated those who continued to adhere to the earlier teachings the Lesser Vehicle (Hinayana)—an epithet to this day widely loathed by non-Mahayanists. One of the eighteen original schools, the Theravada (the speech of the elders) has survived with great vigor in the modern world; it is the undisputed form of Buddhism in the countries of Southeast Asia—Burma, Sri Lanka, Cambodia, Laos, and Thailand. Theravada

Buddhism does not teach sunyata. Sunyata is, however, the founda-tion of Mahayana Buddhism (the form that spread to China, Korea, and Japan) and of the Vajrayana, the Buddhism of Tibet.

In approximately the first half of the second century CE, the Prajnaparamita teachings were put into a form of philosophical argu-ment by Nagarjuna (according to some Mahayana schools and many, but not all, Western scholars).[5] Nagarjuna's stature in Mahayana and Varjayana Buddhism is enormous. His method was to work solely by means of refutation of the positions and assertions of others. His followers soon split into those who continued this method, which is very demanding for the listener as well as for the speaker (the Prasangikas) and those who made positive arguments about empti-ness (Svatantrikas).

The Madhyamika tradition, although it delighted in debate and logical argument, is not to be taken as abstract philosophy in the modern sense. For one thing, the debate was considered so mean-ingful in the social context of the courts and universities of early India that the losing side in a debate was expected to convert. More im-portant, the philosophy was never to be divorced from meditation practice or from the daily activities of life. The point was to realize egolessness in one's own experience and manifest it in action to others. Texts discussing the philosophy included meditation manuals for how to contemplate, meditate, and act on the topic.

In exposition of Nagarjuna in the present day, there is a split between Buddhist practitioners (including traditionally trained prac-titioner scholars) and Western academic scholars. Practitioners say that Western scholars are making up issues, interpretations, and confusions that have nothing to do with the texts or with Buddhism. Western scholars feel that the opinions (and teachings) of "believers" are not an appropriate source for textual exegesis. Since in this book we wish to bring into contact the living tradition of mindfulness/awareness meditation with the living tradition of phenomenology and of cognitive science, for our exposition of the Madhyamika we will draw from the practitioner as well as from the scholarly side of this interesting sociological detente.

Sunyata literally means "emptiness" (sometimes misleadingly trans-lated as "the void" or "voidness"). In the Tibetan tradition, it is said that sunyata may be expounded from three perspectives—sunyata with respect to codependent arising, sunyata with respect to compassion, and sunyata with respect to naturalness. It is the first of these, sunyata with respect to codependent arising, that most naturally fits with the logic we have been exploring in the discovery of groundlessness and its relationship to cognitive science and the concept of enaction.

Nagarjuna's most well known work is the *Stanzas of the Middle Way* (*Mulamadhyamikakarikas*). From the perspective that we will now examine, it carries through the logic of codependent arising to its logical conclusion.

In the Abhidharma analysis of consciousness, each moment of experience takes the form of a particular consciousness that has a particular object to which it is tied by particular relations. For example, a moment of seeing consciousness is composed of a seer (the subject) who sees (the relation) a sight (the object); in a moment of anger consciousness, the one who is angry (the subject) experiences (the relation) anger (the object). (This is what we have called protointentionality.) The force of the analysis was to show that there was no truly existing subject (a self) continuing unchangingly through a series of moments. But what of the objects of consciousness? And what of the relations? The Abhidharma schools had assumed that there were material properties that were taken as objects by five of the senses—seeing, hearing, smelling, tasting, and touching—and that there were thoughts that were taken as an object by the mind consciousness. Such an analysis is still partially subjectivist/objectivist because (1) many schools, such as the basic element analysis discussed in chapters 4 and 6, took moments of consciousness as ultimate realities, and (2) the external world had been left in a relatively unproblematic, objectivist, independent state.

The Mahayana tradition talks about not just one but two senses of ego-self: ego of self and ego of phenomena (dharmas). Ego of self is the habitual grasping after a self that we have been discussing. Mahayanists claim that the earlier traditions attacked this sense of self but did not challenge the reliance on an independently existing world or the mind's (momentary) relations to that world. Nagarjuna attacks the independent existence of all three terms—the subject, the relation, and the object. What follows will be a (synthetically constructed) example of the kind of argument that Nagarjuna makes.[6]

What is it that we mean when we say that the one who sees exists independently or when we say that that which is seen exists independently? Surely we mean that the one who sees exists even when she is not seeing the sight; she exists prior to and/or after seeing the sight. And likewise we mean that the sight exists prior to and/or after it is seen by the seer. That is, if I am the seer of a sight and I truly exist, it means that I can walk away and not see that sight—I can go hear something or think something instead. And if the sight truly exists, it should be able to stay there even when I am not seeing it—for example, it could have someone else see it at a future moment.

Upon closer examination, however, Nagarjuna points out that this makes little sense. How can we talk about the seer of a sight who is not seeing its sight? Conversely how can we speak of a sight that is not being seen by its seer? Nor does it make any sense to say that there is an independently existing seeing going on somewhere without any seer and without any sight being seen. The very position of a seer, the very idea of a seer, cannot be separated from the sights it sees. And vice versa, how can the sight that is being seen be separated from the seer that sees it?

We might try a negative tack and reply that all this is true and that the seer does not exist prior to the sight and the seeing of it. But then how can a nonexistent seer give rise to an existing seeing and an existing sight? Or if we try to argue the other way round and say that the sight didn't exist until the seer saw it, the reply is, How can a nonexistent sight be seen by a seer?

Let us try the argument that the seer and the sight arise simultaneously. In that case, they are either one and the same thing, or they are different things. If they are one and the same thing, then this cannot be a case of seeing, since seeing requires that there be one who sees, a sight, and the seeing of the sight. We do not say that the eye sees itself. Then they must be two separate, independent things. But in that case, if they are truly independent things, each existing in its own right independently of the relations in which it happens to figure, then there could be many relations beside seeing between them. But it makes no sense to say that a seer hears a sight; only a hearer can hear a sound.

We might give in and agree that there is no truly existent independent seer, sight, or seeing but claim that all three put together form a truly existent moment of consciousness that is the ultimate reality. But if you add one nonexistent thing to another nonexistent thing, how can you say that that makes a truly existent thing? Indeed, how can you say that a moment of time is a truly existent thing when to be truly existent, it would have to exist independently of other moments in the past and future? Furthermore, since one moment is but an aspect of time itself, that moment would have to exist independently of time itself (this is an argument about the codependence of things and their attributes); and time itself would have to exist independently of that one moment.

At this point, we might be seized with the terrible feeling that indeed these things do not exist. But surely it makes even less sense to assert that a nonexistent seer either sees or does not see a nonexistent sight at a nonexistent moment than to make these claims about an existent seer. (That this argument has actual psychological force is illustrated by an Israeli joke: Man 1 says, "Things are getting worse and worse; better never to have existed at all." Man 2 says, "How true. But who should be so lucky?—one in ten thousand!") Nagarjuna's point is not to say that things are nonexistent in an absolute way any more than to say that they are existent. Things are codependently originated; they are completely groundless.

Nagarjuna's arguments for complete codependence (or more properly his arguments against any other conceivable view than codependence) are applied to three main classes of topics: subjects and their objects, things and their attributes, and causes and their effects.[7] By these means, he disposes of the idea of noncodependent existence for virtually everything—subject and object for each of the senses; material objects; the primal elements (earth, water, fire, air, and space); passion, aggression, and ignorance; space, time, and motion; the agent, his doing, and what he does; conditions and outcomes; the self as perceiver, doer, or anything else; suffering; the causes of suffering, cessation of suffering, and the path to cessation (known as the Four Noble Truths); the Buddha; and nirvana. Nagarjuna finally concludes, "Nothing is found that is not dependently arisen. For that reason, nothing is found that is not empty."[8]

It is important to remember the context within which these arguments are employed. Nagarjuna's arguments fasten on psychologically real habits of mind and demonstrate their groundlessness within the context of mindfulness/awareness meditation and Abhidharma psychology. A modern philosopher might believe himself able to find faults with Nagarjuna's logic. Even if this were the case, however, it would not overturn the epistemological and psychological force of Nagarjuna's argumentation within the context of his concerns. In fact,

Nagarjuna's arguments can be summarized in a way that makes this point apparent:

1. If subjects and their objects, things and their attributes, and causes and their effects exist independently as we habitually take them to, or exist intrinsically and absolutely as basic element analysis holds, then they must not depend on any kind of condition or relation. This point basically amounts to a philosophical insistence on the meanings of *independent, intrinsic,* and *absolute.* By definition, something is independent, intrinsic, or absolute only if it does not depend on anything else; it must have an identity that transcends its relations.

2. Nothing in our experience can be found that satisfies this criterion of independence or ultimacy. The earlier Abhidharma tradition had expressed this insight as dependent coarising: nothing can be found apart from its conditions of arising, formation, and decay. In our modern context this point is rather obvious when considering the causes and conditions of the material world and is expressed in our scientific tradition. Nagarjuna took the understanding of codependence considerably further. Causes and their effects, things and their attributes, and the very mind of the inquiring subject and the objects of mind are each *equally* codependent on the other. Nagarjuna's logic addresses itself penetratingly to the mind of the inquiring subject (recall our fundamental circularity), to the ways in which what are actually codependent factors are taken by that subject to be the ultimate founding blocks of a supposed objective and a supposed subjective reality.

3. Therefore, nothing can be found that has an ultimate or independent existence. Or to use Buddhist language, everything is "empty" of an independent existence, for it is codependently originated.

We now have a context for understanding emptiness with respect to codependent origination: all things are empty of any independent intrinsic nature. This may sound like an abstract statement, but it has far-ranging implications for experience.

We explained in chapter 4 how the categories of the Abhidharma were both descriptions and contemplative directives for the way the mind is actually experienced when one is mindful. It is important to realize that Nagarjuna is not rejecting the Abhidharma, as he is sometimes interpreted as doing in Western scholarship.[9] His entire analysis is based on the categories of the Abhidharma: what sense would arguments such as that of the seer, the sight, and the seeing have except in that context? (If the reader thinks that Nagarjuna's argument is a linguistic one, that is because he has not seen the force of the Abhidharma.) It is a very precise argument, not just a general handwaving that everything is dependent on everything. Nagarjuna is extending the Abhidharma, but that extension makes an incisive difference to experience.

Why should it make any difference at all to experience? One might say, So what if the world and the self change moment to moment—whoever thought that they were permanent? And so what if they are mutually dependent on each other—whoever thought they were isolated? The answer (as we have seen throughout the book) is that as one becomes mindful of one's own experience, one realizes the power of the urge to grasp after foundations—to grasp the sense of foundation of a real, separate self, the sense of foundation of a real, separate world, and the sense of foundation of an actual relation between self and world.

It is said that emptiness is a natural discovery that one would make by oneself with sufficient mindfulness/awareness—natural but shocking. Previously we have been talking about examining the mind with meditation. There may not have been a self, but there was still a mind to examine itself, even if a momentary one. But now we discover that we have no mind; after all, a mind must be something that is separate from and knows the world. We also don't have a world. There is neither an objective nor subjective pole. Nor is there any knowing because there is nothing hidden. Knowing sunyata (more accurately knowing the world as sunyata) is surely not an intentional act. Rather (to use traditional imagery), it is like a reflection in a mirror—pure, brilliant, but with no additional reality apart from itself. As mind/world keeps happening in its interdependent continuity, there is nothing extra on the side of mind or on the side of world to know or be known further. Whatever experience happens is open (Buddhist teachers use the word *exposed*), perfectly revealed just as it is.

We can now see why Madhyamika is called the middle way. It avoids the extreme of either objectivism or subjectivism, of absolutism or nihilism. As is said by the Tibetan commentators, "Through ascertaining the reason—that all phenomena are dependent arisings—the extreme of annihilation (nihilism) is avoided, and realization of dependent-arising of causes and effects is gained. Through ascertaining the thesis—that all phenomena do not inherently exist—the extreme of permanence (absolutism) is avoided, and realization of the emptiness of all phenomena is gained."[10]

But what does all this mean for the everyday world? I still have a name, a job, memories, and plans. The sun still rises in the morning, and scientists still work to explain that. What of all this?

The Two Truths

The Abhidharma analysis of the mind into basic elements and mental factors already contained within it the distinction between two kinds of truth: ultimate truth, which consisted of the basic elements of existence into which experience could be analyzed, and relative or conventional truth, which was our ordinary, compounded (out of basic elements) experience. Nagarjuna invoked this distinction, gave it new meaning, and insisted on its importance.

> The teaching of the doctrine by the Buddha is based upon two truths: the truth of worldly convention (samvrti) and the ultimate, supreme truth (paramartha).
>
> Those who do not discern the distinction between these two truths, do not understand the profound nature of the Buddha's teaching (XXIV: 8–9).

Relative truth (samvrti, which literally means covered or concealed) is the phenomenal world just as it appears—with chairs, people, species, and the coherence of those through time. Ultimate truth (paramartha) is the emptiness of that very same phenomenal world. The Tibetan term for relative truth, *kundzop*, captures the relation between the two imagistically; *kundzop* means all dressed up, outfitted, or costumed—that is, relative truth is sunyata (absolute truth) costumed in the brilliant colors of the phenomenal world.

By now it should be obvious that the distinction between the two truths, like the analysis of the Abhidharma, was not intended as a metaphysical theory of truth. It is a description of the experience of the practitioner who experiences his mind, its objects, and their relation as codependently originated and thus as empty of any actual, independent, or abiding existence. Like the Abhidharma categories, the description also functions as a recommendation and contemplative aid. This can be seen very clearly in the discourse of Buddhist communities. For example, many of the forms that Westerners take as poetry or irrationality in Zen are actually contemplative exercises directing the mind toward codependent emptiness.

The term for relative truth, *samvrti*, is also often translated as "convention" (within Buddhism as well as by academic scholars), which gives rise to much interpretative confusion. It is important to understand in what sense convention is meant. "Relative" or "conventional" should not be taken in a superficial sense. Convention does not mean subjective, arbitrary, or unlawful. And relative does not mean culturally relative. The relative phenomenal world was always taken to operate by very clear laws regardless of the conventions of any individual or society, such as the laws of karmic cause and effect.

Furthermore, it is very important to understand that the use of convention here is not an invitation to decenter the self and/or world into language as is so popular at present in the humanities. As the founder of the Gelugpa lineage in Tibetan Buddhism puts it, ". . . since nominally designated things are artificial, that is, established as existent in conventional terms, there is no referent to which names are attached which (itself) is not established as merely conventionally existent. And since that is not to say that in general there is no phenomenal basis for using names, the statement of the existence of that (conventional referent) and the statement that (all things) are mere nominal designations are not contradictory."[11] Thus in Buddhism one can perfectly well make distinctions in the relative world between true statements and false ones, and it is recommended that one make true ones.

The sense in which the things designated, as well as the designations, are only conventional may be explained by an example: when I call someone *John*, I have the deep assumption that there is some abiding independent thing that I am designating, but Madhyamika analysis shows there to be no such truly existing thing. John, however, continues to act just the way a perfectly good designatum is supposed to, so in relative or conventional truth he is indeed John. This claim may remind the reader of our discussion of color. Although the experience of color can be shown to have no absolute ground either in the physical world or the visual observer, color is nonetheless a perfectly commensurable designable. Thus such scientific analysis can perfectly well be joined by the far more radical presentation of groundlessness in the Madhyamika.

Because this relative, conventional, codependently originated world is lawful, science is possible—just as possible as daily life. In fact, perfectly functional pragmatic science and engineering are possible even when they are based on theories that make unjustifiable metaphysical assumptions—just as daily life continues coherently even when one believes in the actual reality of oneself. We offer the vision of enactive cognitive science and of evolution as natural drift neither as a claim that this is the only way science can be done nor as a claim that this is the very same thing as Madhyamika. Concepts such as embodiment or structural coupling are *concepts* and as such are always historical. They do not convey that at this very moment—personally—one has no independently existing mind and no independently existing world.

This is a crucially important point. There is a powerful reason why some Madhyamika schools only refute the arguments of others and refuse to make assertions. Any conceptual position can become a ground (a resting point, a nest), which vitiates the force of the Madhyamika. In particular, the view of cognition as embodied action (enaction), although it stresses the interdependence of mind and world, tends to treat the relationship between those (the interaction, the action, the enaction) as though it had some form of independent actual existence. As one's mind grasps the concept of enaction as something real and solid, it automatically generates a sense of the other two terms of the argument, the subject and object of the embodied action. (As we shall discuss, this is why pragmatism is also not the same as thing as the middle way of Madhyamika.) We would be doing a great disservice to everyone concerned—mindfulness/awareness practitioners, scientists, scholars, and any other interested persons—were we to lead anyone to believe that making assertions about enactive cognitive science was the same thing as allowing one's mind to be experientially processed by the Madhyamika dialectic, particularly when this is combined with mindfulness/awareness training. But just as the Madhyamika dialectic, a provisional and conventional activity of the relative world, points beyond itself, so we might hope that our concept of enaction could, at least for some cognitive scientists and perhaps even for the more general milieu of scientific thought, point beyond itself to a truer understanding of groundlessness.

Groundlessness in Contemporary Thought

We began this chapter by evoking the sense of loss of foundations in contemporary science and philosophy. In particular, we cited one important trend in contemporary Anglo-American thought based on a revival of pragmatist philosophy.[12] In Europe—particularly France, Germany, and Italy—an analogous critique of foundations has been pursued, largely as a result of the continuing influence of Nietszche and Heidegger—a trend that includes both poststructuralism[13] and postmodern thought.[14] The Italian philosopher Gianni Vattimo describes this trend as "weak thought" (*pensiero debole*)—that is, a kind of thought that would give up the modernist quest for foundations, yet without criticizing this quest in the name of another, truer foundation.[15] Vattimo defends the positive possibilities of this trend in the introduction to a recent work:

> The ideas of Nietzsche and Heidegger, more than any others, offer us the chance to pass from a purely critical and negative description of the post-modern condition . . . to an approach that treats it as a positive possibility and opportunity. Nietzsche mentions all of this—although not altogether clearly—in his theory of a possibly active, or positive, nihilism. Heidegger alludes to the same thing with his idea of a *Verwindung* of metaphysics which is not a critical overcoming in the 'modern' sense of the term. . . . In both Nietzsche and Heidegger, what I have elsewhere called the "weakening" of Being allows thought to situate itself in a constructive manner within the post-modern condition. For only if we take seriously the outcome of the "destruction of ontology" undertaken by Heidegger, and before him by Nietzsche, is it possible to gain access to the positive opportunities for the very essence of man that are found in post-modern conditions of existence. It will not be possible for thought to live positively in that truly post-metaphysical era as long as man and Being are conceived of—metaphysically, Platonically, etc.—in terms of stable structures. Such conceptions require thought and existence to "ground" themselves, or in other words to stabilize themselves (with logic or with ethics), in the domain of non-becoming and are reflected in a whole-scale mythization of strong structures in every field of experience. This is not to say that everything in such an era will be accepted as equally beneficial for humanity; but the capacity to choose and discriminate between the possibilities that the post-modern condition offers us can be developed only on the basis of an

analysis of post-modernity that captures its own innate characteristics, and that recognizes post-modernity as a field of possibility and not simply as a hellish negation of all that is human.[16]

It is thus clear that our contemporary world has become highly
sensitized to the issue of groundlessness for a number of reasons in
history, politics, art, science, and philosophical reflection. We certainly cannot delve into these developments here. We do find remarkable, however, the extent to which the Western tradition, based on
the reasoning of philosophy and scientific practices, and the Buddhist
tradition and thought, based on experiencing the world with mind-
fulness/awareness, have converged. Nevertheless this convergence
might be a trompe l'oeil; indeed many meditation practitioners would
argue that the very appearance of similarity of the two traditions is
spurious. In this regard, we wish to point out what we believe are
three major differences between the contemporary sense of groundlessness and that of Madhyamika. Then in the next and final chapter
we will consider the ethical dimensions of groundlessness.

The Lack of an Entre-deux
In the first place, contemporary Western views have been unable to
articulate together the loss of foundations for the self and for the
world. There is no methodological basis for a middle way between
objectivism and subjectivism (both forms of absolutism). In cognitive
science and in experimental psychology, the fragmentation of the self
occurs because the field is trying to be scientifically objective. Precisely because the self is taken as an object, like any other external
object in the world, as an object of scientific scrutiny—precisely for
that reason—it disappears from view. That is, the very foundation for
challenging the subjective leaves intact the objective as a foundation.
In an exactly analogous fashion, challenges to the objective status of
the world depend upon leaving the subjective unproblematical. To
espouse that an organism's (or scientist's) perception is never entirely
objective because it is always influenced by past experience and
goals—the scientist's top-down processes—is precisely the result of
taking an independent subject as given and then discovering and
arguing from the subjective nature of his representations.

Nowhere is slight of hand between the inner and the outer more
evident than in the work of David Hume, whose classic passage on
his inability to observe a self we have already quoted. Hume also

noted that there was a contradiction between his idea that outer bodies (the outer world) have a "continued and distinct existence" and his sense impressions of bodies that were discontinuous. In his contemplation of this issue, he suggests that the idea of a continuous external world (like that of a continuous self) is a psychological construction: "There being here an opposition betwixt the notion of the identity of resembling perceptions, and the interruption of their appearance, the mind must be uneasy in that situation, and will naturally seek relief from the uneasiness. . . . In order to free our- selves from this difficulty, we disguise, as much as possible, the interruption, or rather remove it entirely, by supposing that these interrup- ted perceptions are connected by a real existence, of which we are insensible."[17] The interesting point for our present purposes is that there is no evidence that Hume ever thought to put together his empiricist doubts about the self and about the world. He had all the intellectual materials needed for an entre-deux, but with neither an intellectual tradition to suggest it nor an experiential method to discover it, he never considered the possibility.

Our final example is a particularly telling one as it comes from the heart of cognitive science itself. What does a modern cognitivist do if his experience does lead him to approach the entre-deux—the fact that lived experience of the world is actually between what we think of as the world and what we think of as the mind? He takes flight into theory—the current scientific milieu gives him no other option. We are thinking of Jackendoff, a sensitive phenomenologist who seemed led to construct the pièce de résistance of his book, the intermediate-level theory of consciousness, out of his perception of the betweenness of the phenomenological mind:

> On the one hand, intuition suggests that awareness reveals what is going on in the mind, including thought. On the other hand, intuition suggests that awareness reveals what is going on out in the world, that is, the result of sensation or perception. Ac- cording to the Intermediate-Level Theory, it reveals neither. Rather, awareness reflects a curious amalgam of the effects on the mind of both thought and the real world, while leaving totally opaque the means by which these effects come about. *It is only by developing a formal theory of levels of representation* that we could have come to suspect the existence of a part of the compu- tational mind that has these characteristics [our emphasis].[18]

Interpretationism

One of the most seductive forms of subjectivism in contemporary thought is the use made of the concepts of interpretation, whether by pragmatists or hermeneuticists. To its credit, interpretationism provides a penetrating critique of objectivism that is worth pursuing in some detail. To be objective, the interpretationist points out, one would have to have some set of mind-independent objects to be designated by language or known by science. But can we find any such objects? Let us look at an extended example from the philosopher Nelson Goodman.

A point in space seems to be perfectly objective. But how are we to define the points of our everyday world? Points can be taken either as primitive elements, as intersecting lines, as certain triples of intersecting planes, or as certain classes of nesting volumes. These definitions are equally adequate, and yet they are incompatible: what a point is will vary with each form of description. For example, only in the first "version," to use Goodman's term, will a point be a primitive element. The objectivist, however, demands, "What are points really?" Goodman's response to this demand is worth quoting at length:

> If the composition of points out of lines or of lines out of points is conventional rather than factual, points and lines themselves are no less so. . . . If we say that our sample space is a combination of points, or of lines, or of regions, or a combination of combinations of points, or lines, or regions, or a combination of all these together, or is a single lump, then since none is identical with any of the rest, we are giving one among countless alternative conflicting descriptions of what the space is. And so we may regard the disagreements as not about the facts but as due to differences in the conventions—adopted in organizing or describing the space. What, then, is the neutral fact or thing described in these different terms? Neither the space (a) as an undivided whole nor (b) as a combination of everything involved in the several accounts; for (a) and (b) are but two among the various ways of organizing it. But what is *it* that is so organized? When we strip off as layers of convention all differences among ways of describing *it*, what is left? The onion is peeled down to its empty core.[19]

The appearance of the word *empty* here is of interest. Contemporary philosophy is replete with such examples of how things are empty of any intrinsic identity because they depend on forms of designation.

Hilary Putnam has even devised a theorem in formal semantics to show that there can be no unique mapping between words and the world: even if we know the conditions under which sentences are true, we cannot fix the way their terms refer.[20] Putnam concludes that we cannot understand meaning if we hold on to the idea that there is some privileged set of mind-independent objects to which language refers. Instead, he writes, "'Objects' do not exist independently of conceptual schemes. *We* cut up the world into objects when we introduce one or another scheme of description. Since the objects *and* the signs are alike *internal* to the scheme of description, it is possible to say what matches what."[21]

Interestingly, Putnam argues not only that we cannot understand meaning if we suppose language refers to mind-independent objects; he also argues against the very notion of properties that exist intrinsically (i.e., nondependently), a notion that lies at the basis of objectivism: "The problem with the 'Objectivist' picture of the world . . . [t]he deep systemic root of the disease, I want to suggest, lies in the notion of an 'intrinsic' property, a property something has 'in itself,' apart from any contribution made by language or the mind."[22] Putnam argues that this classical idea, combined with contemporary scientific realism, leads to the complete devaluation of experience, for virtually all of the features of our life-world become mere "projections" of the mind. The irony of this stance—which we should nonetheless expect from our discussion of the Cartesian anxiety—is that it becomes indistinguishable from idealism, for it makes the lived world a result of subjective representation.

Yet despite this thorough critique of objectivism, the argument is never turned the other way round. Mind-independent objects are challenged, but object-independent minds never are. (It is actually more obvious and psychologically easier to attack the independence of objects than of minds.) The interpretationists—pragmatist or otherwise—also do not challenge the groundedness of the concepts and interpretations themselves; rather, they take these as the ground on which they stand. This is far from an entre-deux and far from Madhyamika.

Transformative Potential

When contemporary traditions of thought discover groundlessness, it is viewed as negative, a breakdown of an ideal for doing science, for establishing philosophical truth with reason, or for living a meaningful life. Enactive cognitive science and, in a certain sense, contemporary Western pragmatism require that we confront the lack of ultimate foundations. Both, while challenging theoretical foundations, wish to affirm the everyday lived world. Enactive cognitive science and pragmatism, however, are both theoretical; neither offers insight into how we are to live in a world without foundations. In the Madhyamika tradition, on the other hand, as in all Buddhism, the intimation of egolessness is a great blessing; it opens up the lived world as path, as the locus for realization. Thus Nagarjuna writes, "Ultimate truth cannot be taught apart from everyday practices. Without understanding the ultimate truth, freedom (nirvana) is not attained," (XXIV: 10). On the Buddhist path, one needs to be embodied to attain realization. Mindfulness, awareness, and emptiness are not abstractions; there has to be something to be mindful of, aware of, and to realize the emptiness of (and as we will see in chapter 11, to realize the intrinsic goodness of and to be compassionate for). One's very habitual patterns of grasping, anxiety, and frustration are the contents of mindfulness and awareness. The recognition that those are empty of any actual existence manifests itself experientially as an ever-growing openness and lack of fixation. An open-hearted sense of compassionate interest in others can replace the constant anxiety and irritation of egoistic concern.

In early Buddhism, freedom was equated with escape from samsara (the everyday lived world of fixation, habit, and suffering) to the unconditional realm of nirvana. With the teaching of emptiness in the Mahayana, a radical change occurred. Nagarjuna puts it,

> There is no distinction at all between the everyday world (samsara) and freedom (nirvana). There is no distinction at all between freedom and the everyday world.
> The range of the everyday world is the range of freedom. Between them not even the most subtle difference can be found. (XXV: 19, 20)

Freedom is not the same as living in the everyday world conditioned by ignorance and confusion; it is living and acting in the everyday world with realization. Freedom does not mean escape from the world; it means transformation of our entire way of being, our mode of embodiment, within the lived world itself.

This stance is not an easy one for anyone to understand—in cultures where Buddhism flourishes let alone in the modern world. We think that the denial of an ultimate ground is tantamount to the denial of there being any ultimate truth or goodness about our world and experience. The reason that we almost automatically draw this conclusion is that we have not been able to disentangle ourselves from the extremes of absolutism and nihilism and to take seriously the possibilities inherent in a mindful, open-ended stance toward human experience. These two extremes of absolutism and nihilism both lead us away from the lived world; in the case of absolutism, we try to escape actual experience by invoking foundations to supply our lives with a sense of justification and purpose; in the case of nihilism, failing in that search, we deny the possibility of working with our everyday experience in a way that is liberating and transformative.

11

Laying Down a Path in Walking

Science and Experience in Circulation

In the preface we announced that the theme of this book would be the circulation between cognitive science and human experience. In this final chapter we wish to situate this circulation within a wider contemporary context. In particular we wish to consider some of the ethical dimensions of groundlessness in relation to the concern with nihilism that is typical of much post-Nietzschean thought. This is not the place to consider the many points that animate current North American and European discussions; our concern, rather, is to indicate how we see our project in relation to these discussions and to suggest further directions for investigation.

The back-and-forth communication between cognitive science and experience that we have explored can be envisioned as a circle. The circle begins with the experience of the cognitive scientist, a human being who can conceive of a mind operating without a self. This becomes embodied in a scientific theory. Emboldened by the theory, one can discover, with a disciplined, mindful approach to experience, that although there is constant struggle to maintain a self, there is no actual self in experience. The natural scientific inquisitiveness of the mind then queries, But how can there seem to be a coherent self when there is none? For an answer one can turn to mechanisms such as emergence and societies of mind. Ideally that could lead one to penetrate further into the causal relationships in one's experience, seeing the causes and effects of ego grasping and enabling one to begin to relax the struggle of ego grasping. As perceptions, relationships, and the activity of mind expand into awareness, one might have insight into the codependent lack of ultimate foundations either for one's mind or for its objects, the world. The inquisitive scientist then asks, How can we imagine, embodied in a mechanism, that relation of codependence between mind and world? The mechanism that we have created (the embodied metaphor of groundlessness) is that of enactive cognition, with its image of structural coupling through a history of natural drift. Ideally such an image can influence the scientific society and the larger society, loosening the hold of both objectivism and subjectivism and encouraging further communication between science and experience, experience and science.

The logic of this back-and-forth circle exemplified the fundamental circularity in the mind of the reflective scientist. The fundamental axis of this circulation is the embodiment of experience and cognition. It should be recalled that embodiment in our sense, as for Merleau-Ponty, encompasses both the body as a lived, experiential structure and the body as the context or milieu of cognitive mechanisms. Thus in the communication we have portrayed in this book between cognitive science and the tradition of mindfulness/awareness, we have systematically juxtaposed the descriptions of experience taken from mindfulness/awareness practice with descriptions of cognitive architecture taken from cognitive science.

Like Merleau-Ponty, we have emphasized that a proper appreciation of this twofold sense of embodiment provides a middle way or entre-deux between the extremes of absolutism and nihilism. Both of these two extremes can be found in contemporary cognitive science. The absolutist extreme is easy to find, for despite other differences, the varieties of cognitive realism share the conviction that cognition is grounded in the representation of a pregiven world by a pregiven subject. The nihilist extreme is less apparent, but we have seen how it arises when cognitive science uncovers the nonunity of the self yet ignores the possibility of a transformative approach to human experience.

So far we have devoted less attention to this nihilist extreme, but it is in fact far more indicative of our contemporary cultural situation. Thus in the humanities—in art, literature, and philosophy—the growing awareness of groundlessness has taken form not through a confrontation with objectivism but rather with nihilism, skepticism, and extreme relativism. Indeed, this concern with nihilism is typical of late-twentieth-century life. Its visible manifestations are the increasing fragmentation of life, the revival of and continuing adherence to a variety of religious and political dogmatisms, and a pervasive yet intangible feeling of anxiety, which writers such as Milan Kundera in *The Unbearable Lightness of Being* depict so vividly. It is for this reason (and because nihilism and objectivism are actually deeply connected) that we turn to consider in more detail the nihilistic extreme. We have reserved this issue until now because it is both general and far reaching. Our discussion must accordingly become more centrally concerned with the ethical dimension of groundlessness than it has been so far. In the final section of this chapter we will be more explicit about this ethical dimension. Before doing so, however, we wish to examine in more detail the nihilist extreme.

Nihilism and the Need for Planetary Thinking

Let us begin not by attempting to engage nihilism directly but rather by asking how nihilism arises. Where and at what point does the nihilist tendency first manifest itself?

We have been led to face groundlessness or the lack of stable foundations in both enactive cognitive science and in the mindful, open-ended approach to experience. In both settings we began naively but were forced to suspend our deep-seated conviction that the world is grounded independently of embodied perceptual and cognitive capacities. This deep-seated conviction is the motivation for objectivism—even in its most refined philosophical forms. Nihilism, however, is in a sense based on no analogous conviction, for it arises initially in reaction to the loss of faith in objectivism. Nihilism can, of course, be cultivated to a point where it takes on a life of its own, but in its first moment its form is one of *response*. Thus we can already see that nihilism is in fact deeply linked to objectivism, for nihilism is an extreme response to the collapse of what had seemed to provide a sure and absolute reference point.

We have already provided an example of this link between objectivism and nihilism when we examined the discovery within cognitive science of selfless minds. This deep and profound discovery requires the cognitive scientist to acknowledge that consciousness and self-identity do not provide the ground or foundation for cognitive processes; yet she feels that we do believe, and must continue to believe, in an efficacious self. The usual response of the cognitive scientist is to ignore the experiential aspect when she does science and ignore the scientific discovery when she leads her life. As a result, the nonexistence of a self that would answer to our objectivist representations is typically confused with the nonexistence of the relative (practical) self altogether. Indeed, without the resources provided by a progressive approach to experience, there is little choice but to respond to the collapse of an objective self (objectivism) by asserting the objective nonexistence of the self (nihilism).

This response indicates that objectivism and nihilism, despite their apparent differences, are deeply connected—indeed the actual source of nihilism is objectivism. We have already discussed how the basis of objectivism is to be found in our habitual tendency to grasp after regularities that are stable but ungrounded. In fact, nihilism too arises from this grasping mind. Thus faced with the discovery of ground-lessness, we nonetheless continue to grasp after a ground because we have not relinquished the deep-seated reflex to grasp that lies at the root of objectivism. This reflex is so strong that the absence of a solid ground is immediately reified into the objectivist abyss. This act of reification performed by the grasping mind is the root of nihilism. The mode of repudiation or denial that is characteristic of nihilism is actually a very subtle and refined form of objectivism: the mere absence of an objective ground is reified into an objective groundless-ness that might continue to serve as an ultimate reference point. Thus although we have been speaking of objectivism and nihilism as op-posed extremes with differing consequences, they ultimately share a common basis in the grasping mind.

An appreciation of the common source of objectivism and nihilism lies at the heart of the philosophy and practice of the middle way in Buddhism. For this reason, we are simply misinformed when we as-sume that concern with nihilism is a modern phenomenon of Greco-European origin. To appreciate the resources offered by these other traditions, however, we must not lose sight of the specificity of our present situation. Whereas in Buddhism, as anywhere else, there is always the danger of individuals experiencing nihilism (losing heart, as it is called in Buddhism) or of commentators straying into nihilistic errors of interpretation, nihilism has never become full blown or embodied in societal institutions.

Today nihilism is a tangible issue not only for our Western culture but for the planet as a whole. And yet as we have seen throughout this book, the groundlessness of the middle way in Mahayana Bud-dhism offers considerable resources for human experience in our present scientific culture. The mere recognition of this fact should indicate that the imaginative geography of "West" and "East" is no longer appropriate for the tasks we face today. Although we can begin from the premises and concerns of our own tradition, we need no longer proceed in ignorance of other traditions, especially of those that continually strived to distinguish rigorously between the ground-lessness of nihilism and the groundlessness of the middle way.

Unlike Richard Rorty, then, we are not inspired in our attempt to face the issue of groundlessness and nihilism by the ideal of simply "continuing the conversation of the West."[1] Instead, our project throughout this book owes far more to Martin Heidegger's invocation of "planetary thinking." As Heidegger wrote in *The Question of Being*,

> We are obliged not to give up the effort to practice planetary thinking along a stretch of the road, be it ever so short. Here too no prophetic talents and demeanor are needed to realize that there are in store for planetary building encounters for which the participants are by no means equal today. This is equally true of the European and of the East Asiatic languages and, above all, for the area of a possible conversation between them. Neither one of the two is able by itself to open up this area and to establish it.[2]

Our guiding metaphor is that a path exists only in walking, and our conviction has been that as a first step we must face the issue of groundlessness in our scientific culture and learn to embody that groundlessness in the openness of sunyata. One of the central figures of twentieth-century Japanese philosophy, Nishitani Keiji, has in fact made precisely this claim.[3] Nishitani is exemplary for us because he was not only raised and personally immersed in the Zen tradition of mindfulness/awareness but was also one of Heidegger's students and so is thoroughly familiar with European thought in general and Heidegger's invocation of planetary thinking in particular. Nishitani's endeavor to develop a truly planetary form of philosophical yet em-bodied, progressive reflection is impressive. Let us pause to examine a few of the essential points of his thinking.

Nishitani Keiji

In our discussion of the Cartesian anxiety, we saw that there is an oscillation between objectivism and subjectivism that is linked to the concept of representation. Thus representation can be construed ei-ther as the "projection" (subjectivism) or "recovery" (objectivism) of the world. (Usually, of course, both aspects of representation are incorporated in accounts of perception and cognition.)

For Nishitani, this oscillation between subjectivism and objectivism arises for any philosophical stance that is based on what he calls "the field of consciousness." With this phrase Nishitani refers to the philosophical construal of the world as an objective or pregiven realm and of the self as a pregiven knowing subject that somehow achieves contact with this pregiven world. Since consciousness is here understood as subjectivity, the problem arises of how to link consciousness with the supposedly objective realm in which it is situated. As we have already discussed, however, the subject cannot step outside of its representations to behold the pregiven world as it really is in itself. Therefore given this basically Cartesian stance, the objective becomes what is represented as such by the subject. In Nishitani's words, "The mode of being which is said to have rid itself of its relationship to the subjective has simply been constituted through a covert inclusion of a relationship to the subjective, and so cannot, after all, escape the charge of constituting a mode of being defined through its appearance *to us.*"[4]

When the notion of objectivity becomes problematic in this way, so too does the notion of subjectivity. If everything is ultimately specified through its appearance to us, then so is the knowing subject. Since the subject can represent itself to itself, it becomes an object for representation but is different from all other objects. Thus in the end the self becomes both an objectified subject and a subjectified object. This predicament discloses the shiftiness, the instability of the entire subjective/objective polarity.

Nishitani's next move, however, displays the deep influence of the Buddhist philosophical tradition and mindfulness/awareness practice on his thinking. He argues that to realize the fundamental instability or groundlessness of the subjective/objective dualism is in a sense to slip out of the "field of consciousness." We do not "overcome" or "step out" of this dualism as if we knew in advance where we are going, but we do see the arbitrariness and futility of going back and forth between the poles of a fundamentally groundless opposition. Instead our concern shifts to the very disclosure of this groundlessness. Nishitani then follows the pragmatic intention of mindfulness/ awareness by emphasizing the existential role that this disclosure plays. The realization that we do not stand on solid ground, that things incessantly arise and pass away without our being able to pin them down to a stable objective or subjective ground, affects our very life and being. Within this existential context, we can be said to *realize* groundlessness not only in the sense of *understanding* but also in the sense of *actualization*: human life or existence turns into a question, doubt, or uncertainty.

In Zen Buddhism, the Japanese adaptation of mindfulness/awareness in which Nishitani was raised, this uncertainty is called the "Great Doubt." This doubt is not about any particular matter but is rather the basic uncertainty that arises from the disclosure of groundlessness. Unlike the hyperbolic and hypothetical doubt of Descartes, which is merely entertained by the subject on the field of consciousness, the Great Doubt points to the impermanence of existence itself and so marks an existential transformation within human experience. This transformation consists of a conversion away from the subjective/objective standpoint to what is called in the English translation of Nishitani's work the "field of nihility." *Nihility* is a term used to refer to groundlessness in relation to the subjective/objective polarity; it is a relative, negative notion of groundlessness that Nishitani wishes to distinguish from the groundlessness of the middle way.

Nishitani distinguishes between these two kinds of groundlessness because his fundamental point is that European thought in its largely successful critique of objectivism has become trapped in nihilism. Here Nishitani's assessment of our situation actually follows Nietzsche's. As we mentioned in chapter 6, nihilism arises for Nietzsche when we realize that our most cherished beliefs are untenable and yet we are incapable of living without them. Nietzsche devoted considerable attention to the manifestation of nihilism in our discovery that we do not stand on solid ground, that what we take to be an absolute reference point is really an interpretation foisted on an ever-shifting impersonal process. His famous aphorism announcing "the death of God" is a dramatic statement of this collapse of fixed reference points. Nietzsche also understood nihilism to be rooted in our craving for a ground, in our continual search for some ultimate reference point, even when we realize that none can be found: "What does nihilism mean? That the highest values devaluate themselves. The aim is lacking; 'why' finds no answer."[5] The philosophical challenge that Nietzsche faced, which has come to characterize the task of postmodern thought, is to lay down a path of thinking and practice that gives up foundations without transforming itself into a search for new foundations.[6] Nietzsche's attempt is well known: he tried to undercut nihilism by affirming groundlessness through his notions of eternal return and the will to power.

Nishitani deeply admires Nietzsche's attempt but claims that it actually perpetuates the nihilistic predicament by not letting go of the grasping mind that lies at the souce of both objectivism and nihlism. Nishitani's argument is that nihilism cannot be overcome by assimilating groundlessness to a notion of the *will*—no matter how decentered and impersonal. Nishitani's diagnosis is even more radical than Nietzsche's, for he claims that the real problem with Western nihilism is that it is halfhearted: it does not consistently follow through its own inner logic and motivation and so stops short of transforming its partial realization of groundlessness into the philosophical and experiential possiblities of sunyata. The reason why Western nihilism stops short is that Western thought in general has no tradition that works with cognition and lived experience in a direct and pragmatic way. (The one possible exception is psychoanalysis, but in most of its current manifestations it has been unable to confront the basic contradictions in our experience of the self or to offer a transformative reembodiment.) Indeed, our scientific culture has only just begun to consider the possibility of pragmatic and progressive approaches to experience that would enable us to learn to transform our deep-seated and emotional grasping after a ground. Without such a pragmatic approach to the transformation of experience in everyday life—especially within our developing scientific culture—human existence will remain confined to the undecidable choice between objectivism and nihilism.

We should note that Nishitani's point when he claims that Western nihilism stops short of the groundlessness of the middle way is not that we should adopt Buddhism in the sense of a particular tradition with various cultural trappings. It is, rather, that we must achieve an understanding of groundlessness as a middle way by working from our own cultural premises. These premises are largely determined by science, for we live in a scientific culture. We have therefore chosen to follow Nishitani's lead by building a bridge between cognitive science and mindfulness/awareness as a specific practice that embodies an open-ended approach to experience. Furthermore, since we cannot embody groundlessness in a scientific culture without reconceptualizing science itself as beyond the need of foundations, we have followed through the inner logic of research in cognitive science to develop the enactive approach. This approach should serve to demonstrate that a commitment to science need not include as a premise a commitment to objectivism or to subjectivism.

Objectivist science, by its very ideals as well as its historical context in our society, has maintained a role of ethical neutrality. This neutrality has been increasingly challenged in the social discourse of our time. The need for planetary thinking behooves us to consider groundlessness, whether evoked by cognitive science or experience, in its full light in the total human context. Is it not the self that has been considered the bearer of moral and ethical potency? If we challenge the idea of such a self, what have we loosed on the world? Such a concern, we feel, is the result of the failure in Western discourse to analyze the self and its product, self-interest, with experiential acumen. In contrast, the ethical dimension of ego and egolessness are at the very heart of the Buddhist tradition. We turn now to take up, as our final consideration, the issue of what the mindfulness/awareness tradition might have to offer social science for a vision of human action at its best.

Ethics and Human Transformation

The View from Social Science
A parable called "The Tragedy of the Commons" haunts social research on ethical concerns.[7] The parable describes a situation in which a number of herdsmen graze their herds on a common pasturage. Each herdsman knows that it is in his self-interest to increase the size of his herd because, whereas each additional animal brings profit to him, the cost of grazing the animal and the damage done to the pasturage is shared by all the herdsmen. As a result, each of the herdsmen rationally increases his herd size until the commons is destroyed and, with it, all of the herds that grazed on it. The concern of the social scientist is how one can get a group of rationally self-interested herdsmen to cooperate in maintaining the vanishing commons.

This disarmingly disingenuous metaphor for our world situation embodies a long tradition of modern thought about the self and its relation to others, which may be called the economic view of the mind. The goal of the self is assumed to be profit—getting the most at least cost. The unconstrained economic man,[8] such as Hobbes's despot,[9] continues his acquisitions until there is nothing left for anyone else. Therefore, constraints are needed: overt social force, internalized socialization, subtle psychological mechanisms. A general theory called social exchange theory, widely used in social psychology, decision theory, sociology, economics, and political science, views all of human activity, individually and in groups, in terms of input and output calculations, paying and receiving. We believe that this implicit vision of motivation underlies not only social science but many contemporary people's views of their own action. Even altruism is defined in terms of an individual obtaining (psychological) utility from benefiting another.

Is such a view experientially validated? Practitioners in the mindfulness/awareness tradition, as they begin to become mindful, are often amazed to discover the extent of their egotism, the increasingly subtle levels at which they find themselves operating with just such a business-deal mentality. They are also led to question whether such a stance toward the world makes sense.

We believe that the view of the self as an economic man, which is the view the social sciences hold, is quite consonant with the unexamined view of our own motivation that we hold as ordinary, nonmindful people. Let us state that view clearly. The self is seen as a territory with boundaries. The goal of the self is to bring inside the boundaries all of the good things while paying out as few goods as possible and conversely to remove to the outside of the boundaries all of the bad things while letting in as little bad as possible. Since goods are scarce, each autonomous self is in competition with other selves to get them. Since cooperation between individuals and whole societies may be needed to get more goods, uneasy and unstable alliances are formed between autonomous selves. Some selves (altruists) and many selves in some roles (parents, teachers) may get (immaterial) goods by helping other selves, but they will become disappointed (even disillusioned) if those other selves do not reciprocate by being properly helped.

What does the mindfulness/awareness tradition or enactive cognitive science have to contribute to this portrait of self-interest?[10] The mindful, open-ended approach to experience reveals that moment by moment this so-called self occurs only in relation to the other. If I want praise, love, fame, or power, there has to be another (even if only a mental one) to praise, love, know about, or submit to me. If I want to obtain things, they have to be things that I don't already have. Even with respect to the desire for pleasure, the pleasure is something to which I am in a relation. Because self is always codependent with other (even at the gross level we are now discussing), the force of self-interest is always other-directed in the very same respect with which it is self-directed.

What, then, are people doing who appear so self-interested as opposed to other-interested? Mindfulness/awareness meditators suggest that those people are struggling, in a confused way, to maintain the sense of a separate self by engaging in self-referential relationships with the other. Whether I gain or lose, there can be a sense of I; if there is nothing to be gained or lost, I am groundless. If Hobbes's despot were actually to succeed in obtaining everything in the universe, he would have to find some other preoccupation quickly, or he would be in a woeful state: he would be unable to maintain his sense of himself. Of course, as we have seen with nihilism, one can always turn that groundlessness into a ground; then one can maintain oneself in relation to it by feeling despair.

We believe that this insight is important to the social sciences if they are to explain the egoistic behavior of individuals and groups. Even more important, however, is what the mindful, open-ended approach to experience has to contribute to the transformation of that egotism.

Compassion: Worlds without Ground

If planetary thinking requires that we embody the realization of groundlessness in a scientific culture, planetary building requires the embodiment of concern for the other with whom we enact a world. The tradition of mindfulness/awareness offers a path by which this may actually be brought about.

The mindfulness/awareness student first begins to see in a precise fashion what the mind is doing, its restless, perpetual grasping, moment to moment. This enables the student to cut some of the automaticity of his habitual patterns, which leads to further mindfulness, and he begins to realize that there is no self in any of his actual experience. This can be disturbing and offers the temptation to swing to the other extreme, producing moments of loss of heart. The philosophical flight into nihilism that we saw earlier in this chapter mirrors a psychological process: the reflex to grasp is so strong and deep seated that we reify the absence of a solid foundation into a solid absence or abyss.

As the student goes on, however, and his mind relaxes further into awareness, a sense of warmth and inclusiveness dawns. The street fighter mentality of watchful self-interest can be let go somewhat to be replaced by interest in others. We are already other-directed even at our most negative, and we already feel warmth toward some people, such as family and friends. The conscious realization of the sense of relatedness and the development of a more impartial sense of warmth are encouraged in the mindfulness/awareness tradition by various contemplative practices such as the generation of loving-kindness. It is said that the full realization of groundlessness (sunyata) cannot occur if there is no warmth.

For this reason, in the Mahayana tradition, which we have so far presented as being centrally concerned with groundlessness as sunyata, there is an equally central and complementary concern with groundlessness as compassion.[11] In fact, most of the traditional Mahayana presentations do not begin with groundlessness but rather with the cultivation of compassion for all sentient beings. Nagarjuna, for example, states in one of his works that the Mahayana teaching has "an essence of emptiness and compassion."[12] This statement is sometimes paraphrased by saying that emptiness (sunyata) is full of compassion (karuna).[13]

Thus sunyata, the loss of a fixed reference point or ground in either self, other, or a relationship between them, is said to be inseparable from compassion like the two sides of a coin or the two wings of a bird. Our natural impulse, in this view, is one of compassion, but it has been obscured by habits of ego-clinging like the sun obscured by a passing cloud.

This is by no means the end of the path, however. For some traditions, there is a further step to be made in understanding beyond the sunyata of codependent origination—that is, the sunyata of naturalness. Up to now, we have been talking about the contents of realization in primarily negative terms: *no*-self, ego*less*ness, *no* world, *non*duality, emptiness, ground*less*ness. In actual fact, the majority of the world's Buddhists do not speak of their deepest concerns in negative terms; these negatives are preliminaries—necessary to remove habitual patterns of grasping, unsurpassably important and precious, but nonetheless premlinaries—that are pointing toward the realization of a positively conceived state. The Western world—for example, Christianity—although pleased to engage in dialogue with the negating aspects of Buddhism (perhaps as a way of speaking to the nihilism in our own tradition), steadfastly (at times even self-consciously) tends to ignore the Buddhist positive.[14]

To be sure, the Buddhist positive is threatening. It is no ground whatsoever; it cannot be grasped as ground, reference point, or nest for a sense of ego. It does not exist—nor does it not exist.[15] It cannot be an object of mind or of the conceptualizing process; it cannot be seen, heard, or thought—thus the many traditional images for it: the sight of a blind man, a flower blooming in the sky. When the conceptual mind tries to grasp it, it finds nothing, and so it experiences it as emptiness. It can be known (and can only be known) directly. It is called Buddha nature, no mind, primordial mind, absolute bodhicitta, wisdom mind, warrior's mind, all goodness, great perfection, that which cannot be fabricated by mind, naturalness. It is not a hair's breadth different from the ordinary world; it is that very same ordinary, conditional, impermanent, painful, groundless world experienced (known) as the unconditional, supreme state. And the natural manifestation, the embodiment, of this state is compassion—unconditional, fearless, ruthless, spontaneous compassion. "When the reasoning mind no longer clings and grasps, . . . one awakens into the wisdom with which one was born, and compassionate energy arises without pretense."[16]

What do we mean by unconditional compassion? We need to backtrack and consider the development of compassion from the more mundane point of view of the student. The possibility for compassionate concern for others, which is present in all humans, is usually mixed with the sense of ego and so becomes confused with the need to satisfy one's own cravings for recognition and self-evaluation. The spontaneous compassion that arises when one is not caught in the habitual patterns—when one is not performing volitional actions out of karmic cause and effect—is not done with a sense of need for feedback from its recipient. It is the anxiety about feedback—the response of the other—that causes us tension and inhibition in our action. When action is done without the business-deal mentality, there can be relaxation. This is called supreme (or transcendental) generosity.[17]

If this seems abstract, the reader might try a brief exercise. We usually read books like this with some heavy-handed sense of purpose. Imagine for a moment that you are reading this solely in order to benefit others. Does that change the feeling tone of the task?

When discussing wisdom from the point of view of compassion, the Sanskrit term often used is *bodhicitta*, which has been variously translated as "enlightened mind," "the heart of the enlightened state of mind," or simply "awakened heart." Bodhicitta is said to have two aspects, one absolute and one relative. Absolute bodhicitta is the term applied to whatever state is considered ultimate or fundamental in a given Buddhist tradition—the experience of the groundlessness of sunyata or the (positively defined) sudden glimpse of the natural, awake state itself.[18] Relative bodhicitta is that fundamental warmth toward the phenomenal world that practitioners report arises from absolute experience and that manifests itself as concern for the welfare of others beyond merely naive compassion. As opposed to the order in which we have previously described these experiences, it is said that the development of a sense of unproblematical warmth toward the world leads to the experience of the flash of absolute bodhicitta.

Buddhist practitioners obviously do not realize any of these things (even mindfulness) all at once. They report that they catch glimpses that encourage them to make further efforts. One of the most important steps consists in developing compassion toward one's own grasping fixation on ego-self. The idea behind this attitude is that confronting one's own grasping tendencies is a friendly act toward oneself. As this friendliness develops, one's awareness and concern for those around one enlarges as well. It is at this point that one can begin to envision a more open-ended and nonegocentric compassion.

Another characteristic of the spontaneous compassion that does not arise out of the volitional action of habitual patterns is that it follows no rules. It is not derived from an axiomatic ethical system nor even from pragmatic moral injunctions. It is completely responsive to the needs of the particular situation. Nagarjuna conveys this attitude of responsiveness:

> Just as the grammarian makes one study grammar,
> A Buddha teaches according to the tolerance of his students;
> Some he urges to refrain from sins, others to do good,
> Some to rely on dualism, others on non-dualism;
> And to some he teaches the profound,
> The terrifying, the practice of enlightenment,
> Whose essence is emptiness that is compassion.[19]

Unrealized practioners, of course, cannot dispense with rules and moral injunctions. There are many ethical rules in Buddhism whose aim is to put the body and mind into a form that imitates as nearly as possible how genuine compassion might become manifest in that situation (just as the meditative sitting posture is said to be an imitation of enlightenment).

With respect to its situational specificity and its responsiveness, this view of nonegocentric compassion might seem similar to what has been discussed in certain recent psychoanalytic writings as "ethical know-how."[20] In the case of compassionate concern as generated in the context of mindfulness/awareness, this know-how could be said to be based in responsiveness to oneself and others as sentient beings without ego-selves who suffer because they grasp after ego-selves. And this attitude of responsiveness is in turn rooted in an ongoing concern: How can groundlessness be revealed ethically as nonegocentric compassion?

Compassionate action is also called skillful means (upaya) in Buddhism. Skillful means are inseparable from wisdom. It is interesting to consider the relationship of skillful means to ordinary skills such as learning to drive a car or learning to play the violin. Is ethical action (compassionate action) in Buddhism to be considered a skill—perhaps analogous to the Heidegger/Dreyfus account of ethical action as a non-rule-based, developed skill?[21] As we discussed at some length with respect to meditation practice, in some ways skillful means in Buddhism could be seen as similar to our notion of a skill: the student practices ("plants good seeds")—that is, avoids harmful actions, performs beneficial ones, meditates. Unlike an ordinary skill, however, in skillful means the ultimate effect of these practices is to remove all egocentric habits so that the practitioner can realize the wisdom state, and compassionate action can arise directly and spontaneously out of wisdom. It is as if one were born already knowing how to play the violin and had to practice with great exertion only to remove the habits that prevented one from displaying that virtuosity.

It should by now be obvious that the ethics of compassion has nothing to do with satisfying some pleasure principle. Fom the standpoint of mindfulness/awareness, it is fundamentally impossible to satisfy desires that are born within the grasping mind. A sense of unconditional well-being arises only through letting go of the grasping mind. There is, however, no reason for asceticism. Material and social goods are to be employed however the situation warrants. (The middle way between the extremes of asceticism and indulgence is actually the historically earliest sense in which the term middle way was employed in Buddhism.)

The results of the path of mindful, open-ended learning are profoundly transformative. Instead of being embodied (more accurately, reembodied moment after moment) out of struggle, habit, and sense of self, the goal is to become embodied out of compassion for the world.[22] The Tibetan tradition even talks about the five aggregates being transformed into the five wisdoms. Notice that this sense of transformation does not mean going away from the world—getting out of the five aggregates. The aggregates may be the constituents on which the inaccurate sense of self and world are based, but (more properly *and*) they are also the basis of wisdom. The means of transforming the aggregates into wisdom is knowledge, realizing the aggregates accurately—empty of any egoistic ground whatsoever yet filled with unconditional goodness (Buddha nature, etc.), intrinsically just as they are in themselves.

How can such an attitude of all encompassing, decentered, responsive, compassionate concern be fostered and embodied in our culture? It obviously cannot be created merely through norms and rationalistic injunctions. It must be developed and embodied through a discipline that facilitates letting go of ego-centered habits and enables compassion to become spontaneous and self-sustaining. The point is not that there is no need for normative rules in the relative world—clearly such rules are a necessity in any society. It is that unless such rules are informed by the wisdom that enables them to be dissolved in the demands of responsivity to the particularity and immediacy of lived situations, the rules will become sterile, scholastic hindrances to compassionate action rather than conduits for its manifestation.

Perhaps less obvious but even more strongly enjoined by the mindfulness/awareness tradition is that meditations and practices undertaken simply as self-improvement schemes will foster only egohood. Because of the strength of egocentric habitual conditioning, there is a constant tendency, as practitioners in all contemplative traditions are aware, to try to grasp, possess, and become proud of the slightest insight, glimpse of openness, or understanding. Unless such tendencies become part of the path of letting go that leads to compassion, then insights can actually do more harm than good. Buddhist teachers have often written that it is far better to remain as an ordinary person and believe in ultimate foundations than to cling to some remembered experience of groundlessnes without manifesting compassion.

Finally, talk alone will certainly not suffice to engender spontaneous nonegocentric concern. Even more than experiences of insight, words and concepts can be easily grasped at, taken as ground, and woven into a cloak of egohood. Teachers in all contemplative traditions warn against fixed views and concepts taken as reality. Indeed, our promulgations of the concept of enactive cogntive science give us some pause. We would surely not want to trade the relative humility of objectivism for the hubris of thinking that we construct our world. Better by far a straightforward cognitivist than a bloated and solipsistic enactivist.

We simply cannot overlook the need for some form of sustained, disciplined practice. This is not something that one can make up for oneself—any more than one can make up the history of Western science for oneself. Nothing will take its place; one cannot just do one form of science rather than another and think that one is gaining wisdom or becoming ethical. Individuals must personally discover and admit their own sense of ego in order to go beyond it. Although this happens at the individual level, it has implications for science and for society.

In Conclusion

Let us restate why we think ethics in the mindfulness/awareness tradition, and indeed, the mindfulness/awareness tradition itself, are so important to the modern world. There is a profound discovery of groundlessness in our culture—in science, in the humanities, in society, and in the uncertainties of people's daily lives. This is generally seen as something negative—by everyone from the prophets of our time to ordinary people struggling to find meaning in their lives. Taking groundlessness as negative, as a loss, leads to a sense of alienation, despair, loss of heart, and nihilism. The cure that is generally espoused in our culture is to find a new grounding (or return to older grounds). The mindfulness/awareness tradition points the way to a radically different resolution. In Buddhism, we have a case study showing that when groundlessness is embraced and followed through to its ultimate conclusions, the outcome is an unconditional sense of intrinsic goodness that manifests itself in the world as spontaneous compassion. We feel, therefore, that the solution for the sense of nihilistic alienation in our culture is not to try to find a new ground; it is to find a disciplined and genuine means to pursue groundlessness, to go further into groundlessness. Because of the preeminent place science occupies in our culture, science must be involved in this pursuit.

Although late-twentieth-century science repeatedly undermines our conviction in an ultimate ground, we nonetheless continue to seek one. We have laid down a path in both cognitive science and human experience that would lead us away from this dilemma. We repeat that this is not a merely philosophical dilemma; it is also ethical, religious, and political. Grasping can be expressed not only individually as fixation on ego-self but also collectively as fixation on racial or tribal self-identity, as well as grasping for a ground as the territory that separates one group of people from another or that one group would appropriate as its own. The idolatry of supposing not only that there is a ground but that one can appropriate it as one's own acknowledges the other only in a purely negative, exclusionary way. The realization of groundlessness as nonegocentric responsiveness, however, requires that we acknowledge the other with whom we dependently cooriginate. If our task in the years ahead, as we believe, is to build and dwell in a planetary world, then we must learn to uproot and release the grasping tendency, especially in its collective manifestations.

When we widen our horizon to include transformative approaches to experience, especially those concerned not with escape from the world or the discovery of some hidden, true self but with releasing the everyday world from the clutches of the grasping mind and its desire for an absolute ground, we gain a sense of perspective on the world that might be brought forth by learning to embody groundlessness as compassion in a scientific culture. Since we have been most affected by the Buddhist tradition and its approach to experience through mindfulness/awareness, we were naturally led to rely on this tradition in relation to the task of scientific and planetary building. Science is already deeply embedded in our culture. Buddhism from all the world's cultures is now taking root and beginning to develop in the West. When these two planetary forces, science and Buddhism, come genuinely together, what might not happen? At the very least, the journey of Buddhism to the West provides some of the resources we need to pursue consistently our own cultural and scientific premises to the point where we no longer need and desire foundations and so can take up the further tasks of building and dwelling in worlds without ground.

Appendix A
Meditation Terminology

Shamatha (Sanscrit) *shine* (Tibetan)   Meditation for stilling and calming the mind. Traditionally, a concentration technique. It is rarely practiced in its most pure, radical form.

Vipassana (Pali)   The meditation technique practiced today in the Theravada tradition of Buddhism. Its purpose is both to calm the mind and arouse insight. The general technique is for the mind to remain mindfully with its object, whatever that object may be. There are many specific techniques.

Vispashyana (Sanscrit) *Lhagthong* (Tibetan)   Insight. The term is used in at least two major senses:

> 1. Specific techniques used within meditation for examining the calmed mind to obtain insight into its nature. For example, one might be directed to investigate the point of the arising, dwelling, and vanishing of one's thoughts.
> 2. The panoramic awareness in meditation or daily life that enables the practitioner to see with a sense of mature wisdom whatever is occurring.

Shamatha/vispashyana (Sanscrit)   A variety of techniques in which the functions of calming the mind and obtaining insight are combined.

Shikan taza (Japanese)   Just sitting. No technique. Somewhat equivalent to the second sense of vispashyana.

The reader should note that various modern schools of Buddhism refer to similar techniques by different terms and different techniques by the same term, so one cannot tell from terminology alone what meditation is being practiced.

A bibliography for meditation techniques is provided in appendix C. To practice meditation, one should obtain the guidance of a qualified teacher.

Appendix B
Categories of Experiential Events Used in Mindfulness/Awareness[1]

The Five Aggregates (*skandhas*)

1. Forms (*rupa*)
2. Feelings/sensations (*vedana*)
3. Perceptions (discernments)/impulses (*samjña*)
4. Dispositional formations (*samskara*)
5. Consciousnesses (*vijñana*)

The Twelve-fold Cycle of Dependent Origination (*pratityasamutpada*)

1. Ignorance (*avidya*)
2. Dispositional formations (the fourth aggregate)
3. Consciousness (the fifth aggregate)
4. The Psychophysical Complex (*nama-rupa*)
5. The Six Senses (*sad-ayatana*)
6. Contact (*sparsa*)
7. Feeling (the second aggregate)
8. Craving (*trsna*)
9. Grasping (*upadana*)
10. Becoming (*bhava*)
11. Birth (*jati*)
12. Decay and death (*jara-marana*)

The Processes of Mind (*citta/caitta*)

A. Consciousness (the fifth aggregate)

1. Visual consciousness
2. Auditory consciousness
3. Olfactory consciousness

4. Gustatory consciousness
5. Tactile consciousness
6. Mental consciousness

B. Mental factors (the fourth aggregate, here treated as including the second and third aggregates)

Five Ever-present Mental Factors:
1. Contact (the sixth motif in situational patterning)
2. Feeling (the second aggregate)
3. Perception/Discernment (the third aggregate)
4. Intention (*cetana*)
5. Attention (*manas*)

Five Object-ascertaining Factors:
1. Interest (*chandra*)
2. Intensified interest (*adhimoksa*)
3. Inspection/mindfulness (*smrti*)
4. Intense concentration (*samadhi*)
5. Insight/discrimative wisdom (*prajña*)

Eleven Positive Mental Factors:
1. Confidence-trust (*sraddha*)
2. Self-respect (*hri*)
3. Consideration for others (*apatrapya*)
4. Nonattachment (*alobha*)
5. Nonhatred (*advesa*)
6. Nondeludedness (*amoha*)
7. Diligence (*virya*)
8. Alertness (*prasrabdhi*)
9. Concern (*apramada*)
10. Equanimity (*apeksa*)
11. Nonviolence (*ahimsa*)

Six Basic Unwholesome Emotions
1. Attachment (*raga*)
2. Anger (*pratigha*)
3. Arrogance (*mana*)
4. Ignorance (the first motif of situational patterning)
5. Indecision (*vicikitsa*)
6. Opinionatedness (*drsti*)

Twenty Derivative Unwholesome Factors
1. Indignation (*krodha*)
2. Resentment (*upanaha*)
3. Slyness concealment (*mraksa*)
4. Spite (*pradasa*)
5. Jealousy (*irsya*)
6. Avarice (*matsarya*)
7. Deceit (*maya*)
8. Dishonesty (*sathya*)
9. Mental inflation (*mada*)
10. Malice (*vihimsa*)
11. Shamelessness (*ahri*)
12. Inconsideration for others (*anapatrapya*)
13. Gloominess/dullness (*styana*)
14. Restlessness (*auddhatya*)
15. Lack of trust (*asraddhya*)
16. Laziness (*kausidya*)
17. Unconcern (*pramada*)
18. Forgetfulness (*musitasmritita*)
19. Inattentiveness (*viksepa*)
20. Nondiscernment (*asamprajā*)

Four Variable or Indeterminate Factors
1. Drowsiness (*middha*)
2. Worry (*kaukrtya*)
3. Reflection (*vitarka*)
4. Investigation/analysis (*vicara*)

Appendix C

Works on Buddhism and

Mindfulness/Awareness

The following works were chosen to represent a minimal sample of the major living Buddhist traditions of mindfulness/awareness meditation.

Therevada

(One of the original eighteen schools of Buddhism, still prevalent today in Southeast Asia)

Buddhaghosa, B. 1976. *The Path of Purification* (Visuddhimagga). 2 vols. Boston: Shambhala.

Goldstein, J., and J. Kornfield. 1987. *Seeking the Heart of Wisdom: The Path of Insight Meditation*. Boston: Shambhala. This work is Vipassana but not strictly Theravada.

Kornfield, J. 1977. *Living Buddhist Masters*. Santa Cruz: Unity Press.

Narada, M. T., trans. 1975. *A Manual of Abhidhamma (Abhidammattha Sangaha)*. Kandy, Sri Lanka: Buddhist Publication Society.

Silandanda, U. 1990. *The Four Foundations of Mindfulness.* Boston: Wisdom Publications.

Thera, N. 1962. *The Heart of Buddhist Meditation*. New York: Samuel Weiser.

Mahayana and Zen

(Mahayana Buddhism originated in India roughly five hundred years after the Buddha's death. It is the form that spread to China, Korea, and Japan.)

Transitional to Mahayana: Vasubhandhu. 1923. *L' Abdhidharmakosa de Vasubandhu*, 6 Vols. Trans. Louis de La Vallée. Paris and Louvain: Institut Belges des Hautes Etudes Chinoises. Reprinted Paris: Guether 1971.

Vietnamese: Nhat Hanh, T. 1975. *The Miracle of Mindfulness: A Manual on Meditation.* Boston: Beacon Press.

Chinese: Sheng-Yan, M. 1982. *Getting the Buddha Mind.* Elmhurst, N.Y.: Dharma Drum Publications.

Korean: Sahn, S. *Bone of Space.* 1982. San Francisco: Four Seasons Foundation.

Japanese: Suzuki, S. 1970. *Zen Mind, Beginner's Mind.* New York: Weatherhill.

Vajrayana

(Vajrayana is the form of Buddhism indiginous to Tibet. There are four major lineages: Kagyu, Nyingma, Gelugpa, and Sakya. We list at least one reference from each.)

Dorje, W. 1979. *Mahmudra: Eliminating the Darkness of Ignorance.* Dharamsala, India: Library of Tibetan Works and Archives.

Kalu, K. D. C. 1986. *The Dharma.* Buffalo: State University Press of New York.

Khapa, T. 1978. *Calming the Mind and Discerning the Real: Buddhist Meditation and the Middle View.* New York: Columbia University Press.

Khyentse, D. 1988. *The Wish-Fulfilling Jewel.* Boston: Shambhala.

Trizin, K. S. 1986. Parting from the four clingings. In *Essence of Buddhism: Teachings at Tibet House.* New Delhi: Tibet House.

Trungpa, C. 1973. *Cutting Through Spiritual Materialism.* Boston: Shambhala.

Trungpa, C. 1976. *The Myth of Freedom.* Boston: Shambhala.

Trungpa, C. 1981. *Glimpses of Abhidharma.* Boulder: Prajna Press.

Notes

Introduction

1. We are thinking particularly of Merleau-Ponty's early works: *The Structure of Behavior* and *Phenomenology of Perception*.
2. See, for example, Foucault, *The Order of Things*; Derrida, *Speech and Phenomena*; Bourdieu, *The Logic of Practice*.
3. Dreyfus, *What Computers Can't Do*.
4. Winograd and Flores, *Understanding Computers and Cognition*.
5. Globus, *Dream Life, Wake Life*; Globus, Heidegger and cognitive science; Globus, Derrida and connectionism; Globus, Deconstructing the Chinese room.
6. Haugeland, The nature and plausibility of cognitivism.
7. Sudnow, *Ways of the Hand*.
8. The key works here are those of Jaspers, *Allgemeine psychopathologie*, and Binswanger, *Zur phänomenologischen Anthrhopologie*. For a recent review of the state of the art from a Continental perspective, see Jonckheere, *Phénomenologie et analyse existentielle*. For representative works from this school in the Anglo-American world see for example: Lecky, *Self-consistency*; Rogers, *On Becoming a Person*; Snygg and Combs, *Individual Behavior*.
9. Hofstadter and Dennett, *The Mind's Eye*; Turkle, *The Second Self*.
10. Jackendoff, *Consciousness and the Computational Mind*.

Chapter 1

1. Merleau-Ponty, *Phenomenology of Perception*, x–xi.
2. Ibid., 430.
3. For an introductory historical account see Gardner, *The Mind's New Science*. For a textbook presentation see Stillings et al., *Cognitive Science*.
4. This designation is justified by Haugeland, The nature and plausibility of cognitivism. Sometimes cognitivism is described as the "symbolic paradigm" or the "computational approach." We take these designations as synonyms for our purposes here.
5. See Goodman, *Ways of Worldmaking*.
6. See Rorty, *Philosophy and the Mirror of Nature*.
7. This notion of a *background* is a well-developed philosophical idea due especially to Heidegger, *Being and Time*. See sections 29, 31, 58, 68. We shall return to this notion in various ways throughout the book rather than expand on it here.
8. Taylor, The significance of significance.
9. Dennett, Toward a cognitive theory of consciousness.

10. See Stich, *From Folk Psychology to Cognitive Science;* Churchland, *Scientific Realism and the Plasticity of Mind;* Churchland, *Neurophilosophy.* See also Lyons, *The Disappearance of Instrospection.*

11. See H. Dreyfus, *What Computers Can't Do;* C. Taylor, The significance of significance. Dreyfus seems to have modified his stance when it comes to recent connectionism; see his essay with S. Dreyfus, Making a mind versus modeling the brain.

Chapter 2

1. Merleau-Ponty, *The Structure of Behavior.*

2. Brentano, *Psychology from an Empirical Standpoint,* 88.

3. Husserl, *Ideas.*

4. This problem is one of the themes of Husserl's *Cartesian Meditations.*

5. Husserl, *The Crisis of European Sciences and Transcendental Phenomenology.*

6. See David Carr's introduction to Husserl, *The Crisis,* xxxix.

7. See H. Dreyfus's introduction to H. Dreyfus, *Husserl.*

8. Thus Husserl exemplifies one of the "doubles" or ambiguities at the heart of the human sciences. See Dreyfus and Rabinow, *Michel Foucault,* 35–36.

9. See Dreyfus and Rabinow, *Michel Foucault,* 32–34; and the discussion of Merleau-Ponty in Descombes, *Modern French Philosophy.*

10. Fodor, The present status of the innateness controversy, 298.

11. The work of Nagarjuna will be discussed at length in chapter 10.

12. For a recent study of the ethnocentrism in Western philosophy from an insider's perspective see Pol-Droit, *L'amnesie philosophique.* For an extensive recent study of non-Western thought, see Loy, *Non-Duality.*

13. The word *mindfulness* has recently been used in a non-Buddhist and nonmeditative sense by the psychologist Ellen Langer in her book *Mindfulness.* The basic Buddhist meaning of mindfulness is simply to be present with one's experience. Langer uses the word to refer to the human ability to be thoughtful, rather than automatic, about one's experience and actions, and to be cognizant of alternative modes of construal of situations. From the Buddhist point of view, what Langer is describing is not mindfulness but rather, perhaps, being in the "human realm." It is only in human states of mind that one can reflect on one's experience and consider alternatives. Other states of mind, such as intense aggression (hell realm) or stupidity (animal realm) are too habitually automatic to allow reflection. But just because one is in the human realm doesn't mean that one is actually mindful in the Buddhist sense of being present.

14. See Rosch, *The Original Psychology.*

15. Our linguistic intuitions about the use of the word *meditation* were reinforced by a content analysis of 189 U. C. Berkeley students' descriptions of their understanding of the concept of meditation written prior to their taking a class in Buddhist psychology.

16. For works on meditation see appendix C.

17. Cf. Thurman, *The Holy Teaching of Vimalakirti,* 161: "The grasping mind cannot grasp its ultimate inability to grasp; it can only cultivate its tolerance of that inability."

18. Nagel, *The View from Nowhere.*

19. There were also more formal discussions of the mind-body issue in terms of causal relationships between transitory events. See chapters 4, 6, and 10 and Griffiths, *On Being Mindless*.

20. To wed the spiritual-evolution theory of Sri Aurobindo to the mindfulness/awareness tradition as is done in Wilber, Engler, and Brown, *Transformations of Consciousness*, we feel seriously misrepresents the mindfulness/awareness tradition.

21. See, for example, the introductory discussion in Churchland, *Matter and Consciousness*, and the discussion of various positions in the second part of Churchland, *Neurophilosophy*.

22. See Yuasa, *The Body*, 18.

23. See Rorty, *Consequences of Pragmatism*; Margolis, *Pragmatism without Foundations*. See our discussion in chapter 10.

Chapter 3

1. This section owes much to the recent work on the neglected history of early cybernetics, self-organization, and cognition published in the *Cahiers de la Centre de Recherche en Epistémologie Appliqué*, 7–9 (Paris, France). The only other useful source is Heims, *John von Neumann and Norbert Wiener*. The recent book by Gardner, *The Mind's New Science*, discusses this period only rather briefly.

2. The best source for this work is the often-cited Macy Conferences, published by the Josiah Macy Jr. Foundation as *Cybernetics*.

3. McCulloch and Pitts, A logical calculus of ideas immanent in nervous activity.

4. For an interesting perspective on this historical/conceptual moment see Hodges, *Alan Turing*.

5. McCulloch, *Embodiments of Mind*.

6. See Gardner, *The Mind's New Science*, chapter 5, for this period.

7. See Newell, Physical symbol systems; Newell and Simon, Computer science as empirical inquiry; Pylyshyn, *Computation and Cognition*.

8. The irreducibility of the semantic level is actually the subject of some dispute among cognitivists. See Stich, *From Folk Psychology to Cognitive Science*; Fodor, *Psychosemantics*.

9. See Fodor, Special sciences; Fodor, Computation and reduction.

10. For an argument from within analytic philosophy, see Putnam, Computational psychology and interpretation theory. For an enactivist critique of this idea, see Winograd and Flores, *Understanding Computers and Cognition*. This problem is also the basis of Searle's ingenious and now famous "Chinese Room" thought experiment in Searle, Minds, brains, and programs.

11. This is the opening line of a popular textbook in neuroscience: "The brain is an unresting assembly of cells that continually receives information, elaborates and perceives it, and makes decisions." Kuffler and Nichols, *From Neuron to Brain*, 3.

12. For a recent account of this widely known work see Hubel, *Eye, Brain and Mind*.

13. Barlow, Single units and sensation.

14. See, for example, Marr's criticism of Barlow in Marr, *Vision*.

15. Segal, *Imagery*.

16. Kosslyn, *Image and Mind*.

17. Shepard and Metzler, Mental rotation of three dimensional objects.

18. Brown, *A First Language*.
19. Miller, Galanter, and Pribram, *Plans and the Structure of Behavior*; Schank and Abelson, *Scripts, Plans, Goals and Understanding*.
20. Schank and Abelson, *Scripts, Plans, Goals and Understanding*.
21. Kahneman, Slovic, and Tversky, *Judgement Under Uncertainty*; Nisbett and Ross, *Human Inference*.
22. See Pylyshyn, *Computation and Cognition*, chapter 8. For discussions about the controversies surrounding imagery, see Gardner, *The Mind's New Science*, chapter 11; Stillings, et al., *Cognitive Science*, 36–48.
23. Kosslyn, The medium and the message in mental imagery.
24. Palmer, *Visual Information Processing*.
25. H. Dreyfus, Alternative philosophical conceptualizations of psychpathology.
26. Freud, The unconscious, quoted in Dreyfus, Alternative philosophical conceptualizations of psychopathology.
27. Dolard and Miller, *Personality and Psychotherapy*.
28. Erdelyi, *Psychoanalysis*.
29. Fodor, *The Modularity of Mind*.
30. Hofstadter and Dennett, *The Mind's Eye*, 12.
31. Ibid., 13.
32. See Dennett, Toward a cognitive theory of consciousness; Dennett, Artificial intelligence as philosophy and psychology.
33. Pylyshyn, *Computation and Cognition*, 265.
34. Dennett, *Elbow Room*, 74–75.
35. See Fodor, *The Language of Thought*, 52.
36. Jackendoff, *Consciousness and the Computational Mind*. All page references in the next section are to this work.

Chapter 4

1. Hume, *A Treatise of Human Nature*, I, VI, iv.
2. Kant, *Critique of Pure Reason*, 136.
3. Epstein, The self-concept.
4. Gyamtso, *Progressive Stages of Meditation on Emptiness*, 20–21.
5. The categories that we are about to present are ubiquitous in Buddhist teachings, both written and oral. See appendixes A, B, and C, and Narada, *A Manual of Abhidhamma (Abhidammattha Sangaha)*; Buddhaghosa, *The Path of Purification* (Visuddhimagga); Vasubhandhu, *L'Abhidharmakosa de Vasubandhu*; Trungpa, *Glimpses of Abhidharma*; Kalu, *The Dharma*.
6. It is often said that in Buddhist "philosophy" there is little interest in "ontology" or that ontology and epistemology are "not distinguished." This somewhat misses the point about what Buddhism is attempting to do and its orientation toward immediate, everyday experience. From the Buddhist point of view, ontology is simply a very strange category.
7. Translations of these terms unfortunately vary considerably. The Sanscrit terms are *rupa, vedana, samjna, samskara, and vijnana*. The third and fourth terms are particularly difficult to translate. Thus *samjna*, for which we use "perception(discernment)/impulse," has also been translated as "conceptualization," "discernment,"

"discrimination," "perception," and "recognition." *Samskara* is even more problematic, having been rendered as "compositional factors," "dispositions," "emotional creations," "formations," "mental constructions," "motivations," and "volitions." Since the basic idea behind this category is that of the mental tendencies that are formative of one's experiences, we have coined the term "dispositional formations."

8. Kalupahana, *Principles of Buddhist Psychology*, presents an interesting but idiosyncratic account of the psychophysical complex *(nama-rupa)* as the basic category of the Abhidharma. Both sides of the complex, the physical as well as the psychological, are defined in terms of experience: the basic experiential operation that defines the psychological is contact with concepts; that which defines the physical is contact with resistance (the meaning of *contact* in the Abhidharma will be discussed in chapter 6). Phenomenologists might say that the nature of each of these is *distinction*, that is, the emergence of something distinguishable from a background: in the physical modality, distinctions based on sensory resistance, in the psychological modality, distinctions based on concepts.

9. These are known as the *ayatanas*.

10. Philosophers will also be aware of just how tricky these problems can sometimes get. See, for example, the essays collected in Perry, *Personal Identity* and Rorty, *The Identitites of Persons*.

11. Rabten, *The Mind and its Functions*.

12. See Rosch, Proto-intentionality.

13. See Sajama and Kamppinen, *A Historical Introduction to Phenomenology*.

14. The realms are intrepreted both literally (one can be born into existence as a human, hell realm being, hungry ghost, animal, jealous god, or god) or psychologically (as states of mind varying in duration). Consciousness (vijnana) occurs only in some realm in which an emotional disposition (aggression, poverty, ignoring, etc.) generates the logic, color, and entrapment of the continuing enactment of self and world. See Freemantle, *The Tibetan Book of the Dead;* Trungpa, *Cutting Through Spiritual Materialism;* Trungpa, *The Myth of Freedom.*

15. Kant, *Critique of Pure Reason,* 136.

16. Gyamtso, *Progressive Stages of Meditation on Emptiness,* 32, our emphasis.

17. One might think to reverse the figure and ground of one's investigations and ask whether there are not gaps as well as discontinuities between the moments of arising of consciousness. This question touches a crucial difference among Buddhist schools. According to the Theravada Abhidhamma, thought moments are contiguous, even between one lifetime and the next. At the other extreme, there are schools which teach that there can be an absolute gap in the habitual thought process in which one can experience fully awakened mind. The research that we are about to describe can certainly *not* lay claim to relevance for that issue. In the Buddhist literature there are also mentions of the actual moments of time that it takes to switch from one moment to the next, which range anywhere from 13 to 100 milliseconds; see E Conze, *Buddhist Thought in India,* 282; this matter is also discussed by Hayward, *Shifting Worlds, Changing Minds,* chapter 12. This is the general kind of issue that we are going to investigate.

18. For a summary of this literature, see Varela et al., Perceptual framing and cortical alpha rhythm; Gho and Varela, Quantitative assesment of the dependency of the

visual temporal frame upon the alpha rhythm. See also Steriade and Deschenes, The thalamus as a neuronal oscillator; Pöppel, Time perception.

19. For a recent review on this fascinating theme see Llinás, The intrinsic electrophysiological properties of mammalian neurons.

20. Creutzfeld, Watanabe, and Lux, Relations between EEG phenomena and potentials of single cortical cells; Purpura, Functional studies of thalamic internuclear interactions; Jahnsen and Llinas, Ionic basis for the electroresponsiveness and oscillatory properties of guinea-pig thalamic neurones in vitro; Steriade and Deschenes, The thalamus as a neuronal oscillator.

21. Andersen and Andersson, *The Physiological Basis of Alpha Rhythm;* Aoli, McLachlan, and Gloor, Simultaneous recording of cortical and thalamic EEG and single neuron activity in the cat association system during spindles; Connor, Initiation of synchronized neuronal bursting in neocortex.

22. Gevins et al., Shadows of thought.

23. For instance the contemporary author C. Trungpa describes the aggregate in sequencelike terms in one book, *Glimpses of Abhidharma,* and as simultaneously appearing layers of experience in another book, *Mandala.*

24. For instance the classical textbook by Vasubhandu, *L' Abdhidharmakosa de Vasubandhu.*

25. In the last essay he wrote, Merleau-Ponty began by remarking, "La science manipule les choses et renonce à les habiter" ("Science manipulates things and gives up living in them.") See Merleau-Ponty, Eye and mind.

26. See Hayward, *Shifting Worlds, Changing Minds.*

Chapter 5

1. See chapter 3, note 1 for sources on these early years.

2. Rosenblatt, *Principles of Neurodynamics.*

3. For more on the complex early origins of self-organization ideas see Stengers, Les généalogies de l'auto-organisation.

4. Dennett, Computer models and the mind. For a different view of these historical issues see also Minsky and Papert, *Perceptrons,* prologue and epilogue to the 1987 revised edition.

5. The name was proposed in Feldman and Ballard, Connectionist models and their properties. For extensive discussion of current models see Rummelhart and McClelland, *Parallel Distributed Processing.*

6. The main idea here is due to Hopfield, Neural networks and physical systems with emergent computational abilities. See also Tank and Hopfield, Collective computation in neuronlike circuits.

7. There are many variants on these ideas. See Hinton, Sejnowsky, and Ackley, A learning algorithm for Boltzman machines; and Tolouse, Dehaene, and Changeux, *Proceedings of the National Academy of Sciences.*

8. For an extensive discussion of this point of view see Dumouchel and Dupuy, *L'Auto-Organisation.*

9. See for example, von Foerster, *Principles of Self-Organization.*

10. In the United States the Santa Fe Institute for the Study of Complex Systems, and the creation of a new journal, *Complex Systems,* are clear symptoms of this growing tendency. The reader is referred to these sources for more details.

11. An accesible introduction to the modern theory of dynamical systems is Abraham and Shaw, *Dynamics.* For less technical introductions see also Crutchfield et al., Chaos; Gleick, *Chaos.*

12. See Wolfram, Statistical mechanics of cellular automata; Wolfram, Cellular automata as models of complexity.

13. For a recent and representative survey see Rosenbaum, *Readings in Neurocomputing.*

14. The idea in its modern form is due to Rummelhart, Hinton, and Williams, in Rummelhart and McClelland, *Parallel Distributed Processing,* chapter 8.

15. See Sejnowski and Rosenbaum, NetTalk.

16. For an interesting collection of recent examples and discussions see Palm and Aersten, *Brain Theory.*

17. For the effects of bodily tilt, see Horn and Hill, Modifications of the receptive field of cells in the visual cortex occurring spontaneously and associated with bodily tilt. For the effects of auditory stimulation, see Fishman and Michael, Integration of auditory information in the cat's visual cortex; Morell, Visual system's view of acoustic space.

18. See Allman, Meizen, and McGuiness, *Annual Review of Neuroscience.*

19. Abeles, *Local Circuits.*

20. For more on this issue see Churchland and Sejnowski, Perspectives on cognitive neuroscience.

21. For a detailed examination of this for the case of binocular rivalry see Varela and Singer, Neuronal dynamics in the cortico-thalamic pathway as revealed through binocular rivalry.

22. Singer, Extraretinal influences in the geniculate.

23. Grossberg, *Studies in Mind and Brain.* For a recent update of the idea, see Carpenter and Grossberg, A massively parallel architecture for a self-organizing neural pattern recognition machine.

24. Smolensky, On the proper treatment of connectionism.

25. For the distinction between symbolic and emergent description and explanation in biological systems see Varela, *Principles of Biological Autonomy,* chapter 7; and more recently Oyama, *The Ontogeny of Information.*

26. See Hillis, Intelligence as an emergent behavior; Smolensky, On the proper treatment of connectionism. In a different vein, see Feldman, Neural representation of conceptual knowledge. Feldman proposes a middle ground between "punctuate" and distributed systems.

27. This position is extensively argued in Fodor and Pylyshyn, Connectionism and cognitive architecture. For a philosophical position in favor of connectionism, see H. Dreyfus and S. Dreyfus, Making a mind versus modeling the brain.

28. Fodor and Pylyshyn, Connectionism and cognitive architecture.

29. See Varela, Coutinho, and Dupire, Cognitive networks.

30. For two important examples, see Amitt, Neural networks counting chimes; Smolensky, Tensor product variable binding and the representation of symbolic structures in connectionist networks.

Chapter 6

1. Minsky, *The Society of Mind;* Papert, *Mindstorms.*
2. For specific examples and discussion see Minsky and Papert's prologue and epilogue to their new edition of *Perceptrons.*
3. For example, in their epilogue to the new edition of *Perceptrons,* they write, "How, then, could networks support symbolic forms of activities? We conjecture that, inside the brain, agencies with different jobs are usually constrained to communicate with one another only through *neurological* [our emphasis] bottlenecks (i.e., connections between relatively small numbers of units that are specialized to serve as symbolic recognizers and memorizers)." But if these bottlenecks are essential for symbolic activities, they would presumably have to exist for artificial minds too, thus it is not clear why they are neurological instead of being features of the abstract, cognitive architecture.
4. This idea has also been extensively explored, though in a somewhat different context, in Fodor, *The Modularity of Mind.*
5. Minsky, *The Society of Mind,* 44–45, 54, 97, 134, 184.
6. Jackendoff, *Consciousness and the Computational Mind,* 27.
7. Kuhn, *The Structure of Scientific Revolutions.*
8. Segal, *Introduction to the Work of Melanie Klein.*
9. Greenburg and Mitchel, *Object Relations in Psychoanalytic Theory.*
10. Horowitz, *Introduction to Psychodynamics.*
11. Turkle, Artifical intelligence and psychoanalysis.
12. Schafer, *A New Language for Psychoanalysis.*
13. Turkle, *Psychoanalytic Politics.*
14. For a striking example of the open-ended quality of the analytic journey, see Marie, *Que est-ce que la psychoanalyse;* Marie, *L'experience psychoanalytique.*
15. The references we have already given for the Abhidharma also supply information about codependent arising *(pratityasamutpada).* See chapter 4, note 5. Evocative presentations of the Wheel of Life are given in Trungpa, *Karma Seminar,* and Goodman, Situational patterning. The latter attempts the provocative task of translating the Wheel into phenomenological language; in the process, however, he markedly alters the original meaning.
16. See for example O'Flaherty, *Karma and Rebirth in Classical Indian Traditions;* Neufeldt, *Karma and Rebirth.*
17. Our discussion in this section draws on the following works: Conze, *Buddhist Thought in India;* Griffiths, *On Being Mindless;* Guenther, *Philosophy and Psychology in the Abhidharma;* Guenther, *From Reductionism to Creativity;* Guenther and Kawamura, *Mind in Buddhist Psychology;* Kalupahana, *The Principles of Buddhist Psychology;* Klein, *Knowledge and Liberation;* Rabten, *The Mind and its Functions;* Sopa and Hopkins, *Practice and Theory of Tibetan Buddhism;* Stcherbatski, *The Central Conception of Buddhism and the Meaning of the Word "Dharma";* Trungpa, *Glimpses of Abhidharma.*
18. The only complete translation of Vasubhandu, *L'Abhidharmakosa de Vasubhandu,* into a Western language is by Louis de La Vallée Poussin. There is no scholary consensus on the exact dates of Vasubandhu, and some scholars conjecture that there were actually two different philosophers named Vasubandhu.

19. Minsky, *The Society of Mind*, 19.
20. Guenther, *Philosophy and Psychology in the Abhidharma*.
21. Rabten, *The Mind and its Functions*, 52.
22. Trungpa, *The Myth of Freedom*.
23. Minsky, *The Society of Mind*, 39–40.
24. Ibid., 50.
25. Jackendoff, *Consciousness and the Computational Mind*, 300.
26. See Fodor, Observation reconsidered; Churchland, Perceptual plasticity and theoretical neutrality.
27. For studies of the implications of such a perspective see Yuasa, *The Body*; Wilber, Engler, and Brown, *Transformations of Consciousness*. From our point of view, however, the latter book has many problems. Meditation is presented largely as a matter of special "altered" states. See also chapter 2, note 20.
28. Globus, *Dream Life, Wake Life*.
29. Turkle, Artificial intelligence and psychoanalysis.
30. Nietzsche, *The Will to Power*, 9.
31. See Popper and Eccles, *The Self and its Brain*.
32. Penrose, *The Emperor's New Mind*.

Chapter 7

1. R. Rorty, *Philosophy and the Mirror of Nature*.
2. See Searle, *Intentionality*.
3. This conception of vision is, of course, due to David Marr. See Marr, *Vision*, especially the introduction. For a philosophical explication of the idea of information involved in the representationist approach, see Dretske, *Knowledge and the Flow of Information*.
4. See Quine, Epistemology naturalized; and the other essays collected in Kornblith, *Naturalizing Epistemology*.
5. See R. Rorty, *Philosophy and the Mirror of Nature*, 246.
6. Fodor, Fodor's guide to mental representations.
7. Minsky, *The Society of Mind*, 287.
8. Ibid., 288. The italics are Minsky's.
9. For a detailed discussion of this notion of operational closure, see Varela, *Principals of Biological Autonomy*.
10. See ibid.; Kelso and Kay, Information and control.
11. Bernstein, *Beyond Objectivism and Relativism*, part III.
12. Kant, *Critique of Pure Reason*, 257.
13. In his replies to Hobbes's objections, Descartes wrote, "I take the term idea to stand for whatever the mind directly perceives. . . . I employed this term because it was the term currently used by the Philosophers for the forms of perception of the Divine mind, though we can discern no imagery in God; besides I had no more suitable term." *The Philosophical Works of Descartes, Volume II*, 67–68.
14. See R. Rorty, *Philosophy and the Mirror of Nature*, chapter 1.
15. Minsky, *The Society of Mind*, 304.
16. Ibid.

Chapter 8

1. H. Dreyfus and S. Dreyfus, *Mind over Machine.*
2. See Winograd and Flores, *Understanding Computers and Cognition.* Our argument in this section owes a great deal to this work.
3. For an account of regularization theory, see Poggio, Torre, and Koch, Computational vision and regularization theory.
4. For a sample of discussions in AI about these themes, see the multiple reviews of Winograd and Flores, *Understanding Computers and Cognition,* in *Artifical Intelligence* 31 (1987): 213–261.
5. This point was first made by H. Dreyfus, *What Computers Can't Do.* For a more recent argument to this effect, see Putnam, Much ado about not very much.
6. See Heidegger, *Being and Time;* Gadamer, *Truth and Method.* For an introduction to hermeneutics see Palmer, *Hermeneutics.*
7. For references to phenomenology see chapter 2. In this connection, the work of M. Foucault is also essential. See Foucault, *The Order of Things;* Foucault, *Discipline and Punish.* For a critical discussion of Foucault in relation to both hermeneutics and phenomenology, see Dreyfus and Rabinow, *Michel Foucault.*
8. For an exception to this view of folk psychology, one that defends a "first-person" approach in which folk-psychology is not a "third-person" casual-explanatory theory, see Thornton, *Folk Psychology.*
9. Johnson, *The Body in the Mind,* 175.
10. Ibid., 14.
11. This model was first introduced in Varela, Structural coupling and the origin of meaning in a simple cellular automata.
12. For more details, see Varela, *Principles of Biological Autonomy.*
13. Hurvich and Jameson, An opponent-process theory of color vision. For more recent developments, see the articles by Hurvich and Jameson in Ottoson and Zeki, *Central and Peripheral Mechanisms of Colour Vision.*
14. The most recent demostrations are due to E. Land. See Land, The retinex theory of color vision; and for recent developments, Land, Recent advances in retinex theory and some implications for cortical computations. For earlier discussions, see Helson, Fundamental problems in color vision. I; Helson and Jeffers, Fundamental problems in color vision. II; Judd, Hue, saturation, and lightness of surface colors with chromatic illumination.
15. For a vivid demonstration of these two phenomena, see Brou et al., The colors of things.
16. This experiment belongs to the kind of phenomena made popular by E. Land. See Land, Experiments in color vision; Land, The retinex. The use of rotations of gray checkerboards, as described here, was first presented in Maturana, Uribe, and Frenck, A biological theory of relativistic color coding in the primate retina.
17. See Gouras and Zenner, Color vision.
18. Zeki, Colour coding in the cerebral cortex.
19. Kandinsky, *Concerning the Spiritual in Art,* 57. As quoted in Johnson, *The Body in the Mind,* 83–84.
20. Johnson, *The Body in the Mind.,* 84.

21. For an excellent recent review see DeYoe and Van Essen, Concurrent processing streams in monkey visual cortex.

22. Sacks and Wasserman, The case of the colorblind painter.

23. Ibid., 26.

24. Ibid., 33.

25. Maloney, *Computational Approaches to Color Constancy*; Maloney and Wandell, Color constancy; see also Gershon, *The Use of Color in Computational Vision*.

26. See Maloney, *Computational Approaches to Color Constancy*, 119. For a philosophical discussion, see Hilbert, *Color and Color Perception*; Matthen, Biological functions and perceptual content. For extensive discussion and criticism of this view, see Thompson, *Colour Vision*.

27. For detailed arguments, see Hardin, *Color for Philosophers*; Thompson, *Colour Vision*.

28. See Jameson and Hurvich, Essay concerning color constancy.

29. Gouras and Zenner, Color vision, 172.

30. Consider, for example, this passage from a well-known text by Gleason, *An Introduction to Descriptive Linguistics*, 4: "There is a continuous gradation of color from one end of the spectrum to the other. Yet an American describing it will list the hues as red, orange, yellow, green, blue, purple, or something of the kind. There is nothing inherent either in the spectrum or the human perception of it which would compel its division in this way."

31. Berlin and Kay, *Basic Color Terms*.

32. Ibid., 109.

33. E.R. Heider [Rosch], Universals in color naming and memory.

34. Brown and Lenneberg, A study in language and cognition; Lantz and Steffire, Language and cognition revisited; Steffire, Castillo Vales, and Morely, Language and cognition in yucatan.

35. Heider [Rosch], Universals in color naming and memory; Heider [Rosch], Linguistic Relativity; Rosch, On the internal structure of perceptual and semantic categories; Heider [Rosch] and Olivier, The structure of the color space in naming and memory for two languages.

36. Heider [Rosch], Focal color areas and the development of color names.

37. Lakoff, *Women, Fire and Dangerous Things*.

38. Kay and McDaniel, The linguistic significance of the meanings of basic color terms.

39. DeValois and Jacobs, Primate color vision.

40. Kay and Kempton, What is the Sapir-Whorf hypothesis?

41. As reported in Lakoff, *Women, Fire and Dangerous Things*, 29.

42. MacLaury, Color-category evolution and Shuswap yellow-with-green.

43. This conception of embodiment has been most emphasized in cognitive science by H. Dreyfus, *What Computers Can't Do*; Johnson, *The Body in the Mind*; and Lakoff, *Women, Fire, and Dangerous Things*.

44. See Kelso and Kay, Information and control.

45. Merleau-Ponty, *The Structure of Behavior*, 13.

46. Held and Hein, Adaptation of disarranged hand-eye coordination contingent upon re-afferent stimulation.

47. Bach y Rita, *Brain Mechanisms in Sensory Substitution*, as described in Livingstone, *Sensory Processing, Perception, and Behavior*.

48. Freeman, *Mass Action in the Nervous System*.

49. Freeman and Skarda, Spatial EEG patterns, nonlinear dynamics, and perception.

50. For a recent review see Bressler, The gamma wave; the work of Gray and Singer, Stimulus-specific neuronal oscillations in orientation columns in cat visual cortex, has been largely responsible for the wider acceptance of this hypothesis; for Hermissenda see Gelperin and Tank, Odour-modulated collective network oscillations of olfactory interneurons in a terrestrial mollusc; and for the results on the avian brain see Neuenschwander and Varela, Sensori-triggered and spontaneous oscillations in the avian brain.

51. It should also be noted that this fast dynamics is not restricted to sensorial trigger: the oscillations appear and disappear quickly and quite spontaneously in various places of the brain. This suggests that such fast dynamics involve all those subnetworks that give rise to the entire readiness-to-hand in the next moment. They involve not only sensory interpretation and motor action but also the entire gamut of cognitive expectations and emotional tonality, which are central to the shaping of a moment of action. Between breakdown these oscillations are the symptoms of (rapid) reciprocal cooperation and competition among distinct agents that are activated by the current situation, vying with each other for differing modes of interpretation for a coherent cognitive framework and readiness for action. On the basis of this fast dynamics, as in an evolutionary process, one neuronal ensemble (one cognitive subnetwork) finally becomes more prevalent and becomes the behavioral mode for the next cognitive moment. When we say "becomes prevalent," we do not mean a process of optimization but rather a process of consolidation out of a chaotic dynamic.

52. All of Piaget's books are relevant. We are particularly indebted to Piaget, *The Construction of Reality in the Child*.

53. See for example Bourne, Dominowski, and Loftus, *Cognitive Processes*.

54. E. Rosch et al., Basic objects in natural categories; Rosch, Principles of categorization; Rosch, Wittgenstein and categorization research in cognitve psychology; Mervis and Rosch, Categorization of natural objects.

55. Rosch et al., Basic objects in natural categories.

56. Johnson, *The Body in the Mind*.

57. Sweetzer, *Semantic Structure and Semantic Change*.

58. Lakoff, *Women, Fire and Dangerous Things*.

59. Lakoff, Cognitive semantics. This article provides a concise overview of Lakoff and Johnson's experientialist approach.

60. Berofski, *Making History*.

61. Merleau-Ponty, *Phenomenology of Perception*; Jaspers, *Allgemeine psychopathologie*; Binswanger, *Zur phänomenologischen Anthropologie*.

62. H. Dreyfus, Alternative philosophical conceptualizations of psychopathology.

63. This is reminiscent of the Buddhist view that consciousness is always born into a total realm. See chapter 4, note 12.

64. The classic statement is May, *Existential Psychoanalysis*.

65. Wilber, Engler, and Brown, *Transformations of Consciousness*; Wellwood, *Awakening the Heart*.

66. Marr, *Vision;* Poggio, Torre, and Koch, Computational vision and regularization theory.
67. Gibson, *The Ecological Approach to Visual Perception.*
68. Kornblith, *Naturalizing Epistemology.*
69. This tendency can occassionally be discerned in both Lakoff, *Women, Fire and Dangerous Things* and Johnson, *The Body in the Mind.*
70. For comparative discussions of color vision, see Jacobs, *Comparative Color Vision;* Nuboer, A comparative review on colour vision. For insect color vision, see Menzel, Spectral sensitivity and colour vision in invertebrates. For discussion in the context of cognitive science, see Thompson, Palacios, and Varela, Ways of coloring.
71. For tetrachromacy in fishes, see Harosi and Hashimoto, Ultraviolet visual pigment in a vertebrate; Neumeyer, *Das Farbensehen des Goldfisches.* For birds, see Jane and Bowmaker, Tetrachromatic colour vision in the duck; Burkhardt, UV vision; Palacios et al., Color mixing in the pigeon; Palacios and Varela, Color mixing in the pigeon.II.
72. These mechanisms have still not been studied with the detail that has been devoted to the those in the primate group. See Varela et al., The neurophysiology of avian color vision.
73. For extensive discussion of these and other implications of comparative color vision in a philosophical context, see Thompson, *Colour Vision;* and Thompson et al., Ways of coloring.

Chapter 9

1. See in particular Gould, Darwinism and the expansion of evolutionary theory; Gould and Lewontin, The spandrels of San Marco and the Panglossian paradigm. For more general discussion, see Sober, *The Nature of Selection;* Ho and Saunders, *Beyond Neo-Darwinism;* Endler, The newer synthesis? For a recent *defense* of neo-Darwinism in the face of these various challenges see Hecht and Hoffman, Why not neo-Darwinism? Piatelli-Palmarini, Evolution, selection, and cognition, explores similar themes, though in the context of a defense of cognitivism.
2. This term is from Sober, *The Nature of Selection.*
3. The idea of evolution as natural drift was first introduced in Maturana and Varela, *The Tree of Knowledge.* In this chapter we expand and modify this idea significantly in relation to its original presentation.
4. Geschwind and Galaburda, *Cerebral Lateralization.*
5. Gould and Eldredge, Punctuated equilibria.
6. Packard, An intrinsic model of adaptation.
7. For a concise comparison between these two extremes see Lambert and Hughes, Keywords and concepts in structuralist and functionalist biology.
8. For this topic see the articles in Goodwin, Holder, and Wyles, *Development and Evolution.*
9. de Beer, *Embryos and Ancestors,* 163.
10. Kauffman, Developmental constraints.
11. Crow and Kimura, *An Introduction to Population Genetics.*
12. Our discussion here owes much to Wake, Roth, and Wake, On the problem of stasis in organismal evolution.

13. Dawkins, *The Selfish Gene*.

14. Wynne-Edwards, *Animal Dispersion in Relation to Social Behaviour*.

15. Eldredge and Salthe, Hierarchy and evolution.

16. For a recent discussion see Brandon and Burian, *Genes, Organisms, and Populations*.

17. Lewontin, A natural selection.

18. An interesting example of this revisionist mood is the critical study of the classic example of industrial melanism in moths as a textbook case of natural selection. According to Lambert, Millar, and Hughes, On the classic case of natural selection, this example can be transformed into a classic study against neo-Darwinism by considering a substantial amount of ignored extant literature.

19. For a thorough and technical discussion of this point see Oster and Rocklin, Optimization models in evolutionary biology. For recent general discussion see Dupré, *The Latest on the Best*.

20. This analogy was first proposed in Edelman and Gall, The antibody problem. It is also used by Piatelli-Palmarini, Evolution, selection, and cognition. We use the analogy here with an extension which is not in line with the intention of either of these authors.

21. This point can be made in greatest detail for the immune system. See Varela et al., Cognitive networks.

22. For the concept of "satisficing" see Stearns, On fitness.

23. Jacob, Evolution and tinkering.

24. This notion of viability, that is, a set of possible trajectories as opposed to a unique optimal one, can be made mathematically precise. See Aubin and Cellina, *Differential Inclusions;* and the discussion in Varela, Sanchez-Leighton, and Coutinho, Adaptive strategies gleaned from networks.

25. Lewontin, The organism as the subject and object of evolution.

26. Ibid.

27. Oyama, *The Onotgeny of Information*.

28. Ibid., 22.

29. Ibid., 122.

30. See Edelman, *Neural Darwinism*; Reeke and Edelman, Real brains and artificial intelligence. For similar expositions see Changeux, *L'Homme Neuronal;* Cowan and Fawcett, Regressive events in neurogenesis; Piatelli-Palmarini, Evolution, selection, and cognition.

31. Hellerstein, Plotting a theory of the brain, 61.

32. See Menzel, Spectral sensitivity and colour vision in invertebrates; Menzel, Colour pathways and colour vision in the honey bee.

33. See Lythgoe, *The Ecology of Vision*, 188–193.

34. Lewontin, The organism as the subject and object of evolution.

35. Gibson, *The Ecological Approach to Visual Perception*. For a more recent statement of the Gibsonian project, see Turvey et al., Ecological laws of perceiving and acting. This paper defends the Gibsonian project against the extensive cognitivist criticisms in Fodor and Pylyshyn, How direct is visual perception?

36. See Turvey, et al., Ecological laws of perceiving and acting, 283.

37. Gibson, A direct theory of visual perception, 239.

38. Gibson, *The Ecological Approach to Visual Perception*, 139. We should note that there appears to be a subtle difference between Gibson and some of his followers over

the precise ontological status of affordances. Thus whereas Gibson construes them as in no way depending on the perceiver, Turvey et al., Ecological laws of perceiving and acting, construe them as emergent properties of the animal-environment system, that is, as properties that in our terms are enacted or brought forth from a history of coupling. This idea is obviously compatible with our enactive approach. A difference, however, would still remain, for unlike Gibson we would not claim that the proper explanation of how affordances are perceived is to be given in entirely optical terms—even if these were the terms of a distinctly ecological optics.

39. See Prindle, Carello and Turvey, Animal-environment mutuality and direct perception. This article is in response to Ullman, Against direct perception.

40. We have stressed the differences between our approach and Gibson's for the sake of conceptual clarity. For an excellent discussion that combines both our emphasis on the autonomy (operational closure) of the animal and the Gibsonian emphasis on optical invariants, see Kelso and Kay, Information and control.

41. See Searle, *Intentionality*.

42. Readers familiar with the early work of Heidegger will recognize here a considerable echo of Heidegger's notion that intentionality consists in an existential structure of being-in-the-world, which Heidegger calls *transcendence*. Very roughly, the idea here is that intentionality consists of the fact that our existence continually surpasses or transcends present situations for the sake of future possibilities. One of Heidegger's most focused discussions of this idea can be found in his book *The Essence of Reasons*. For discussion of the intentionality of action in the context of cognitive science, see Winograd and Flores, *Understanding Computers and Cognition*.

43. For an interesting collection of recent papers on this topic see *Evolution, Games and Learning*. Many of these contributors would not, of course, agree with our readings of their work.

44. See Holland, Escaping brittleness.

45. See Moravec, *Mind Children*.

46. Brooks, Achieving artificial intelligence through building robots; Brooks, Intelligence without representation; Brooks, A Robot that walks; Brooks, A robust layered control system for a mobile robot.

47. Brooks, Intelligence without representation, 7.

48. Ibid., 9.

49. Ibid., 11.

Chapter 10

1. Putnam, *The Faces of Realism*, 29.

2. Ibid.

3. R. Rorty, *Philosophy and the Mirror of Nature*, 394.

4. Hopkins, *Meditation on Emptiness*; Inada, *Nagarjuna*; Iida, *Reason and Emptiness*; Kalupahana, *Nagarjuna*. The reader is warned that the interpretation given by Kalupahana is not shared by anyone else, neither within Buddhist communities nor amongst scholars. Gymatso, *Progressive Stages of Meditation on Emptiness*; Murti, *The Central Philosophy of Buddhism*; Sprung, *Lucid Exposition of the Middle Way*; Streng, *Emptiness*; Thurman, *Tsong Khapa's Speech of Gold in the Essence of True Eloquence*. A

surprisingly good discussion of Madhyamika is included in a work devoted to other topics: Beyer, *The Cult of Tara*.

5. See the references in note 4. All discuss Nagarjuna.

6. This example is constructed out of many others. It is designed to show the force, clarity, and potential personal relevance of Nagarjuna's reasoning. We find it remarkable how Western scholarship has generally missed the understanding of sunyata with respect to codependence; we hope that this discussion can provide additional clarity.

7. A discussion of the application of the Madhyamika attack on causality to cognitive science is found in Rosch, What does the tiny vajra refute?

8. Kalupahana, *Nagarjuna*, XXIV, 18–19.

9. This point should be self-evident from our presentation of Abhidharma in chapters 4 and 6. It is controversial, however, because many Western scholars see Nagarjuna as rejecting the Abhidharma. On this point we find ourselves allied with Kalupahana, *Nagarjuna*.

10. Hopkins, *Meditation on Emptiness*, 168.

11. Thurman, *Tsong Khapa's Speech of Gold in the Essence of True Eloquence*, 357.

12. Putnam, *The Faces of Realism*; R. Rorty, *Philosophy and the Mirror of Nature*; and R. Rorty, *Consequences of Pragmatism*; Margolis, *Pragmatism without Foundations*.

13. See Derrida, *Of Grammatology*; Derrida, *Margins of Philosophy*; Foucault, *The Order of Things*; Foucault, *Discipline and Punish*; Dreyfus and Rabinow, *Michel Foucault*.

14. Lyotard, *The Postmodern Condition*; Vattimo, *The End of Modernity*.

15. Vattimo, *The End of Modernity*.

16. Ibid., 11–12.

17. Hume, *A Treatise of Human Nature*, 199, 206.

18. Jackendoff, *Consciousness and the Computational Mind*, 300.

19. Goodman, *Ways of Worldmaking*, 117–118.

20. See Putnam, *Reason, Truth and History*, chapter 2. For discussion of Putnam's theorem in the context of cognitive science, see Lakoff, *Women, Fire, and Dangerous Things*; chapter 15.

21. Putnam, *Reason, Truth and History.*, 52.

22. Putnam, *The Faces of Realism*, 8.

Chapter 11

1. R. Rorty, *Philosophy and the Mirror of Nature*, 394.

2. Heidegger, *The Question of Being*, 107. For a detailed discussion of this passage in the overall context of Heidegger's thought see Thompson, Planetary thinking/planetary building..

3. Nishitani, *Religion and Nothingness*. Nishitani belongs to a current in contemporary Japanese philosophy known as the Kyoto school. For an introduction to this school see Franck, *The Buddha Eye*.

4. Nishitani, *Religion and Nothingness*, 120.

5. Nietzsche, *The Will to Power*, 9.

6. See Vattimo, *The End of Modernity*.

7. Hardin, The tragedy of the commons.

8. We use the term *man* here rather than *person* deliberately.

9. Hobbes, *Leviathan*.

10. See Rosch, The micropsychology of self interest.

11. The Sanscrit term translated here as "compassion" is *karuna*. This translation has some shortcomings, but there is no other satisfactory English term.

12. Hopkins, *Precious Garland and Song of the Four Mindfulness*, 76.

13. Nishitani echoes this statement when he writes that "the nature of the task of the *ought* is the other-directedness of the *is*." Nishitani, *Religion and Nothingness*, 260.

14. For a living example, see the transcribed discussion in Theological encounter III in *Buddhist Christian Studies* 8, 1988.

15. To say that something exists is not a compliment in any of the Sanscritic traditions.

16. Trungpa, *Sadhana of Mahamudra*.

17. The classic exposition is by the Indian philosopher Shantideva (c. 8th century CE). See Batchelor, *A Guide to the Bodhisattva's Way of Life*. For an extensive commentary and discussion of this text by a contemporary Tibetan teacher, see Gyatso, *Meaningful to Behold*.

18. Not all traditions, of course, employ either the terminology or the concept of *bodhicitta*.

19. This translation is R. Thurman's. For Hopkins's translation, see Hopkins, *Precious Garland and Song of the Four Mindfulnesses*, 76.

20. Rajchman, *Le savoir-faire avec l'inconscient*.

21. H. Dreyfus and S. Dreyfus, What is morality? A deeper analysis of the relation between the concept of ethics as a skill and the Buddhist concept of skillful means would take us too far afield at this point.

22. This is the image of the *bodhisattva*, a being who vows to continue to be reborn endlessly for the sake of others rather than out of his own karma (and rather than departing to nirvana). Practitioners in the Mahayana and Vajrayana traditions take this idea seriously and themselves take bodhisattva ordinations and vows. Historians who treat the development of the bodhisattva ideal in Mahayana Buddhism as the degeneration of Buddhism into polytheism might do well to look at the way this ideal is treated in actual Buddhist communities.

Appendix B

1. In compiling this list we have drawn on several sources: Guenther and Kawamura, *Mind in Buddhist Psyhology*; Rabten, *The Mind and Its Functions*; Stcherbatski, *The Central Conception of Buddhism and the Meaning of the Word "Dharma."*

References

Abeles, M. 1984. *Local Circuits*. New York: Springer Verlag.

Abraham, R., and C. Shaw. 1985. *Dynamics: The Geometry of Behavior*. 3 vols. Santa-Cruz: Aerial Press.

Allman, J., F. Meizen, and E. McGuiness. 1985. *Annual Review of Neuroscience* 8: 407–430.

Amitt, D. 1988. Neural networks counting chimes. *Proceedings of the National Academy of Sciences* (USA) 85: 2141–2144.

Andersen, P., and S. A. Andersson. 1968. *The Physiological Basis of Alpha Rhythm*. New York: Appleton-Century Croft.

Aoli, M., R. S. McLachlan, and P. Gloor. 1984. Simultaneous recording of cortical and thalamic EEG and single neuron activity in the cat association system during spindles. *Neuroscience Letters* 47: 29–36.

Artifical Intelligence. 1987. 31: 213–261.

Aubin, J. P., and A. Cellina. 1984. *Differential Inclusions*. New York: Springer-Verlag.

Bach y Rita, P. 1962. *Brain Mechanisms in Sensory Substitution*. New York: Academic Press.

Barlow, H. 1972. Single units and sensation: A neuron doctrine for perceptual psychology. *Perception* 1: 371–394.

Batchelor, S., trans. 1979. *A Guide to the Bodhisattva's Way of Life*. Dharamsala, India: Library of Tibetan Works and Archives.

Berlin, B., and P. Kay. 1969. *Basic Color Terms: Their Universality and Evolution*. Berkeley: University of California Press.

Bernstein, R. 1983. *Beyond Objectivism and Relativism: Science, Hermeneutics, and Praxis*. Philadelphia: University of Pennsylvania Press.

Berofski, R. 1987. *Making History: Pukapukan and Anthropological Constructions of Knowledge*. Cambridge: Cambridge University Press.

Beyer, S. *The Cult of Tara*. Berkeley: University of California Press.

Binswanger, L. 1947. *Zur phänomenologischen Anthropologie*.

Bourdieu, P. 1989. *The Logic of Practice*. Oxford: Basil Blackwell.

Bourne, L. E., R. L. Dominowski, and E. F. Loftus. 1979. *Cognitive Processes*. Englewood Cliffs, New Jersey: Prentice Hall.

Brandon, R., and R. Burian, eds. 1984. *Genes, Organisms, and Populations: Controversies over the Units of Selection*. Cambridge, Massachusetts: The MIT Press.

Brentano, F. 1973. *Psychology from an Empirical Standpoint*. London: Routledge and Kegan Paul.

Bressler, S. 1990. The gamma wave: a cortical information carrier. *Trends in Neuroscience* 13:161–162.

Brooks, R. A. 1986. Achieving artificial intelligence through building robots. A.I. Memo 899, MIT Artificial Intelligence Laboratory, May.

Brooks, R. A. 1987. Intelligence without representation. MIT Artificial Intelligence Report.

Brooks, R. A. 1989a. A robot that walks: Emergent behaviors from a carefully evolved network. A.I. Memo 1091, MIT, February.

Brooks, R. A. 1989b. A robust layered control system for a mobile robot. *IEEE Journal Robotics Automation* RA-2:14–23.

Brou, P., T. R. Sciascia, L. Linden, and J. Y. Lettvin. 1986. The colors of things. *Scientific American* 255:84–91.

Brown, R. 1980. *A First Language.* Cambridge, Massachusetts: Harvard University Press.

Brown, R. W., and E. H. Lenneberg. 1954. A study in language and cognition. *Journal of Abnormal and Social Psychology* 49:454–462.

Buddhaghosa, B. 1976. *The Path of Purification* (Visuddhimagga). 2 vols. Boston: Shambhala.

Buddhist Christian Studies. 1988. Vol. 8.

Burkhardt, D. 1989. UV vision: A bird's eye view of feathers. *Journal of Comparative Physiology* 164:787–796.

Cahiers de la Centre de Recherche en Epistémologie Appliqué 7–9. 1985. Paris: Ecole Polytechnique.

Carpenter, G., and S. Grossberg. 1987. A massively parallel architecture for a self-organizing neural pattern recognition machine. *Computer Vision, Graphics and Image Processing* 37:54–115.

Changeux, J. P. 1982. *L'homme neuronal.* Paris: Fayarad.

Churchland, P. M. 1979. *Scientific Realism and the Plasticity of Mind.* Cambridge: Cambridge University Press.

Churchland, P. M. 1984. *Matter and Consciousness: A Contemporary Introduction to the Philosophy of Mind.* Cambridge, Massachusetts: The MIT Press, A Bradford Book.

Churchland, P. M. 1988. Perceptual plasticity and theoretical neutrality: A reply to Jerry Fodor. *Philosophy of Science* 55:167–187.

Churchland, P. S. 1986. *Neurophilosophy.* Cambridge, Massachusetts: The MIT Press, A Bradford Book.

Churchland, P. S., and T. J. Sejnowski. 1988. Perspectives on cognitive neuroscience. *Science* 242:741–745.

Clemens, H. 1983. *Alfred R. Wallace: Biologist and Social Reformer.* London: Hutchinson.

Connor, B. W. 1984. Initiation of synchronized neuronal bursting in neocortex. *Nature* 310:686–687.

Conze, E. 1970. *Buddhist Thought in India.* Ann Arbor: University of Michigan Press.

Cowan, M., and J. Fawcett. 1984. Regressive events in neurogenesis. *Science* 225:1258–1265.

Creutzfeld, O. D., S. Watanabe, and H. D. Lux. 1986. Relations between EEG phenomena and potentials of single cortical cells. I. Evoked responses after thalamic and epicortical stimulation. *EEG Clinical Neurophysiology* 20:1–18.

Crow, J., and M. Kimura. 1980. *An Introduction to Population Genetics.* Minneapolis: Burgess.

Crutchfield, J., J. D. Farmer, N. H. Packard, and R. S. Shaw. 1986. Chaos. *Scientific American* 255 (6):46–57.

Dawkins, R. 1976. *The Selfish Gene*. New York: Oxford University Press.

de Beer, G. 1953. *Embryos and Ancestors*. Oxford: Oxford University Press.

Dennett, D. 1978a. Artificial intelligence as philosophy and psychology. In *Brainstorms*. Cambridge, Massachusetts: The MIT Press, A Bradford Book.

Dennett, D. 1978b. *Brainstorms*. Cambridge, Massachusetts: The MIT Press, A Bradford Book.

Dennett, D. 1978c. Toward a cognitive theory of consciousness. In *Brainstorms*. Cambridge, Massachusetts: The MIT Press, A Bradford Book.

Dennett, D. 1984a. Computer models and the mind—a view from the East Pole. *Times Literary Supplement*, December 14. (Also reprinted in 1986 as The logical geography of computational approaches: A view from the East Pole. In *The Representation of Knowledge*, ed. M. Brand and M. Harnish. Tucson: University of Arizona Press.)

Dennett, D. 1984b. *Elbow Room: The Varieities of Free Will Worth Wanting*. Cambridge, Massachusetts: The MIT Press, A Bradford Book.

Derrida, J. 1974a. *Of Grammatology*. Trans. G. Spivak. Baltimore: Johns Hopkins University Press.

Derrida, J. 1974b. *Speech and Phenomena*. Evanston, Illinois: Northwestern University Press.

Derrida, J. 1978. *Writing and Difference*. Trans. Alan Bass. Chicago: University of Chicago Press.

Derrida, J. 1982. *Margins of Philosophy*. Trans. Alan Bass. Chicago: University of Chicago Press.

Descartes, R. 1911. *The Philosophical Works of Descartes*, Vol. 2. Trans. Elizabeth S. Haldane and G. R. T. Ross. Cambridge: Cambridge University Press.

Descombes, V. 1980. *Modern French Philosophy*. Cambridge: Cambridge University Press.

DeValois, R. L., and G. H. Jacobs. 1968. Primate color vision. *Science* 162:533–540.

DeYoe, E., and D. C. Van Essen. 1988. Concurrent processing streams in monkey visual cortex. *Trends in Neuroscience* 11:219–226.

Dolard, J., and N. Miller. 1950. *Personality and Psychotherapy*. New York: McGraw-Hill.

Dorje, W. 1979. *Mahmudra: Eliminating the Darkness of Ignorance*. Dharamsala, India: Library of Tibetan Works and Archives.

Dretske, F. I. 1981. *Knowledge and the Flow of Information*. Cambridge, Massachusetts: The MIT Press, A Bradford Book.

Dreyfus, H. 1979. *What Computers Can't Do*. Revised edition. New York: Harper and Row.

Dreyfus, H., ed. 1982. *Husserl: Intentionality and Cognitive Science*. Cambridge, Massachusetts: The MIT Press, A Bradford Book.

Dreyfus, H. 1989. Alternative philosophical conceptualizations of psychopathology. In *Phenomenology and Beyond: The Self and Its Language*, ed. H. A. Durfee and D. F. T. Rodier, 41–50. Dordrecht: Kluwer Academic Publishers.

Dreyfus, H., and S. Dreyfus. 1986. *Mind over Machine*. New York: Macmillan, Free Press.

Dreyfus, H., and S. Dreyfus. 1988. Making a mind versus modeling the brain: Artificial intelligence back at a branchpoint. *Daedulus* (Winter): 15–43.

Dreyfus, H., and S. E Dreyfus. 1990. What is morality? A phenomenological account of the development of ethical expertise. In *Universalism versus Communitarianism*, ed. D. Rassmussen. Cambridge, Massachusetts: The MIT Press.

Dreyfus, H., and P. Rabinow. 1983. *Michel Foucault: Beyond Structuralism and Hermeneutics*. Chicago: University of Chicago Press.

Dumouchel, P., and J. P. Dupuy, eds. 1983. *L'auto-organisation: De la physique au politique*. Paris: Editions du Seuil.

Dupré, J., ed. 1987. *The Latest on the Best*. Cambridge, Massachusetts: The MIT Press, A Bradford Book.

Edelman, G. 1987. *Neural Darwinism*. New York: Basic Books.

Edelman, G., and W. Gall. 1979. The antibody problem. *Annual Review of Biochemistry* 38:699–766.

Eldredge, N., and S. Salthe. 1984. Hierarchy and evolution. *Oxford Surveys in Evolutionary Biology* 1:184–208.

Endler, J. 1986. The newer synthesis? Some conceptual problems in evolutionary biology. *Oxford Surveys in Evolutionary Biology* 3:224–243.

Epstein, S. 1980. The self-concept: A review and the proposal of an integrated theory of personality. In *Personality: Basic Issues and Current Research*, ed. E. Staub Englewood Cliffs, New Jersey: Prentice Hall.

Erdelyi, M. H. 1985. *Psychoanalysis: Freud's Cognitive Psychology*. New York: W. H. Freeman.

Evolution, Games and Learning: Models for Adaptation in Machines and Nature. 1986. *Physics* 220.

Feldman, J. 1986. Neural representation of conceptual knowledge. University of Rochester Technical Report 189.

Feldman, J., and D. Ballard. 1982. Connectionist models and their properties. *Cognitive Science* 6:205–254.

Fishman, M., and C. Michael. 1973. Integration of auditory information in the cat's visual cortex. *Vision Research* 13:1415.

Fodor, J. 1975. *The Language of Thought*. Cambridge, Massachusetts: Harvard University Press.

Fodor, J. 1981a. Computation and reduction. In *RePresentations: Philosophical Essays on the Foundations of Cognitive Science*. Cambridge, Massachusetts: The MIT Press, A Bradford Book.

Fodor, J. 1981b. The present status of the innateness controversy. In *RePresentations: Philosophical Essays on the Foundations of Cognitive Science*. Cambridge, Massachusetts: The MIT Press, A Bradford Book.

Fodor, J. 1981c. *RePresentations: Philosophical Essays on the Foundations of Cognitive Science*. Cambridge, Massachusetts: The MIT Press, A Bradford Book.

Fodor, J. 1981d. Special sciences; or, the disunity of science as a working hypothesis. In *RePresentations: Philosophical Essays on the Foundations of Cognitive Science*. Cambridge, Massachusetts: The MIT Press, A Bradford Book.

Fodor, J. 1983. *The Modularity of Mind*. Cambridge, Massachusetts: The MIT Press, A Bradford Book.

Fodor, J. 1984. Observation reconsidered. *Philosophy of Science* 51:23–43.

Fodor, J. 1985. Fodor's guide to mental representations: The intelligent auntie's vademecum. *Mind* 94:76–100.

Fodor, J. 1987. *Psychosemantics: The Problem of Meaning in the Philosophy of Mind*. Cambridge, Massachusetts: The MIT Press, A Bradford Book.

Fodor, J., and Z. Pylyshyn. 1981. How direct is visual perception? Some reflections on Gibson's ecological approach. *Cognition* 9:139–196.

Fodor, J., and Z. Pylyshyn. 1988. Connectionism and cognitive architecture: A critical review. *Cognition* 28:3–71.

Foucault, M. 1973. *The Order of Things: An Archaelogy of the Human Sciences.* New York: Random House, Vintage.

Foucault, M. 1979. *Discipline and Punish: The Birth of the Prison.* New York: Random House, Vintage.

Franck, F., ed. 1980. *The Buddha Eye: An Anthology of the Kyoto School.* New York: Crossroads.

Freeman, W. 1975. *Mass Action in the Nervous System.* New York: Academic Press.

Freeman, W., and C. Skarda. 1985. Spatial EEG patterns, nonlinear dynamics, and perception: The neo-Sherringtonian view. *Brain Research Reviews* 10:145–175.

Freemantle, F., trans. 1975. *The Tibetan Book of the Dead.* Boston: Shambhala.

Gadamer, H. G. 1975. *Truth and Method.* Boston: Seabury Press.

Gardner, H. 1985. *The Mind's New Science: A History of the Cognitive Revolution.* New York: Basic Books.

Gelperin, A., and D. Tank. 1990. Odour-modulated collective network oscillations of olfactory interneurons in a terrestrial mollusc. *Nature* 345:437–439.

Gershon, R. 1986. *The Use of Color in Computational Vision.* University of Toronto Technical Reports on Research in Biological and Computational Vision: RCBV-86–4. Department of Computer Science.

Geschwind, N., and A. Galaburda. 1986. *Cerebral Lateralization: Biological Mechanisms, Associations, and Pathology.* Cambridge, Massachusetts: The MIT Press.

Gevins, A., R. Shaffer, J. Doyle, B. Cutillo, R. Tannehill, and S. Bressler. 1983. Shadows of thought: Shifting lateralization of human brain electrical patterns during brief visuomotor task. *Science* 220:97–99.

Gho, M., and F. Varela. 1989. Quantitative assesment of the dependency of the visual temporal frame upon the alpha rhythm. *Journal Physiologie* (Paris) 83:95–101.

Gibson, J. J. 1972. A direct theory of visual perception. In *The Psychology of Knowing,* ed. J. R. Royce and W. W. Rozeboom. New York: Gordon and Breach.

Gibson, J. J. 1979. *The Ecological Approach to Visual Perception.* Boston: Houghton Mifflin.

Gleason, H. A. 1961. *An Introduction to Descriptive Linguistics.* New York: Holt, Rinehart and Winston.

Gleick, J. 1987. *Chaos: The Making of a New Science.* New York: Viking Press.

Globus, G. 1987. *Dream Life, Wake Life.* Albany: State University of New York Press.

Globus, G. 1990. Heidegger and cognitive science. *Philosophy Today* (Spring): 20–30.

Globus, G. In press. Deconstructing the Chinese room. *Journal of Mind and Behavior.*

Globus, G. In press. Derrida and connectionism: Differance in neural nets. *Philosophical Psychology.*

Goldstein, J., and J. Kornfield. 1987. *Seeking the Heart of Wisdom: The Path of Insight Meditation.* Boston: Shambhala.

Goodman, N. 1978. *Ways of Worldmaking.* Indianapolis: Hackett Publishing Company.

Goodman, S. 1974. Situational patterning. In *Crystal Mirror III.* Berkeley: Dharma Publishing.

Goodwin, B., N. Holder, and C. Wyles, eds. 1983. *Development and Evolution.* Cambridge: Cambridge University Press.

Gould, S. J. 1982. Darwinism and the expansion of evolutionary theory. *Science* 216:380–387.

Gould, S. J., and N. Eldredge. 1977. Punctuated equilibria: The tempo and mode of evolution reconsidered. *Paleobiology* 3:115.

Gould, S. J., and R. Lewontin. 1979. The spandrels of San Marco and the Panglossian paradigm: A critique of the adaptationist programme. *Proceedings of the Royal Society of London* 205:581–598.

Gouras, P., and E. Zenner. 1981. Color vision: A review from a neurophysiological perspective. *Progress in Sensory Physiology* 1:139–179.

Gray, C., and W. Singer. 1989. Stimulus-specific neuronal oscillations in orientation columns in cat visual cortex. *Proceedings of the National Academy of Sciences* (USA) 86:1698–1702.

Greenburg, J. R. and S. A. Mitchel. 1983. *Object Relations in Psychoanalytic Theory.* Cambridge, Massachusetts: Harvard University Press.

Griffiths, P. J. 1986. *On Being Mindless: Buddhist Meditation and the Mind-Body Problem.* LaSalle, Illinois: Open Court.

Grossberg, S. 1984. *Studies in Mind and Brain.* Boston: D. Reidel.

Guenther, H. 1976. *Philosophy and Psychology in the Abhidharma.* Berkeley: Shambhala Publications.

Guenther, H. 1989. *From Reductionism to Creativity.* Boston: New Science Library.

Guenther, H., and L. S. Kawamura. 1975. *Mind in Buddhist Psychology.* Emeryville, California: Dharma Publishing.

Gyamtso, K. T. 1986. *Progressive Stages of Meditation on Emptiness.* Trans. Shenpen Hookham. New Marsten, Oxford: Longchen Foundation.

Gyatso, K. 1980. *Meaningful to Behold: View, Meditation, and Action in Mahayana Buddhism.* London: Wisdom Publications.

Hardin, C. L. 1988. *Color for Philosophers: Unweaving the Rainbow.* Indianapolis: Hackett Publishing Company.

Hardin, G. 1968. The tragedy of the commons. *Science* 162:1243–1248.

Harosi, F. I., and Y. Hashimoto. 1983. Ultraviolet visual pigment in a vertebrate: A tetrachromatic cone system in the Dace. *Science* 222:1021–1023.

Haugeland, J. 1981. The nature and plausibility of cognitivism. Reprinted in *Mind Design: Philosophy, Psychology, Artifical Intelligence,* ed. J. Haugeland. Cambridge, Massachusetts: The MIT Press, A Bradford Book.

Hayward, J. 1987. *Shifting Worlds, Changing Minds: Where the Sciences and Buddhism Meet.* Boston: New Science Library.

Hecht, M., and A.Hoffman. 1986. Why not neo-Darwinism? A critique of paleobiological challenges. *Oxford Surveys in Evolutionary Biology* 3:1–47.

Heidegger, M. 1958. *The Question of Being.* Trans. William Kluback and Jean T. Wilde. New Haven, Connecticut: College and University Press.

Heidegger, M. 1962. *Being and Time.* New York: Harper and Row.

Heidegger, M. 1969. *The Essence of Reasons.* Trans. T. Malick. Evansville, Illinois: Northwestern University Press.

Heider, E. R. 1971. Focal color areas and the development of color names. *Developmental Psychology* 4:447–455.

Heider, E. R. 1972. Universals in color naming and memory. *Journal of Experimental Psychology* 93:10–20.

Heider, E. R. 1974. Linguistic relativity. In *Human Communication: Theoretical Explorations*, ed. A. L. Silverstein. New York: Halsted Press.

Heider, E. R. and D. C. Olivier. 1972. The structure of the color space in naming and memory for two languages. *Cognitive Psychology* 3:337–354.

Heims, S. 1980. *John von Neumann and Norbert Wiener*. Cambridge, Massachusetts: The MIT Press.

Held, R., and A. Hein. 1958. Adaptation of disarranged hand-eye coordination contingent upon re-afferent stimulation. *Perceptual-Motor Skills* 8:87–90.

Hellerstein, D. 1988. Plotting a theory of the brain. *The New York Times Magazine*, May 22.

Helson, H. 1938. Fundamental problems in color vision. I. The principles governing changes in hue, saturation, and lightness of nonselective samples in chromatic Iilumination. *Journal of Experimental Psychology* 23:439–476.

Helson, H., and V. B. Jeffers. 1940. Fundamental problems in color vision. II. Hue, lightness and saturation of selective samples in chromatic illumination. *Journal of Experimental Psychology* 26:1–27.

Hilbert, D. R. 1987. *Color and Color Perception: A Study in Anthropocentric Realism*. Stanford: Center for the Study of Language and Information.

Hillis, D. 1988. Intelligence as an emergent behavior; or, the songs of Eden. *Dadaelus* (Winter):175–189.

Hinton, G., T. Sejnowsky, and D. Ackley. 1985. A learning algorithm for Boltzman machines. *Cognitive Science* 9:147–169.

Ho, M., and P. Saunders. 1984. *Beyond Neo-Darwinism*. New York: Academic Press.

Hobbes, T. *Leviathan*. New York: Modern Library.

Hodges, A. 1984. *Alan Turing: The Enigma of Intelligence*. New York: Touchstone.

Hofstadter, D. R. and D. Dennett, eds. 1981. *The Mind's Eye: Fantasies and Reflections on Self and Soul*. New York: Basic Books.

Holland, J. 1986. Escaping brittleness. In *Machine Learning*, ed. R. Michalski, J. Carbonnel, and T. Mitchel. Los Altos, California: Morgan Kaufmann.

Hopfield, J. 1982. Neural networks and physical systems with emergent computational abilities. *Proceedings of the National Academy of Sciences* (USA) 79:2554–2558.

Hopkins, P. J., trans. 1975. *Precious Garland and Song of the Four Mindfulnesses*. London: Allen and Unwin.

Hopkins, J. 1983. *Meditation on Emptiness*. London: Wisdom Publications.

Horn, G., and R. Hill. 1974. Modifications of the receptive field of cells in the visual cortex occurring spontaneously and associated with bodily tilt. *Nature* 221:185–187.

Horowitz, M. J. 1988. *Introduction to Psychodynamics: A New Synthesis*. New York: Basic Books.

Hubel, D. 1988. *Eye, Brain and Mind*. New York: W. H. Freeman.

Hume, D. 1964. *A Treatise of Human Nature*. Ed. L. A. Selby-Bigge. Oxford: Clarendon Press.

Hurvich, L. M., and D. Jameson. 1957. An opponent-process theory of color vision. *Psychological Review* 64:384–404.

Husserl, E. 1931. *Ideas: General Introduction to a Pure Phenomenology*. Trans. W. R. Boyce Gibson. London: Allen and Unwin.

Husserl, E. 1960. *Cartesian Meditations: An Introduction to Phenomenology*. Trans. Dorian Cairns. The Hague: Martinus Nijhoff.

Husserl, E. 1970. *The Crisis of European Sciences and Transcendental Phenomenology.* Trans. David Carr. Evanston, Illinois: Northwestern University Press.

Iida, S. 1980. *Reason and Emptiness.* Tokyo: Hokuseido Press.

Inada, K. K. 1970. *Nagarjuna: A Translation of his Mulamadhyamikakarikas.* Tokyo: Hokusiedo Press.

Jackendoff, R. 1987. *Consciousness and the Computational Mind.* Cambridge, Massachusetts: The MIT Press, A Bradford Book.

Jacob, F. 1977. Evolution and tinkering. *Science* 196:1161–1166.

Jacobs, G. H. 1978. *Comparative Color Vision.* New York: Academic Press.

Jahnsen, H., and R. Llinas. 1984. Ionic basis for the electroresponsiveness and oscillatory properties of guinea-pig thalamic neurones in vitro. *Journal of Physiology* 349:227–247.

Jameson, D., and L. Hurvich. 1989. Essay concerning color constancy. *Annual Review of Psychology* 40:1–22.

Jane, S. D., and J. K. Bowmaker. 1988. Tetrachromatic colour vision in the duck. *Journal of Comparative Physiology* 162:225–235.

Jaspers, K. 1913. *Allgemeine psychopathologie.* Frankfurt: R. Mein.

Johnson, M. 1987. *The Body in the Mind: The Bodily Basis of Imagination, Reason, and Meaning.* Chicago: University of Chicago Press.

Jonckheere, P., ed. 1989. *Phénoménologie et analyse existentielle.* Brussels: De Boeck.

Josiah Macy Jr. Foundation. 1950–1954. Cybernetics: Circular Causal and Feedback Mechanisms in Biological and Social Systems. 5 vols. New York: Josiah Macy Jr. Foundation.

Judd, D. B. 1940. Hue, saturation, and lightness of surface colors with chromatic illumination. *Journal of the Optical Society of America* 30:2–32.

Kahneman, D., P. Slovic, and A. Tversky, eds. 1982. *Judgement Under Uncertainty: Heuristics and Biases.* New York: Cambridge University Press.

Kalu, K. D. C. 1986. *The Dharma.* Buffalo: State University of New York Press.

Kalupahana, D. 1986. *Nagarjuna: The Philosophy of the Middle Way.* Albany: State University of New York Press.

Kalupahana, D. 1987. *Principles of Buddhist Psychology.* Albany: State University of New York Press.

Kandinsky, W. 1947. *Concerning the Spiritual in Art.* New York: Wittenborn Art Books.

Kant, I. 1963. *Critique of Pure Reason.* Trans. Norman Kemp Smith. New York: St. Martin's Press.

Kauffman, S. 1983. Developmental constraints: Intrinsic factors in evolution. In *Developmental Evolution*, ed. B. Goodwin, N. Holder, and C. Wyles. Cambridge: Cambridge University Press.

Kay, P., and W. Kempton. 1984. What is the Sapir-Whorf hypothesis? *American Anthropologist* 86:65–79.

Kay, P., and C. McDaniel. 1978. The linguistic significance of the meanings of basic color terms. *Language* 54:610–646.

Kelso, J. A. S., and B. A. Kay. 1987. Information and control: A macroscopic analysis of perception-action coupling. In *Perspectives on Perception and Action*, ed. H. Heuer and A. F. Sanders. New Jersey: Lawrence Erlbaum Associates.

Khapa,T. 1978. *Calming the Mind and Discerning the Real: Buddhist Meditation and the Middle View.* Trans. Alex Wayman. New York: Columbia University Press.

Khyentse, D. 1988. *The Wish-Fulfilling Jewel.* Boston: Shambhala.

Klein, A. 1986. *Knowledge and Liberation: Tibetan Buddhist Epistemology in Support of Transformative Religious Experience.* Ithaca, New York: Snow Lion.

Kornblith, H., ed. 1984. *Naturalizing Epistemology.* Cambridge, Massachusetts: The MIT Press, A Bradford Book.

Kornfield, J. 1977. *Living Buddhist Masters.* Santa Cruz, California: Unity Press.

Kosslyn, S. 1980. *Image and Mind.* Cambridge, Massachusetts: Harvard University Press.

Kosslyn, S. 1981. The medium and the message in mental imagery: A theory. *Psychological Review* 88:46–66.

Kuffler, S., and J. Nichols. 1976. *From Neuron to Brain.* Boston: Sinauer Associates.

Kuhn, T. 1970. *The Structure of Scientific Revolutions.* Chicago: University of Chicago Press.

Lakoff, G. 1987. *Women, Fire and Dangerous Things: What Categories Reveal about the Mind.* Chicago: University of Chicago Press.

Lakoff, G. 1988. Cognitive semantics. In *Meaning and Mental Representations,* ed. Umberto Eco et al. Bloomington: Indiana University Press.

Lambert, D., and A. J. Hughes.1988. Keywords and concepts in structuralist and functionalist biology. *Journal of Theoretical Biology* 133:133–145.

Lambert, D., C. Millar, and T. Hughes. 1986. On the classic case of natural selection. *Biology Forum* 79:11–49.

Land, E. 1959. Experiments in color vision. *Scientific American* 200 (no. 5): 84–99.

Land, E. 1964. The retinex. *American Scientist* 52:247–264.

Land E. 1977. The retinex theory of color vision. *Scientific American,* 237 (no.6): 108–128.

Land, E. 1983. Recent advances in retinex theory and some implications for cortical computations: Color vision and the natural image. *Proceedings of the National Academy of Sciences* (USA) 80:5163–5169.

Langer, E. 1989. *Mindfulness.* New York: Addison Wesley.

Lantz, D., and V. Stefflre. 1964. Language and cognition revisited. *Journal of Abnormal and Social Psychology* 69:472–481.

Lecky, P. 1961. *Self-consistency: A Theory of Personality.* Hamden, Connecticut: The Shoe String Press.

Lewontin, R. 1983. The organism as the subject and object of evolution. *Scientia* 118:63–82.

Lewontin, R. 1989. A natural selection: Review of J. M. Smith's *Evolutionary Genetics. Nature* 339:107.

Livingstone, B. 1978. *Sensory Processing, Perception, and Behavior.* New York: Raven Press.

Llinás, R. 1988. The intrinsic electrophysiological properties of mammalian neurons: Insights into central nervous system function. *Science* 242:1654–1664.

Loy, D. 1989. *Non-Duality.* New Haven, Connecticut: Yale University Press.

Lyons, W. 1986. *The Disappearance of Instrospection.* Cambridge, Massachusetts: The MIT Press, A Bradford Book.

Lyotard, J. F. 1984. *The Postmodern Condition: A Report on Knowledge*. Trans. G. Bennington and B. Massumi. Minneapolis: University of Minnesota Press.

Lythgoe, J. 1979. *The Ecology of Vision*. Oxford: Clarendon Press.

McCulloch, W. S. 1965. *Embodiments of Mind*. Cambridge, Massachusetts: The MIT Press.

McCulloch, W. S., and W. Pitts. 1943. A logical calculus of ideas immanent in nervous activity. *Bulletin of Mathematical Biophysics* 5. Reprinted in McCulloch, W. S. 1965. *Embodiments of Mind*. Cambridge, Massachusetts: The MIT Press.

MacLaury, R. E. 1987. Color-category evolution and Shuswap yellow-with-green. *American Anthropologist* 89:107–124.

Maloney, L. T. 1985. Computational approaches to color constancy, Technical Report 1985-01, Stanford University Applied Psychological Laboratory.

Maloney, L. T., and B. A. Wandell. 1986. Color constancy: A method for recovering surface spectral reflectance. *Journal of the Optical Society of America*, 3 (no. 1): 29–33.

Margolis, J. 1986. *Pragmatism without Foundations*. Oxford: Basil Blackwell.

Marie, P. 1988. *Que est-ce que la psychoanalyse?* Paris: Auber.

Marie, P. 1990. *L'experience psychoanalytique*. Paris: Auber.

Marr, D. 1982. *Vision: A Computational Investigation into the Human Representation and Processing of Visual Information*. New York: W. H. Freeman and Company.

Matthen, M. 1988. Biological functions and perceptual content. *Journal of Philosophy* 85:5–27.

Maturana, H., G. Uribe, and Samy Frenck. 1968. A biological theory of relativistic color coding in the primate retina. *Archivos de biologia y medicina experimentales*, Supplement No. 1. Chile.

Maturana, H. and F. J. Varela. 1987. *The Tree of Knowledge: The Biological Roots of Human Understanding*. Boston: New Science Library.

May, R. 1958. *Existential Psychoanalysis*. New York: Basic Books.

Menzel, R. 1979. Spectral sensitivity and colour vision in invertebrates. In *Comparative Physiology and Evolution of Vision in Invertebrates*, ed. H. Autrum. Berlin: Springer Verlag.

Menzel, R. 1985. Colour pathways and colour vision in the honey bee. In *Central and Peripheral Mechanisms of Colour Vision*, ed. D. Ottoson and S. Zeki. London: Macmillan.

Merleau-Ponty, M. 1962. *Phenomenology of Perception*. Trans. Colin Smith. London: Routledge and Kegan Paul.

Merleau-Ponty, M. 1963. *The Structure of Behavior*. Trans. Alden Fisher. Boston: Beacon Press.

Merleau-Ponty, M. 1964. Eye and mind. In *The Primacy of Perception and Other Essays*, ed. James M. Edie. Evanston, Illinois: Northwestern University Press.

Mervis, C. B., and E. Rosch. 1981. Categorization of natural objects. In *Annual Review of Psychology* 32, ed. M. R. Rosenzweig and L. W. Porter.

Miller, G. A., E. Galanter, and K. H. Pribram. 1960. *Plans and the Structure of Behavior*. New York: Holtz.

Minsky, M. 1986. *The Society of Mind*. New York: Simon and Schuster.

Minsky, M., and S. Papert. 1987. *Perceptrons*. Rev. ed. Cambridge, Massachusetts: The MIT Press.

Moravec, H. 1988. *Mind Children*. Cambridge, Massachusetts: Harvard University Press.

Morell, F. 1972. Visual system's view of acoustic space. *Nature* 238:44–46.

Murti, T. R. V. 1955. *The Central Philosophy of Buddhism*. London: George Allen & Unwin.

Nagel, T. 1986. *The View from Nowhere*. New York: Oxford University Press.

Narada, M. T., trans. 1975. *A Manual of Abhidhamma (Abhidammattha Sangaha)*. Kandy, Sri Lanka: Buddhist Publication Society.

Neuenschwander, S., and F. Varela. 1990. Sensori-triggered and spontaneous oscillations in the avian brain. *Society of Neuroscience Abstracts* 16.

Neufeldt, R. W., ed. 1986. *Karma and Rebirth: Post Classical Developments*. Buffalo: State University of New York Press.

Neumeyer, C. 1986. *Das Farbensehen des Goldfisches*. Ph. D. dissertation, University of Mainz, West Germany.

Newell, A. 1980. Physical symbol systems. *Cognitive Science* 4:135–183.

Newell, A., and Simon, H. Computer science as empirical inquiry: Symbols and search. Reprinted in *Mind Design: Philosophy, Psychology, Artificial Intelligence*, ed. J. Haugeland. Cambridge, Massachusetts: The MIT Press, A Bradford Book.

Nhat Hanh, T. 1975. *The Miracle of Mindfulness: A Manual on Meditation*. Boston: Beacon Press.

Nietzsche, F. 1967. *The Will to Power*. Trans. Walter Kaufmann and R. J. Hollingdale. New York: Random House.

Nisbett, R., and L. Ross. 1980. *Human Inference: Strategies and Shortcomings of Social Judgement*. Englewood Cliffs, New Jersey: Prentice Hall.

Nishitani, K. 1982. *Religion and Nothingness*. Trans. Jan Van Bragt. Berkeley: University of California Press.

Nuboer, J. F. W. 1986. A comparative review on colour vision. *Netherlands Journal of Zoology* 36:344–380.

O'Flaherty, W. D., ed. 1980. *Karma and Rebirth in Classical Indian Traditions*. Berkeley: University of California Press.

Oster, G., and S. Rocklin. 1979. Optimization models in evolutionary biology. In *Lectures in Mathathematical Life Sciences* 11. Rhode Island: American Mathematical Society.

Ottoson, D. and S. Zeki, eds. 1985. *Central and Peripheral Mechanisms of Colour Vision*. London: Macmillan.

Oyama, S. 1985. *The Ontogeny of Information*. Cambridge: Cambridge University Press.

Packard, N. 1988. An intrinsic model of adaptation. In *Artificial Life*, ed. C. H. Langton. New Jersey: Addison Wesley.

Palacios, A., C. Martinoya, S. Bloch, and F. J. Varela. 1990. Color mixing in the pigeon: A psychophysical determination in the longwave spectral range. *Vision Research* 30:587–596.

Palacios, A., and F. Varela. In press. Color mixing in the pigeon. II. A psychophysical determination in the middle and shortwave spectral range. *Vision Research*.

Palm, G., and A. Aersten, eds. 1986. *Brain Theory*. New York: Springer Verlag.

Palmer, R. 1979. *Hermeneutics*. Evanston, Illinois: Nothwestern University Press.

Palmer, S. In press. *Visual Information Processing*. Englewood Cliffs, New Jersey: Lawrence Erlbaum.

Papert, S. 1981. *Mindstorms*. New York: Harper and Row.

Penrose, R. 1990. *The Emperor's New Mind*. New York: Oxford University Press.

Perry, J., ed. 1975. *Personal Identity*. Berkeley: University of California Press.

Piaget, J. 1954. *The Construction of Reality in the Child*. New York: Basic Books.

Piatelli-Palmarini, M. 1987. Evolution, selection, and cognition. In *From Enzyme Adaptation to Natural Philosophy*, ed. E. Quagliariello, G. Gernardi, and A. Ullman. Amsterdam: Elsevier.

Poggio, T., V. Torre, and C. Koch. 1985. Computational vision and regularization theory. *Nature* 317:314–319.

Pol-Droit, R. 1989. *L'amnesie philosophique*. Paris: Presses Universitaires de France.

Pöppel, E. 1989. Time perception. In *Encyclopedia of Neuroscience*. New York: Wiley.

Popper, K., and J. Eccles. 1981. *The Self and its Brain*. New York: Springer International.

Prindle, S. S., C. Carello, and M. T. Turvey. 1980. Animal-environment mutuality and direct perception. *Behavioral and Brain Sciences* 3:395–397.

Purpura, D. P. 1972. Functional studies of thalamic internuclear interactions. *Brain Behavior* 6:203–209.

Putnam, H. 1981. *Reason, Truth and History*. Cambridge: Cambridge University Press.

Putnam, H. 1983. Computational psychology and interpretation theory. Reprinted in *Realism and Reason: Philosophical Papers, Volume 3*, ed. H. Putnam. Cambridge: Cambridge University Press.

Putnam, H. 1987. *The Faces of Realism*. LaSalle, Illinois: Open Court.

Putnam, H. 1988. Much ado about not very much. *Daedulus* (Winter):269–281.

Pylyshyn, Z. 1984. *Computation and Cognition: Toward a Foundation for Cognitive Science*. Cambridge, Massachusetts: The MIT Press, A Bradford Book.

Quine, W. V. 1969. Epistemology naturalized. Reprinted 1984 in *Naturalizing Epistemology*, ed. H. Kornblith. Cambridge, Massachusetts: The MIT Press, A Bradford Book.

Rabten, G. 1981. *The Mind and its Functions*. Mt. Pelverin, Switzerland: Tharpa Choeling.

Rajchman, J. 1986. *Le savoir-faire avec l'inconscient: Ethique et psychoanalyse*. Bourdeaux: W. Blake.

Reeke, G. N., and G. M. Edelman. 1988. Real brains and artificial intelligence. *Daedelus* 117 (no. 1): 143–173.

Rogers, C. 1961. *On Becoming a Person*. Boston: Houghton Mifflin.

Rorty, A. O., ed. 1976. *The Identitites of Persons*. Berkeley: University of California Press.

Rorty, R. 1979. *Philosophy and the Mirror of Nature*. Princeton: Princeton University Press.

Rorty, R. 1982. *Consequences of Pragmatism*. Minneapolis: University of Minnesota Press.

Rosch, E. 1973. On the internal structure of perceptual and semantic categories. In *Cognitive Development and the Acquisition of Language*, ed. T. Moore. New York: Academic Press.

Rosch, E. 1978. Principles of categorization. In *Cognition and Categorization*, ed. E. Rosch and B. B. Lloyd. Hillsdale, New Jersey: Lawrence Erlbaum.

Rosch, E. 1987. Wittgenstein and categorization research in cognitive psychology. In *Meaning and the Growth of Understanding: Wittgenstein's Significance for Developmental*

Psychology, ed. M. Chapman and R. Dixon. Hillsdale, New Jersey: Lawrence Erlbaum.

Rosch, E. 1988. What does the tiny vajra refute? Causality and event structure in Buddhist logic and folk psychology. Berkeley Cognitive Science Report #54.

Rosch, E. Unpublished. The micropsychology of self interest.

Rosch, E. Unpublished. Proto-intentionality: The psychology of philosophy.

Rosch, E. In preparation. *The Original Psychology: Buddhist Views of Mind in Contemporary Society.*

Rosch, E., C. B. Mervis, W. D. Gray, D. M. Johnson, and P. Boyes-Braem. 1976. Basic objects in natural categories. *Cognitive Psychology* 8:382–349.

Rosenbaum, I. 1989. *Readings in Neurocomputing.* Cambridge, Massachusetts: The MIT Press.

Rosenblatt, F. 1962. *Principles of Neurodynamics: Perceptrons and the Theory of Brain Dynamics.* New York: Spartan Books.

Rummelhart, D., and J. McClelland, eds. 1986. *Parallel Distributed Processing: Studies on the Microstructure of Cognition.* 2 vols. Cambridge, Massachusetts: The MIT Press.

Sacks, O., and R. Wasserman. 1987. The case of the colorblind painter. *New York Review of Books,* November 19, 25–34.

Sahn, S. 1982. *Bone of Space.* San Francisco: Four Seasons Foundation.

Sajama, S., and M. Kamppinen. 1987. *A Historical Introduction to Phenomenology.* London: Croom Helm.

Schafer, R. 1976. *A New Language for Psychoanalysis.* New Haven, Connecticut: Yale University Press.

Schank, R. C., and R. Abelson. 1977. *Scripts, Plans, Goals and Understanding.* Hillsdale, New Jersey: Lawrence Erlbaum Associates.

Searle, J. 1980. Minds, brains, and programs. *Behavioral and Brain Sciences* 3:417–457. Reprinted 1981 in *Mind Design: Philosophy Psychology, Artificial Intelligence,* ed. J. Haugeland. Cambridge, Massachusetts: The MIT Press, A Bradford Book.

Searle, J. 1983. *Intentionality: An Essay in the Philosophy of Mind.* Cambridge: Cambridge University Press.

Segal, H. 1976. *Introduction to the Work of Melanie Klein.* London: Hogarth Press.

Segal, S. J. 1971. *Imagery: Current Cognitive Approaches.* New York: Academic Press.

Sejnowski, T., and C. Rosenbaum. 1986. NetTalk: A parallel network that learns to read aloud. Johns Hopkins University. Technical Report JHU/EECS-86.

Sheng-Yan, M. 1982. *Getting the Buddha Mind.* Elmhurst, New York: Dharma Drum Publications.

Shepard, R., and J. Metzler. 1971. Mental rotation of three dimensional objects. *Science* 171:701–703.

Silandanda, U. 1990. *The Four Foundations of Mindfulness.* Boston: Wisdom Publications.

Singer, W. 1980. Extraretinal influences in the geniculate. *Physiology Reviews* 57:386–420.

Smolensky, P. 1988. On the proper treatment of connectionism. *Behavior and Brain Sciences* 11:1–74.

Smolensky, P. In press. Tensor product variable binding and the representation of symbolic structures in connectionist networks. *Artificial Intelligence.*

Snygg, D., and A. W. Combs. 1949. *Individual Behavior.* New York: Harper and Row.

Sober, E. 1984. *The Nature of Selection.* Cambridge, Massachusetts: The MIT Press, A Bradford Book.

Sopa, G. L., and J. Hopkins. 1976. *Practice and Theory of Tibetan Buddhism.* New York: Grove Press.

Sprung, M. 1979. *Lucid Exposition of the Middle Way.* Boulder: Prajna Press.

Stcherbatski, T. 1979. *The Central Conception of Buddhism and the Meaning of the Word "Dharma."* Delhi: Motilal Banarasidass. Originally published by the Royal Asiatic Society.

Stearns, S. 1982. On fitness. In *Environmental Adaptation and Evolution,* ed. D. Mossakowski and G. Roth. Stuttgart: Gustav Fisher.

Steffire, V., V. Castillo Vales, and L. Morely. 1966. Language and cognition in Yucatan: A cross-cultural replication. *Journal of Personality and Social Psychology* 4:112–115.

Stengers, I. 1985. Les généalogies de l'auto-organisation. *Cahiers de la Centre de Recherche en Epistémologie Appliqué* 8:7–105.

Steriade, M., and M. Deschenes. 1985. The thalamus as a neuronal oscillator. *Brain Research Reviews* 8:1–63.

Stich, S. 1983. *From Folk Psychology to Cognitive Science: The Case Against Belief.* Cambridge, Massachusetts: The MIT Press, A Bradford Book.

Stillings, N. A., M. Feinstein, J. L. Garfield, E. L. Rissland, D. A. Rosenbaum, S. Weisler, and L. Baker-Ward. 1987. *Cognitive Science: An Introduction.* Cambridge, Massachusetts: The MIT Press, A Bradford Book.

Streng, F. J. 1967. *Emptiness: A Study in Religious Meaning.* Nashville, Tennessee: Abingdon Press.

Sudnow, D. 1978. *Ways of the Hand: The Organization of Improvised Conduct.* Cambridge, Massachusetts: Harvard University Press.

Suzuki, S. 1970. *Zen Mind, Beginner's Mind.* New York: Weatherhill.

Sweetzer, E. E. 1984. Semantic Structure and Semantic Change. Ph.D. dissertation, University of California at Berkeley.

Tank, D. W. and J. Hopfield. 1987. Collective computation in neuronlike circuits. *Scientific American* 257 (no. 6): 104–114.

Taylor, C. 1983. The significance of significance: The case of cognitive psychology. In *The Need for Interpretation,* ed. Solace Mitchell and Michael Rosen. London: The Athalone Press.

Thera, N. 1962. *The Heart of Buddhist Meditation.* New York: Samuel Weiser.

Thompson, E. 1986. Planetary thinking/planetary building: An essay on Martin Heidegger and Nishitani Keiji. *Philosophy East and West* 36:235–252.

Thompson, E. Forthcoming. *Colour Vision: A Study in Cognitive Science and the Philosophy of Perception.*

Thompson, E., A. Palacios, and F. Varela. In press. Ways of coloring: Comparative color vision as a case study for cognitive science. *Behavioral and Brain Sciences.*

Thornton, M. 1989. *Folk Psychology: An Introduction.* Toronto: University of Toronto Press/Canadian Philosophical Monographs.

Thurman, R. A. F., trans. 1976. *The Holy Teaching of Vimalakirti.* Philadelphia: Pennsylvania University Press.

Thurman, R. A. F. 1984. *Tsong Khapa's Speech of Gold in the Essence of True Eloquence: Reason and Enlightenment in the Central Philosophy of Tibet.* Princeton: Princeton University Press.

Tolouse, G., S. Dehaene, and J. Changeux. 1986. *Proceedings of the National Academy of Sciences* (USA) 83:1695–1698.

Trizin, K. S. 1986. Parting from the four clingings. In *Essence of Buddhism: Teachings at Tibet House*. New Delhi: Tibet House.

Trungpa, C. *Karma Seminar*. Boulder: Vajradhatu Press.

Trungpa, C. 1973. *Cutting Through Spiritual Materialism*. Boston: Shambhala.

Trungpa, C. 1976. *The Myth of Freedom*. Boston: Shambhala.

Trungpa, C. 1978. *Mandala*. Boulder: Vajradhatu Press.

Trungpa, C. 1981. *Glimpses of Abhidharma*. Boulder: Prajna Press.

Trungpa, C. 1986. *Sadhana of Mahamudra*. Boulder: Vajradhatu Press.

Turkle, S. 1979. *Psychoanalytic Politics: Freud's French Revolution*. Cambridge, Massachusetts: The MIT Press.

Turkle, S. 1984. *The Second Self: Computers and the Human Spirit*. New York: Simon and Schuster.

Turkle, S. 1988. Artifical intelligence and psychoanalysis: A new alliance. *Daedelus* (Winter): 241–269.

Turvey, M. T., R. E. Shaw, E. S. Reed, and W. M. Mace. 1981. Ecological laws of perceiving and acting: In reply to Fodor and Pylyshyn. *Cognition* 9:237–304.

Ullman, S. 1980. Against direct perception. *Behavioral and Brain Sciences* 3:373–415.

Varela, F. 1979. *Principles of Biological Autonomy*. New York: Elsevier North Holland.

Varela, F. 1988. Structural coupling and the origin of meaning in a simple cellular automata. In *The Semiotics of Cellular Communications in the Immune System*, ed. E. Secarz, F. Celada, N. A. Mitchinson, and T. Tada. New York: Springer-Verlag.

Varela, F., A. Coutinho, and B. Dupire. 1988. Cognitive networks: Immune, neural, and otherwise. In *Theoretical Immunology*, ed. A. Perelson, vol. 2. New Jersey: Addison-Wesley.

Varela, F., J. C. Letelier, G. Marin, and H. Maturana. 1983. The neurophysiology of avian color vision. *Archivos de biologia y medicina experimentales* 16:291–303.

Varela, F., V. Sanchez-Leighton, and A. Coutinho. 1988. Adaptive strategies gleaned from networks: Viability theory and clasifier systems. In *Evolutionary and Epigenetic Order from Complex Systems: A Waddington Memorial Symposium*, ed. B. Goodwin and P. Saunders. Edinburgh: Edinburgh University Press.

Varela, F., and W. Singer. 1987. Neuronal dynamics in the cortico-thalamic pathway as revealed through binocular rivalry. *Experimental Brain Research* 66:10–20.

Varela, F., A. Toro, E. R. John, and E. L. Schwartz. 1981. Perceptual framing and cortical alpha rhythm. *Neuropsychologia* 19:675–686.

Vasubhandu. 1923. *L'Abhidharmakosa de Vasubandhu*. 6 Vols. Trans. Louis de La Vallée Poussain. Paris and Louvain: Institut Belges des Hautes Etudes Chinoises. Reprinted Paris: Guenther 1971.

Vattimo, G. 1989. *The End of Modernity*. Trans. J. Snyder. Baltimore: Johns Hopkins University Press.

von Foerster, H., ed. 1962. *Principles of Self-Organization*. New York: Pergamon Press.

Wake, D., G. Roth, and M. Wake. On the problem of stasis in organismal evolution. 1983. *Journal of Theoretical Biology* 101:211–224.

Wellwood, J., ed. 1983. *Awakening the Heart: East West Approaches to Psychotherapy and the Healing Relationship*. Boston: Shambhala.

Wilber, K., J. Engler, and D. Brown. 1987. *Transformations of Consciousness: Conventional and Contemplative Perspectives on Development*. Boston: New Science Library.

Winograd, T., and F. Flores. 1986. *Understanding Computers and Cognition: A New Foundation for Design*. New Jersey: Ablex Press.

Wolfram, S. 1983. Statistical mechanics of cellular automata. *Reviews of Modern Physics* 55:601–644.

Wolfram, S. 1984. Cellular automata as models of complexity. *Nature* 311:419.

Wynne-Edwards, V. 1982. *Animal Dispersion in Relation to Social Behaviour*. Edinbugh: Oliver & Boyd.

Yuasa, Y. 1987. *The Body: Toward an Eastern Mind-Body Theory*. Trans. Nagatomi Shigenori and T.P. Kasulis. Albany: State University of New York Press.

Zeki, S. 1983. Colour coding in the cerebral cortex: The reaction of cells in monkey visual cortex to wavelengths and colours. *Neuroscience* 9:741–765.

Index